Reading across the Curriculum: A Research Report for Teachers

Revised and enlarged edition
Reading in the Content Areas:
Research for Teachers

edited by
Mary M. Dupuis
Linda H. Merchant

ERIC Clearinghouse on Reading
and Communication Skills

EDINFO Press

Published 1993 by:
ERIC Clearinghouse on Reading and Communication Skills
Carl B. Smith, Director
2805 East 10th Street, Suite 150
Bloomington, Indiana 47408-2698
and
EDINFO Press

ERIC (an acronym for Educational Resources Information Center) is a national network of 16 clearinghouses, each of which is responsible for building the ERIC database by identifying and abstracting various educational resources, including research reports, curriculum guides, conference papers, journal articles, and government reports. The Clearinghouse on Reading and Communication Skills (ERIC/RCS) collects educational information specifically related to reading, English, journalism, speech, and theater at all levels. ERIC/RCS also covers interdisciplinary areas, such as media studies, reading and writing technology, mass communication, language arts, critical thinking, literature, and many aspects of literacy.

This publication was prepared with funding from the Office of Educational Research and Improvement, U.S. Department of Education, under contract no. RI88062001. Contractors undertaking such projects under government sponsorship are encouraged to express freely their judgment in professional and technical matters. Points of view or opinions, however, do not necessarily represent the official view or opinions of the Office of Educational Research and Improvement.

Library of Congress Cataloging-in-Publication Data
Mary M. Dupuis, Linda H. Merchant, editors.
  Reading across the curriculum: A research report for teachers
     p.   cm.
  Rev. and enl. ed. of: Reading in the content area. 1984.
  Includes bibliographical references.
  ISBN 0-927516-33-0
  1. Content area reading. 2. Reading comprehension. 3.Individualized reading instructions. 4.Teachers —In-service training. I. Dupuis, Mary M. II. Merchant, Linda H. III. Reading in the content area.
LB1050.455.R45 1992
428.4'071'2—dc20

92-10123
CIP

LB1050.455
.R45
1993

ERIC/RCS Advisory Board Members

APR 17 1996

Table of Contents

Mary M. Dupuis is Professor of Education, and formerly the Director of Teacher Education, at the Pennsylvania State University. She studied at Northwestern, George Washington, and Purdue, and completed her doctorate at Penn State. Experience in numerous fields—from assessment to computers, from teacher education to study habits, from composition to videos—contributes directly to Dr. Dupuis' expertise on the "across the curriculum" approach to reading and course content. Widely published on many topics within her disciplines, and always welcome as a speaker at professional gatherings, she is also energetically involved as a consultant in the life of public schools and other community organizations across the Commonwealth of Pennsylvania.

Linda Hamer Merchant is an Assistant Professor of Education, supervisor of student learning, and specialist in reading at the Pennsylvania State University. She studied at Penn State and Johns Hopkins, and she wrote her doctorate at Penn State. She has taught at, administered in, and consulted with schools in Pennsylvania, Maryland, and Virginia. Concerned with the cognitive processes of learning in both able and disabled students, Dr. Merchant emphasizes an individualized approach for every student. She advocates the use of literature and the application of "across the curriculum" methods as ways of individualizing structured learning from discipline to discipline, student to student.

Introduction

Mary M. Dupuis
The Pennsylvania State University

Reading and Writing across the Curriculum

Strong interest has prompted extensive research on reading and writing across the curriculum. At all grade levels, reading teachers are moving into a new role as resource specialist to content teachers. Because content teachers cannot expect to keep up with the research and teaching techniques in their own areas plus the research in reading and writing, we have developed this handy reference to the literature on research and teaching in reading and writing for the major subject areas taught in schools.

Reading teachers and supervisors frequently are asked to provide information to content teachers about teaching reading and writing. Content teachers, especially department heads and coordinators, are asked to provide similar information to the teachers with whom they work. The sources of information about the most recent research in reading and writing, therefore, need to be available to every teacher.

This book is one source of that information. In many ways, it is the successor to *Reading in the Content Areas: Research for Teachers,* published almost a decade ago by the International Reading Association.[1] In the decade since, more research has been forthcoming on reading and writing across the curriculum than in all the years before. Interest in the effective instruction of reading and writing in the content subject areas has never been higher! Therefore, we have greatly revised, extended, and updated that earlier publication.

The research on implementing reading and writing in content classrooms suggests two major problems. First, content teachers often know less than they need to know about reading and writing in general and the specific aspects of teaching these literacies within their own subjects. Second, content teachers often have negative attitudes towards teaching reading and writing. They often feel helpless and frustrated when their students cannot read classroom materials.[2] In our report to teachers, we are aiming at the first problem, and if we hit it, then implications follow for the second problem. With knowledge come more positive attitudes, hence a partial solution to the second problem. In this book, we intend to supply content-area teachers with the information they need to function as reading and writing teachers *within* their subject/academic discipline. Reading and writing are germane to the study of all content areas, and the other way around.

The scope of this book is the full curriculum. Focusing on grades 4-12, we include the typical academic areas: English/language arts, social studies, science, mathematics; foreign languages, art, and music; health and physical education; and the vocational areas of business and vocational-technical education. These subjects are taught not only in the intermediate grades (4-6) but also in junior and senior high school. When the team preparing this book began its work, the task seemed more formidable than ever. Over thirty textbooks are currently in print to teach teachers how to deal with reading in the content classroom. These texts are sharply focused on practical activities that will be useful in the classroom.

Our investigation of the research base of these textbooks revealed circular references but little research. Perhaps this is not an uncommon situation. Certain techniques come to be accepted as useful because other professionals report them to be so, rather than because of careful, controlled study. One of our team's goals was to find the research base for particular techniques in specific content areas where it was available, and to point out where research is needed.

It was clear from the beginning that diverse reading skills and strategies are necessary in all disciplines.[3] All disciplines identify vocabulary and word-attack skills as important. Comprehension is seen across all the disciplines as the key to reading success. The whole-language approach to reading and language study is recognized for its emphasis on the activation of prior knowledge and for development of schema, ways of organizing the information in reading materials. Because vocabulary and comprehension are fundamental to learning in all disciplines, vocabulary- and comprehension-based approaches to teaching reading are essential in a discipline-based approach. Different disciplines treat vocabulary and comprehension differently, however, and study skills vary widely from discipline to discipline.

All disciplines involve students and teachers with vocabulary and comprehension, and in the chapters that follow we deal with these elements of concern within each discipline, and with elements that differ among the disciplines. Although all disciplines need some types of study skills, each chapter is addressed to those skills considered useful in that discipline. We have sought for reading and writing commonalities across the disciplines, but even more we have sought for the differences that make each content area special in the reading and writing demands it places on students.

Each chapter is a review of the research on reading in one content area. The chapters usually begin with a summary or overview, showing the major concerns and unique features of language use in that area. Some chapters have extensive bibliographies of research and/or teaching techniques germane to the subject. Mathematics, in particular, has generated a great deal of research into the reading process, specifically the process of reading mathematical writing. Research on reading and writing in English has focused on reading literature and using the writing process, with more emphasis on attitude and interest than has been the case in the other subjects.[4] Because researchers in reading and writing across the curriculum have paid less attention to other subject areas, some of our reviews are shorter than others. In some content areas, we could find no research on reading or writing.

As for teaching techniques, many references are available in science, mathematics, English, and social studies, and some aspects of vocational education. We found relatively few for other subjects. In both music and foreign language, content teachers face some confusion. Reading has a plural meaning for them: Reading music as text, a technical skill that music teachers teach, is different from reading alphabetic text. We focus on reading *about* music in a music class. Similarly, foreign-language teachers face the technical problem of teaching students to read the other languages. We examine some of the strategies useful for students in reading and comprehending a second language. We found very little research on this kind of reading in either music or foreign-language study. Clearly, these are areas in need of research on effective teaching techniques. In each chapter, we bring out areas of needed research. In each, we review sources of information for teachers in that content area. The review is followed by an annotated bibliography of sources.

Although the sources listed here were up-to-date as of the date we finished writing, we know that more information becomes available as each month's journals arrive in the mail or on the library shelves. The process is never-ending. This review offers a reference and starting point for work with reading and writing across the curriculum.

One of our goals is to stimulate further research, especially in the areas where it is most needed. We believe that subject teachers and reading teachers alike can help one another and other teachers by sharing effective techniques with the profession.

Notes

1. M. Dupuis, editor, *Reading in the Content Areas: Research for Teachers* (Newark, Delaware: International Reading Association, 1984).

2. M. Dupuis, J. Lee, B.J. Badiali, and E.N. Askov, *Teaching Reading and Writing in the Content Areas* (Glenview, Illinois: Scott, Foresman, and Co., 1989).

3. Dupuis, *et al.* 1989; H. Singer and D. Dolan. *Reading and Learning from Text* (Hillsdale, New Jersey: Lawrence Erlbaum Associates, Inc., 1985); D.E. Alvermann, D.W. Moore, and M.W. Conley, *Research within Reach: Secondary School Reading* (Newark, Delaware: International Reading Association, 1987); R.T. Vacca and J.L. Vacca, *Content Area Reading*, third edition (Glenview, Illinois: Scott, Foresman, and Co., 1989); A.V. Manzo and U.C. Manzo, *Content Area Reading: A Heuristic Approach* (Columbus, Ohio: Merrill Publishing Co., 1990); J.L. Vaughn and T.H. Estes, *Reading and Reasoning beyond the Primary Grades* (Boston: Allyn and Bacon, 1986); J.D. McNeil, *Reading Comprehension: New Directions for Classroom Practice,* second edition (Glenview, Illinois: Scott, Foresman, and Co., 1987).

4. G.R. Carlsen, *Books and the Teenage Reader,* second, revised edition (New York: Harper and Row, 1980); D. Fader, *The New Hooked on Books.* (New York: Berkley Publishing Group, 1981).

References

1. Alvermann, D. E., D. W. Moore, and M. W. Conley. *Research within Reach: Secondary School Reading*. Newark, Delaware: International Reading Association, 1987.

2. Carlsen, G. R. *Books and the Teenage Reader*, second, revised edition. New York: Harper and Row, 1980.

3. Dupuis, M. M., J. Lee, B. J. Badiali, and E. N. Askov. *Teaching Reading and Writing in the Content Areas*. Glenview, Illinois: Scott, Foresman, and Co., 1989.

4. Fader, D. *The New Hooked on Books*. New York: Berkley Publishing Group, 1981.

5. Manzo, A. V. and U. C. Manzo. *Content Area Reading: A Heuristic Approach*. Columbus, Ohio: Merrill Publishing Co., 1990.

6. McNeil, J. D. *Reading Comprehension: New Directions for Classroom Practice*, second edition. Glenview, Illinois: Scott, Foresman, and Co., 1987.

7. Singer, H. and D. Dolan. *Reading and Learning from Text*. Hillsdale, New Jersey: Lawrence Erlbaum Associates, Inc., 1985.

8. Vacca, R. T. and J. L. Vacca. *Content Area Reading*, third edition. Glenview, Illinois: Scott, Foresman, and Co., 1989.

9. Vaughn, J. L. and T. H. Estes. *Reading and Reasoning beyond the Primary Grades*. Boston: Allyn and Bacon, 1986.

1

Reading in English

Linda H. Merchant
The Pennsylvania State University

Carol T. Fishel
Arlington Baptist Schools
Baltimore, Maryland

Overview

Is content-area reading in English class a contradiction in terms? Have not reading and writing skills always been within the province of the English teacher? The answers to these questions are not simple.

In the early elementary grades, the language-arts teacher does assume the primary role in students' acquisition of reading and writing skills. By the fourth grade, however, reading for information, enjoyment, and intellectual development increases, often with scant attention being paid to the reading process itself. Even in English class, teachers assume that the student who can read is able efficiently to process and learn from a variety of written materials. In recent years, new attention has been directed to the reading process in English class because the development of the process of reading is integral to the development of thinking skills.

A closer examination of English as a content area reveals its special reading demands. Readers need skills to comprehend different literary genres as well as expository text and periodicals. Although in other content areas, in which rewriting a text in the reader's own words often can assist comprehension, appreciation of fine literature demands that each author's style and linguistic choices be preserved. The problem of maintaining the integrity of an author's artistic composition while enabling the young reader to comprehend and appreciate it, can be met by application of what has been learned about reading in English class.

Research: Vocabulary

Research seems to indicate that many efficient strategies for learning new vocabulary are available for use. Many questions about the efficacy of different strategies for different age groups and reading abilities are yet to be answered; however, the trend seems to be to combine a number of strategies to build as many networks of meaning as possible. A look at the research in comprehension indicates that the interaction among vocabulary knowledge, schema, and comprehension is increasingly being addressed as a whole.

Research in past years has focused on the effects of strategies that facilitate vocabulary development and comprehension for able and less-able readers alike. Joan Gipe investigated the effects of several methods of vocabulary development. For able and less-able readers in the third and fifth grades, the context method was significantly better than any other method. Learning the words in context seemed especially to help readers be able to use the words in context. Gipe was surprised to find that categorization was not effective in vocabulary learning for these young readers.[1]

In related studies, Michael Pressley, Joel Levin, and Gloria Miller investigated a keyword strategy. They instructed some students to take a familiar part of a new word, such as "cat" from "catkin," and form an image that merged the familiar meaning with the obscure meaning. Subjects in control groups were instructed to use whatever strategy they desired. Keyword subjects in all studies performed significantly better than did control subjects.[2]

These investigators also assigned approximately forty college students either to keyword or context approaches to learn 30 obscure English words. All students were required to learn 100 percent of the words. The keyword students learned the vocabulary at a significantly faster rate, but one-week retention rates were nearly equivalent for both groups.[3]

Researchers have examined the relative strengths of several different types of vocabulary development. Maryann Eeds and Ward Cockrum assigned groups of both high- and low-achieving fifth-graders to three treatment groups. In one, teachers helped students relate 85 vocabulary words taken from a novel to their own schemata or background knowledge. A second group looked the words up in the dictionary and wrote definitions, and a third group read the words in context. Teachers were rotated among the three groups during the instructional period. Both immediate testing and delayed testing for vocabulary meanings showed a significant main effect indicating the superiority of the schema-based vocabulary instruction, for both high and low achievers.[4]

A. H. Duin and Michael F. Graves used intensive vocabulary instruction strategies developed at the University of Minnesota (common topic, link to experience, networks of meaning, timed matching games, use of words in student writing) in an experiment with seventh-graders. They found a significant difference between a control group using traditional vocabulary instruction and an experimental group which received intensive vocabulary instruction in the areas of vocabulary knowledge and use of new words in essays. This difference was in favor of intensive instruction.[5]

In addition to investigating instructional strategies to develop vocabulary meanings, some researchers have examined the relationships between vocabulary instruction and comprehension.

Edward Kameenui, Douglas Carnine, and Roger Freschi investigated the effects of vocabulary and vocabulary instruction on comprehension. In two experiments with elementary students, they found that substituting easy words for difficult ones made materials significantly easier to understand, and that instruction on difficult words significantly facilitated comprehension.[6]

A study that combined vocabulary, prereading activities, and comprehension was conducted by Dana Thomas and John Readence. These researchers compared traditional basal vocabulary instruction with two other lesson frameworks: the reconciled reading lesson, which involved vocabulary enrichment activities normally used after reading, and a list-group-label strategy. The subjects in the study were 66 average and above-average second-graders. The reconciled-reading-lesson group outperformed the other two groups on measures of comprehension.[7]

Research: Comprehension

In the area of comprehension research in English, most work has been done with short stories, but a small amount of research has involved teaching the structure of language to facilitate comprehension.

Because connectives are often taught to students who are learning compound and complex sentences, Judith Soltis and Susanne Pflaum investigated the effects of instruction in connectives on the comprehension of seventh- and eighth-grade inner-city students. The experimental treatment involved identifying connectives in text, learning categories of connectives, and completing worksheets with the connectives (for a desired relational meaning). Using the *Standard Test Lessons in Reading* and a cloze-like connectives test, the researchers found significant differences only on the connectives test. The value of the treatment is difficult to ascertain because instruction in one skill usually has little effect on standardized reading test scores.[8]

In an experiment with third-graders, Michael Sampson, William Valmont, and R. V. Allen found that substituting instructional cloze materials and lessons in reading centers for 15 weeks resulted in significantly better comprehension and divergent production for the experimental group when compared to the control group that used traditional reading lessons, although no difference was found in the development of vocabulary meanings. The emphasis in the experiment was on language choices and alternative meanings.[9]

In several comprehension studies, researchers have explored which instructional strategies may facilitate comprehension of short stories for both able and less-able readers. Robert A. Lucking examined the effects of hierarchically ordered comprehension questions based on the Bloom-Clegg taxonomy.[10] In Phase I, students read the short story silently, and then they wrote an essay. In Phase II, students read the story, and then they were led in an unstructured discussion. In Phase III, teachers used hierarchically ordered questions, moving up the Bloom-Clegg taxonomy to question students after reading. After each phase, student attitudes were assessed, and their essays were evaluated by the Purves content analysis scheme. At the end of Phase III, the subjects exhibited more interpretation in their essays and more positive attitudes than they did at the end of either Phase I or II.[11] Our own judgment is that the greater amount of interpretation represents a grasp of broader meanings above the literal-knowledge level.

Dealing with questioning strategies, Dan Donlan and Harry Singer investigated the effects of pre-posed questions on readers' comprehension of short stories. With high-school subjects, the experimenters examined teacher-prepared questions (similar to those used in a directed reading activity), student-prepared questions, and schema-based student-pre-posed questions. Results from a content-based comprehension test indicated that students using self-pre-posed questions based on the short-story schema exhibited the best comprehension. Awareness of short-story structures from general schema questions seemed to be crucial for forming effective questions.[12]

In a subsequent study, Singer and Donlan found similar results. Fifteen eleventh-grade students were randomly assigned to an experimental group in which they were taught to construct story-specific questions from general schema-based questions for short stories. The control group answered teacher-prepared questions. Over a three-week period, the two groups read six complex short stories. Criterion-referenced comprehension tests revealed a significant difference between the two groups; the group of students who constructed story-specific questions had significantly greater comprehension.[13]

In the area of critical comprehension of short stories, New Zealand high-school students scored higher in comprehension than students in nine other countries, according to an internationally based study of critical literary skills under the auspices of the International Association for the Evaluation of Educational Achievement. Part of the study involved having students in ten countries read three internationally acclaimed short stories translated into their own languages. Given twenty questions from three categories (form, content, affect), the students were asked to choose the five questions they considered most critical to the understanding of each story. The New Zealand students demonstrated flexibility when they chose different questions for different stories; this critical flexibility seems to have facilitated comprehension.[14]

In addition to the role of questions, some researchers have investigated the role of different types of prior knowledge on comprehension of narrative material.

Researchers redesigned two reading lessons for third-grade students to emphasize prior knowledge and to sketch a story map of central events and relationships before reading. Comprehension of two stories was measured by story recall and forced-choice questions. The experimental group receiving these revised lessons performed significantly better than a control group.[15]

Amber Prince and Dianne Mancus matched 45 subjects in grades one through five on reading level, age, and sex. Within each level, one group was taught three basal stories in a traditional format while the other group was taught in an altered format (presenting the enrichment activities at the beginning of the lesson). The group receiving the altered format demonstrated significantly higher comprehension.[16]

Dale Dinnel and John Glover found that college students who received advance organizers about a passage in linguistics, and who were required to perform an encoding manipulation such as paraphrasing, performed significantly better on tests of memory than did others who either did not receive advance organizers or who did not perform any encoding manipulations.[17]

Exploring the role of prior knowledge, T. A. Roberts tested both fifth- and ninth-grade students with and without soccer-club experience for their comprehension of a story about a soccer game. Two types of prereading instruction were provided, one involving information about soccer and the other not providing information about the game. Findings seem to indicate that the prior knowledge was more powerful than prereading instruction for older students, but that the younger subjects' experience was externally activated by the relevant knowledge.[18]

In a similar vein, Donna Recht and Lauren Leslie divided 64 junior high school students into four equal groups based on preassessed high and low reading ability and preassessed knowledge of baseball. Each subject read an account of a half-inning of baseball. Students demonstrated their comprehension and memory verbally (by retelling) and nonverbally (by moving figures around). They summarized the game and sorted passage ideas for importance. A significant main effect showing the greater importance of prior knowledge occurred for all measures. In addition, no interaction between the effects of prior knowledge and ability was found.[19]

Many researchers have examined the effects of other factors on comprehension, among which are modes of presentation, repeated readings, and culture.

In 1974, René Weisberg examined the question of whether less-able readers comprehend poorly because of reading difficulties, and whether able and less-able readers, in trying to comprehend, exhibit processing differences when using linguistically coded prior knowledge. She investigated fourth-grade readers' comprehension of six short stories presented through visual and auditory modes, and tested through free and probed recall. Less-able readers recalled significantly less explicit and implicit material, and they could answer significantly fewer probed questions than could the more-able readers. Perhaps the less-able readers had difficulty encoding linguistically, or they may have had inefficient retrieval strategies. Weisberg believed that the difference in memory for idea units between the able and the less-able readers—regardless of modes of presentation—supports a general language-comprehension deficit in less-able readers.[20] One may question whether the comprehension difficulty is general; it may occur more with school-based language structures, such as the short story.

Lawrence O'Shea, Paul Sindelar, and D. J. O'Shea had 30 third-graders read separate passages one, three, or seven times following cues to attend either to reading rate or to meaning. Comprehension was measured by a retelling of the story after the final reading. Fluency and the number of story propositions were analyzed. Both fluency and comprehension increased significantly as the number of readings increased, although young readers cued to fluency read faster, but comprehended less, than did those cued to comprehension.[21] This difference supports the idea that a reader's purposes for reading are influential in directing the reader's efforts.

Another factor that influences comprehension is culture. Gayle Nelson measured the recall of 93 Egyptian adult students who had read four pairs of stories based on different cultures. Stories were matched on the basis of Fry readability measures and by the instructor's review for content, reading level, and length. All students completed the eight readings and quizzes. Student performance was significantly higher on readings based on Egyptian culture, even though the students did not always prefer the Egyptian material.[22]

A further factor affecting comprehension of narrative material is the use of reading guides. Comparing students using hierarchical and nonhierarchical study guides for narrative material, Diane Armstrong and others found a significant difference between the comprehension of students who used study guides, and a control group which did not. No significant difference was evident in levels of comprehension based on the organizational patterns of guides when they included literal, inferential, and evaluative questions.[23] We can conclude that reading guides increased comprehension as long as questions were posed at all levels, but that the order of these questions was not significant.

In the area of interest and motivation, Ruth Cline and George Kretke studied sustained silent reading with several hundred subjects in three junior high schools. An inventory of reading attitudes showed that subjects involved in a three-year sustained silent reading program exhibited significantly more positive attitudes toward reading than did the control subjects; however, reading achievement scores on the *Stanford Achievement Test* revealed no significant differences between the two treatment groups.[24]

English involves students in reading various literary genres, but few readability studies have been done on this aspect. Mary Dupuis investigated the cloze procedure as a means of predicting students' ability to read short stories. A 48 percent cloze score predicted minimum comprehension. Dupuis concluded that the cloze procedure can be helpful to teachers in matching students to appropriate short stories.[25] Extension of these findings to other forms of literature awaits further study.

Strategies for Many Genres

Of all the content areas, English is the most demanding in terms of reading skills needed to understand the variety of genres. Students' understanding and appreciation of all the genres is usually the English teacher's goal. The teacher will need to use every available resource to increase comprehension and appreciation, and to develop efficient reading skills.

To comprehend poetry, students need instruction in inverted syntax, poetic vocabulary, figurative language, poetic patterns, and the use of compressed ideas.[26] Reading skills demanded by drama include visualizing sets and forming action structures based upon careful attention to stage instructions and dialogue. In fiction, such as the novel or short story, comprehending characters, plot, and setting; understanding strategies for reviewing; and learning to locate transitions are necessary reading skills. Biography demands ascertaining and evaluating the author's world view. The essay genre demands the comprehension of arguments and their organization.[27] Reading newspapers involves comprehension of reporting styles and application of standards of media.

In addition to all the genres and media, many English classes use a grammar text that requires literal and inferential comprehension of expository text and efficient study skills. For all genres, word-attack skills and continual development of specialized and general vocabulary are always needed.

Strategies for Readiness

Because English as a content area involves such a variety of reading demands, some writers limit themselves to discussing the reading requirements of a particular genre, such as poetry. Others discuss strategies that they find applicable to more than one genre. Most instructional activities fall into three major areas: readiness, guidance in reading, and extension of understanding.

Readiness activities seem to have two components: motivating students and overcoming initial difficulties. Motivation is often provided by allowing students to select materials.[28] Self-selection can provide the added benefit of controlling for reading difficulty if available materials span many reading levels. A variety of interest inventories can help teachers choose reading materials for grouping or unit building.[29]

E. L. Thomas and H. Alan Robinson detailed activities that build suspense or interest just before reading.[30] Jim Detherage incorporated these activities into an English unit structured around running. Students actually ran, read about running, and wrote about running. The students selected reading materials at various difficulty levels.[31] Similarly, W. R. Heitzman reported that units which included reading newspapers to build vocabulary and comprehension have been shown to be highly motivating for inner-city children.[32] Robert Cooter and Robert Griffith combined literature, projects, writing, group cooperation, and comprehension processes in the Dublin thematic model. The authors provided a number of possible activities related to self-selected reading.[33] Barbara Guzzetti found an increase in positive attitudes toward reading when students were allowed to use trade books and to select a variety of response projects to demonstrate comprehension.[34] Elaine Lutz suggested folk literature as a source of reading and writing activities because it holds high interest for students, and it can be extended to students' own writing.[35]

In addition to building motivation, overcoming initial difficulties is a concern for the English teacher. Initial difficulty in comprehending the plot and differentiating the characters especially impedes the efforts of less-able readers to finish the reading. Preparing students to read and comprehend may be accomplished in several different ways:

- providing advance organizers, such as overviews of characters and plot

- resolving the conflicts involved in fiction and their relationships to the students' experience

- oral reading of the initial parts with explanatory comments and questions by the teacher

Another aspect of building readiness is in the area of vocabulary. Both genre-related vocabulary and general vocabulary are necessary for thorough comprehension. For example, teaching vocabulary concepts (literal and inferential) is especially important in poetry because poetic language is often least similar to student language.[36]

A variety of techniques can be used to teach the necessary vocabulary:

- categorical development of vocabulary through a game format

- dramatization of vocabulary through small skits

- using analogies to show relationships

- using vocabulary guides

- clarifying figurative language

Additional readiness may be built by assessing and building a background in the literary skills that are necessary for students to make appropriate inferences while reading. For example, Susan Davis and Jean Hunter gave gifted eighth-graders the research problem of evaluating for accuracy some area in a historical novel. Students looked up pertinent information in general historical reference books as they evaluated the novels they were reading. The final product was a short research paper. Once the frame for their reading was constructed, the teacher set purposes for the actual reading, and the students were able to perform their evaluation tasks more effectively.[37]

Strategies for Guided Reading

The second phase of reading instruction in English is guidance through the actual reading process. Guidance can involve the use of tapes (with or without comments) for less-able readers to use as they read silently. Guidance can also come in the form of glosses of difficult vocabulary or syntax, and the use of reading guides of various types. Almost all types of guides focus on building different levels of comprehension: literal, interpretive, and applied. Guides may be used with individuals or with small groups. For example, Donald O'Brien and Sheila Schwarzberg's reading and reaction guides provide a sample reading and reaction guide for poetry, and illustrate how it could be used to direct discussion in small groups.[38]

Special types of guides, such as cause-and-effect and sequence guides, may be used to develop needed understanding. Such specialized guides help students focus on a range of comprehension levels beyond the literal, and they assist teachers in organizing their questioning at different levels.

In addition to developing reading guides and glossing difficult texts, some teachers have taught students specific strategies for actively acquiring vocabulary and facilitating comprehension while reading. For example, students can be taught to use different types of clues to build vocabulary.[39] Lou Burmeister proposed teaching older students to use the morphemic elements of English to facilitate vocabulary acquisition and overall comprehension.[40]

Strategies for Comprehension

Various strategies and techniques are used to help students comprehend the English content material. Many teachers develop and use learning centers where students can work individually or in cooperative learning groups to strengthen reading skills.

Dale and Bonnie Johnson discussed different types of inferences needed to comprehend English content material. They recommended teaching vocabulary during prereading, tying it to prior knowledge, and elaborating the students' conceptual schema.[41]

A form of logic in English that may impede comprehension is syntax. M. Lubell and Brenda Townsend identified three major syntactical difficulties for experienced readers of narrative prose, and they illustrated how students can learn these relationships of main clauses in conditional, periodic, and complex modification structures.[42]

Several researchers have proposed the development of internal strategies to help students understand literature. John Readence and David Moore taught secondary English students to use structures such as intimacy and withdrawal to analyze character relationships in short stories as they read.[43] Michelle Commeyras taught students to use six critical-thinking dispositions and abilities to interpret drama and to discover which could be applied to other literature.[44] Sheila McAuliffe and Ruth Brancard illustrated the application of Anderson's profundity scale to literature. Using the frameworks of the physical, mental, moral, psychological, and philosophical planes, McAuliffe and Brancard allowed students to work with reading groups based on their individual interests. Each group approached the novel, its characters, and their actions through the particular plane chosen. For example, one group listed the values of each major character, and then supported their conclusions by referring to the words and actions of the character analyzed.[45]

Similarly, Daniel and Sharon A. Moore recommended different frameworks for self-questioning by students of literature because these self-questions stimulate extensive thinking and divergent responses.[46] William W. Crowder taught students guidelines for evaluating newspapers and magazines to facilitate their critical reading of the print media.[47] All of these belong to the category of metacognitive strategies that students can learn to use in English class to process what they read more effectively.

Strategies for Extension of Understanding

The extension phase of reading involves synthesis and evaluation. There is a growing emphasis on building logical concepts through comprehension of literature and synthesis with other literature, concepts, and experiences. George H. Henry carefully guided students in applying the logical strategies of joining and excluding as they built concepts and higher-order abstractions through literature. He illustrated the techniques in a poetry unit in which students developed a concept of the human relationship to nature through a process of analysis and synthesis.[48]

Related to developing abstractions is the use of analogies to build concepts through logical relationships. Barbara Bellows taught the use of similes, metaphors, maxims, proverbs, and personification as analogies, using the analogies to compare characters, dialogue, setting, and mood.[49]

An effective way to use the activities from the readiness, guidance, and extension phases to develop reading skills is to use, or adapt, the directed reading-thinking activity.[50] As the unit is an efficient way to plan for developing long-range reading skills in English, so the directed reading-thinking activity is an efficient way to develop the reading skills necessary for a particular reading task in English.

Alexa Lindquist developed reading guides for high-school classes for five general types of literature: short story, essay, novel, drama, and poetry. The guides followed a prereading, guidance, and extension pattern, and they were built on Bloom's taxonomy. Lindquist modeled the guides and analyzed them sentence by sentence with students who then used them with other materials. She also provided a sample guide for a novel. The guides were not meant to be exhaustive, but they could effectively focus thinking.[51]

A small-group variation of using guides was proposed by Mollee Sager. In addition to the common-knowledge base provided by the guides, members of small groups were assigned additional, individualized readings in such areas as historical background or the author's life. Each student in a group became an expert on the additional knowledge. The group shared knowledge, vocabulary, and guide information. Then the group wrote a joint story similar to the one studied, with each group member writing an individual ending.[52]

Robert White integrated many of the previously discussed suggestions into a reading development plan for the English classroom. This plan provides a broad outline for instituting and managing reading-skill development for small and large groups.[53]

Resources for the Teacher

What materials are available for the English or reading teacher? Lists of genre-related reading skills are available to guide planning.[54] For the teacher who wishes to move from single-text strategies to multi-text strategies, Stephen and Susan Judy listed several sources of junior-high and senior-high booklists from the National Council of Teachers of English.[55] Columns, such as "What's New in Teaching Materials?" in *The English Journal*, provide more resources. Jessie Moore suggested guidelines for the use of sustained silent reading in the classroom, and Kathleen Reed devised a multidimensional model for assessing the development of student attitudes towards reading.[56] One of the promising aspects of computer-aided English instruction is the publication of programs for individualized vocabulary and comprehension development and for word processing. Interactive fiction is a growing field that engages the reader in unaccustomed ways. Hypertext programs allow readers access to glossed cultural or informational texts or definitions.[57]

In light of what is being done, what needs exist in content-area reading for English? More research needs to be conducted concerning the instructional strategies that will be most helpful for different learning styles and most appropriate for different genres. Additionally, work on handling the reading needs of the exceptional or linguistically different students in English classes should be expanded. Mary Dupuis and Eunice Askov offered a decision-making model for meeting individual needs, and they discussed some of the factors involved for the exceptional or linguistically different child.[58] Like Stanley Levinson, they advocated adaptation of the language-experience approach in the secondary school to meet reading needs.[59] Because language is integral to the teaching of English, and future programs may place greater demands on the classroom teacher, additional research in these areas would be helpful.

A broad look at the literature reveals that reading specialists in the upper grades are taking a stronger role as resource persons for the classroom teacher. The effectiveness of this collaboration needs to be investigated. Examination of present attitudes and practices of English teachers could provide a basis for development and implementation of content-area reading programs.

All these research needs are directed to assisting the classroom teacher in a demanding, but rewarding, task—implementing reading-skill development in the English classroom.

Notes

1. J. P. Gipe, "Use of Relevant Context Helps Kids Learn New Word Meanings," *Reading Teacher 33* (1980): 398-402.

2. M. Pressley, J. R. Levin, and G. E. Miller, "How Does the Keyword Method Affect Vocabulary, Comprehension, and Usage?" *Reading Research Quarterly 16* (1981): 213-26.

3. Pressley, Levin, and Miller. Keyword Method.

4. M. Eeds and W. A. Cockrum, "Teaching Word Meanings by Expanding Schemata vs. Dictionary Work vs. Reading in Context," *Journal of Reading 28* (1985): 492-97.

5. A. H. Duin and M. F. Graves, "Teaching Vocabulary as a Writing Prompt," *Journal of Reading 32* (1988): 204-11.

6. E. J. Kameenui, D. W. Carnine, and R. Freschi, "Effects of Text Construction and Instructional Procedures for Teaching Word Meanings on Comprehension and Recall," *Reading Research Quarterly 17* (1982): 367-99.

7. D. G. Thomas and J. E. Readence, "Effects of Differential Vocabulary Instruction and Lesson Framework on the Reading Comprehension of Primary Children," *Reading Research and Instruction 27* (1988): 1-12.

8. J. M. Soltis and S. W. Pflaum, "The Effects of Instruction in Connectives on Reading Comprehension," *Reading World 19* (1979): 179-84.

9. M. R. Sampson, W. J. Valmont, and R. V. Allen, "The Effects of Instructional Cloze on the Comprehension Vocabulary and Divergent Production of Third Grade Students," *Reading Research Quarterly 17* (1982): 389-99.

10. R. A. Lucking, "A Study of the Effects of Hierarchically Ordered Questioning Techniques on Adolescents' Responses to Short Stories," *Research in the Teaching of English 10* (1976): 269-76.

11. S. C. Purves and V. Rippere, *Elements of Writing about a Literary Work: A Study of Response to Literature*. Champaign, Illinois: NCTE, 1968.

12. D. Donlan and H. Singer, "Active Comprehension of Short Stories," 1979.

13. H. Singer and D. Donlan, "Active Comprehension: Problem-Solving Schema with Question Generation for Comprehension of Complex Short Stories," *Reading Research Quarterly 17* (1982): 166-86.

14. J. T. Guthrie, "Research: Learning to Criticize Literature," *Journal of Reading 24* (1980): 92-94.

15. I. L. Beck, C. A. Perfetti, and M. G. McKeown, "Effects of Long-Term Vocabulary Instruction on Lexical Access and Reading Comprehension," *Journal of Educational Psychology 74* (1982): 506-21.

16. A. T. Prince and D. S. Mancus, "Enriching Comprehensions: A Schema Altered Basal Reading Lesson," *Reading Research and Instruction 27* (1987): 45-54.

17. D. Dinnel and J. Glover, "Advance Organizers: Encoding Manipulations," *Journal of Educational Psychology 77* (1985): 514-21.

18. T. Roberts, "Development of Pre-instruction versus Experience: Effects on Factual and Inferential Comprehension," *Reading Psychology 9* (1988): 141-57.

19. D. E. Recht and L. Leslie, "Effects of Prior Knowledge on Good and Poor Readers' Memory of Text," *Journal of Educational Psychology 80* (1988): 16-20.

20. R. A. Weisberg, "A Comparison of Good and Poor Readers' Ability to Comprehend Explicit and Implicit Information in Short Stories Based on Two Modes of Presentation," *Research in the Teaching of English 13* (1974): 337-51.

21. L. J. O'Shea, P. T. Sindelar, and D.J. O'Shea, "The Effects of Repeated Readings and Additional Cues on Reading Fluency and Comprehension," *Journal of Reading Behavior 17* (1985): 129-40.

22. G. L. Nelson, "Culture's Role in Reading Comprehension: A Schema Theoretical Approach," *Journal of Reading 30* (1987): 424-29.

23. D. P. Armstrong, J. Patberg, and P. Dewitz, "Reading Guides: Helping Students Understand," *Journal of Reading 31* (1988): 532-40.

24. R. J. K. Cline and G. L. Kretke, "An Evaluation of Long Term SSR in the Junior High-School," *Journal of Reading 23* (1980): 503-06.

25. M. M. Dupuis, "The Cloze Procedure: Can It Be Used with Literature?" *Reading Improvement 13* (1976): 199-203.

26. S. A. Chesler, "Integrating the Teaching of Reading and Literature," *Journal of Reading 19* (1976): 360-66.

27. G. E. LaRoque, "Developing Special Skills for Reading Genres," *Reading Improvement 14* (1977): 182-86.

28. D. Elkins, *Teaching Literature: Designs for Cognitive Development*. Columbus, Ohio: Charles E. Merrill, 1976.

29. W. J. Lanberg, "Helping Reluctant Readers Help Themselves: Interest Inventories," *English Journal 66* (1977): 40-44.

30. E. L. Thomas, and H. A. Robinson, *Improving Reading in Every Class*, third edition. Boston: Allyn & Bacon, 1982.

31. J. Detherage, "Reading, Writing, and Running," *English Journal 69* (1980): 38-41.

32. W. R. Heitzmann, *The Newspaper in the Classroom: What Research Says to the Teacher*. Washington, D.C.: National Education Association, 1979, 1986.

33. R. B. Cooter and B. Griffith, "Thematic Units for Middle School," *Journal of Reading 32* (1989): 676-81.

34. B. J. Guzzetti, "Enhancing Comprehension through Trade Books in High School English Classes," *Journal of Reading 33* (1990): 411-13.

35. E. Lutz, "Using Folk Literature in Your Reading Program," *Journal of Reading 30* (1986): 76-78.

36. S. A. Chesler, "Integrating the Teaching of Reading and Literature," *Journal of Reading 19* (1976): 360-66.

37. S. L. Davis and J. Hunter, "Historical Novels: A Context for Gifted Student Research," *Journal of Reading 33* (1990): 602-06.

38. D. O'Brien and S. Schwarzberg, "A Strategy for Improving Teenagers' Understanding and Appreciation of Poetry," *Journal of Reading 30* (1977): 381-86.

39. J. W. Lee, "Increasing Comprehension through the Use of Context Clue Categories," *Journal of Reading 22* (1978): 259-61.

40. L. E. Burmeister, "Vocabulary Development in Content-Area Reading through the Use of Morphemes," *Journal of Reading 19* (1976): 481-86.

41. D. D. Johnson and B. V. Johnson, "Highlighting Vocabulary in Inferential Comprehension Instruction," *Journal of Reading 29* (1986): 622-25.

42. M. Lubell and B. S. Townsend, "A Strategy for Teaching Complex Prose Structures," *Journal of Reading 33* (1989): 102-06.

43. J. E. Readance and D. Moore, "Responding to Literature: An Alternative to Questioning," *Journal of Reading 23* (1979): 107-11.

44. M. Commeyras, "Using Literature to Teach Critical Thinking," *Journal of Reading 32* (1989): 703-07.

45. S. McAuliffe and R. Blanchard, "An Experienced-Based Approach to Evaluating Literature," *Journal of Reading 25* (1982): 501-04.

46. D. W. Moore and S. A. Moore, "Reading Literature Independently," *Journal of Reading 30* (1987): 596-600.

47. W. W. Crowder, "Helping Elementary Students Understand the News through a Study of Reporting Styles," *Reading Improvement 15* (1970): 141-44.

48. G. H. Henry, *Teaching Reading as Concept Development: Emphasis on Affective Thinking.* Newark, Delaware: International Reading Association, 1978: 27-39.

49. B. P. Bellows, "Running Shoes Are to Jogging as Analogies Are to Creative/Critical Thinking," *Journal of Reading 23* (1980): 507-11.

50. J. E. Readence, T. W. Bean, and R. S. Baldwin, *Content Area Reading: An Integrated Approach.* Dubuque, Iowa: Kendall/ Hunt, 1989: 146-48.

51. A. A. Lindquist, "Applying Bloom's Taxonomy in Writing Reading Guides," *Journal of Reading 25* (1982): 768-74.

52. M. Sager, "Exploiting the Reading/Writing Connection to Engage Students in Text," *Journal of Reading 33* (1989): 40-43.

53. R. H. White, "Reading Skills in the English Class," *The Clearing House 51* (1977): 32-35.

54. G. E. LaRocque, "Developing Special Skills for Reading Genres," *Reading Improvement 14* (1977): 182-86.

55. S. N. Tchudi and S. L.Tchudi, *The English Teacher's Handbook,* revised edition. Portsmouth, New Hampshire: Boynton/Cook, 1991.

56. J. C. Moore, *Guidelines for Secondary SSR*. Washington: Department of Health, Education and Welfare, 1980. [ED 195 955]; K. Reed, "Assessing Responses to Reading," *Reading World 19* (1979): 149-56.

57. W. V. Costanzo, "Media, Metaphors, and Models," *English Journal 77* (1988): 28-32.

58. M. M. Dupuis and E. N. Askov, *Content-Area Reading: An Individualized Approach*. Englewood Cliffs, New Jersey: Prentice-Hall, 1982: 282-95.

59. S. Levinson, "Teaching Reading and Writing to Limited and Non-English Speakers in Secondary Schools," *English Journal 68* (1979): 38-42.

Annotated Bibliography

Armstrong, D. P., J. Patberg, and P. Dewitz. "Reading Guides: Helping Students Understand," *Journal of Reading 31* (1988): 532-40.

   Compares experimental students using hierarchical and non-hierarchical study guides for narrative material with control students who used no guides for reading. Reports that comprehension testing revealed a significant difference between experimental groups and the control group, but no significant differences between the organizational patterns of guides when guides covered literal, inferential, and applied comprehension.

Arnold, R. D. "Teaching Cohesive Ties to Children," *The Reading Teacher 42* (1988): 106-10.

   Defines cohesion as certain related elements that help basic clauses hold together, such as reference, substitution, ellipsis, etc. Gives several teaching activities for cohesive elements.

Aulis, M. and F. Gelbert. "Effects of Method of Instruction and Ability of Literal Comprehension of Short Stories," *Research in the Teaching of English 14* (1980): 51-59.

   Investigates the effects of four instructional methods on the literal comprehension of short stories by able and less-able seventh-grade readers. Significant results indicate that vocabulary training and paced reading provided optimal results for the able reader.

Beach, R. "Studying the Relationship between Prior Knowledge and Response to Literature," *English Journal 69* (1980): 93-96.

   Asserts that knowledge of both social and literary conventions is necessary for students to make inferences. Outlines techniques for judging students' knowledge and ascertaining how that knowledge (or lack of it) affects their responses to literature.

Beck, I. L., C. A. Perfetti, and M. G. McKeown. "Effects of Long-Term Vocabulary Instruction on Lexical Access and Reading Comprehension," *Journal of Educational Psychology 74* (1982): 506-21.

Reports that third-grade students who received two reading lessons revised to emphasize prior knowledge and a story map of central events and relations, performed significantly better on measures of comprehension than did a control group.

Bellows, B. P. "Running Shoes are to Jogging as Analogies Are to Creative/Critical Thinking," *Journal of Reading 23* (1980): 507-11.

Explains the rationale behind the use of analogies to guild critical/creative thinking in the content areas. Includes a basic analogies unit with applications to literature comprehension. Teaches similes, metaphors, personification, maxims, and proverbs as analogies. Proposes use of analogies in comprehension activities to compare character, plot, setting, and mood.

Burmeister, L. "Vocabulary Development in Content-Area Reading through the Use of Morphemes," *Journal of Reading 19* (1976): 481-86.

Discusses vocabulary development through study of morphemes; suggests some possible activities for the classroom.

Carr, E. M. "The Vocabulary Overview Guide: A Metacognitive Strategy to Improve Vocabulary Comprehension and Retention," *Journal of Reading 28* (1985): 684-89.

Reports on a vocabulary overview guide to help students recognize the framework of relationships of vocabulary, and a vocabulary overview sheet to help students organize and personalize vocabulary meanings—techniques developed for remedial use.

Cassidy, J. "How to Read in 'English'," *Teacher 95* (1987): 48-52.

Discusses English activities for a learning center where five reading-skill areas for fourth- and fifth-graders are reinforced. Includes detailed directions for the activities.

Chesler, S. A. "Integrating the Teaching of Reading and Literature," *Journal of Reading 19* (1976) 360-66.

Discusses the reading difficulties and skills necessary to handle the poetry genre. Provides sample methods for choosing poems,
preparing for reading, surveying, and facilitating literal and critical comprehension.

Cline, R. J. and G. L. Kretke. "An Evaluation of Long Term SSR
in the Junior High School," *Journal of Reading 23* (1980):
503-06.

Reports of sustained silent reading on junior high school
students' attitudes toward reading: a significantly higher positive
attitude toward reading for those engaged in SSR, but no significant differences in reading achievement, and no interaction of the
treatment with intellectual capacity.

Commeyras, M. "Using Literature to Teach Critical Thinking,"
Journal of Reading 32 (1989): 703-07.

Describes a sample grid for a drama using external clues that
lead to interpretation. Uses six critical-thinking dispositions and
abilities that can be developed through literature.

Cooter, R. B. and B. Griffith. "Thematic Units for Middle School:
An Honorable Seduction," *Journal of Reading 32* (1989):
676-81.

Combines literature, projects, writing, group cooperation, and
comprehension processes into a thematic model. Suggests a number of possible activities related to student-selected reading.

Costanzo, W. V. "Media, Metaphors, and Models," *English Journal*
77 (1988): 28-32.

Discusses using the computer to explore writing as playing
with light, as collaboration with an interactive computer, as an
options process, as an organized process, and as a terrain to be
traversed. Describes two new trends: interactive fiction involving
the reader and hypertext.

Crowder, W. W. "Helping Elementary Students Understand the News through a Study of Reporting Styles," *Reading Improvement 15* (1978): 141-44.

> Describes a four-step procedure to enable elementary language arts students to evaluate news reports that they read and hear. Provides detailed information for the classroom teacher to build a unit based on reporting styles.

Davis, S. L. and J. Hunter. "Historical Novels: A Context for Gifted Student Research," *Journal of Reading 33* (1990): 602-06.

> Gifted middle school students were given the problem of evaluating the accuracy of a historical novel in one particular area, such as clothing or transportation. Students selected three topics from a list of general historical reference books, chose a focus, and collected information. Although frustrated at times, students found the progression helpful and the task relevant.

Detherage, J. "Reading, Writing, and Running," *English Journal 69* (1980): 38-41.

> Reports on a unit in which running, literature, running experiences, and personal journals by runners were used to improve reading, writing, and communication skills. Students selected materials from various levels of difficulty. Linking reading, experience, and responsive writing provided a basis for verbalized concept development.

Dinnel, D. and J. Glover. "Advance Organizers: Encoding Manipulations," *Journal of Educational Psychology 77* (1985): 514-21.

> Reports two experiments in which an encoding manipulation such as paraphrasing increased memorability of advance organizers; true organizers (abstract, logical overviews) facilitated memory of the text for undergraduates.

Donlan, D. and H. Singer. "Active Comprehension of Short Stories," paper presented at the annual meeting of the Claremont Reading Conference, Claremont, California (January 1979). [ED 170 705]

Reports the effects on comprehension of pre-posed questions; schema-based student-prepared questions produced significantly higher comprehension than did either teacher-prepared or general student-prepared questions. Includes general schema questions for a short story; illustrates how to apply them in the classroom.

Duffelmeyer, F. A. and B. B. Duffelmeyer. "Developing Vocabulary through Dramatization," *Journal of Reading 23* (1976): 141-43.

Advocates the teaching of vocabulary in language arts through dramatization of small skits. Student experiences with words in context facilitates deeper processing. Register and the use of words in various social stories can be discussed following dramatizations. Includes a sample dramatization and how it can be used in the classroom.

Duin, A. H. and M. F. Graves. "Teaching Vocabulary as a Writing Prompt," *Journal of Reading 32* (1988): 204-11.

Reports a significant difference in vocabulary knowledge and essay use between a seventh-grade control group using traditional vocabulary instruction, and experimental groups receiving intensive vocabulary instruction: common topic, link to experience, networks of meaning, timed matching, and use of words in student writing.

Dupuis, M. M. "The Cloze Procedure: Can It Be used with Literature?" *Reading Improvement 13* (1976): 199-203.

Concludes that the cloze procedure can help teachers match students to appropriate short stories.

Dupuis, M. M. "The Cloze Procedure As a Predictor of Comprehension in Literature," *Journal of Educational Research 74* (1980): 27-33.

Reports studies using tenth-grade students to investigate whether cloze exercises can help English teachers match students' reading levels to appropriate stories. Results suggest the following: 1) The cloze procedure works with short stories as it does with expository writing. 2) The scoring procedures reported, using controlled synonyms as well as exact word replacement, can make the procedure more flexible. 3) The cutoff scores for predicting comprehension and grouping levels may need adjustment from the 44-57 percent cutoffs reported elsewhere.

Dupuis, M. M. and E. N. Askov. *Content Area Reading: An Individualized Approach.* Englewood Cliffs, New Jersey: Prentice-Hall, 1982.

Provides general information about diagnosing student reading skills, using a variety of grouping plans, applying a decision-making model, and organizing instruction through a unit plan. Strategies for developing vocabulary, comprehension, and study skills are included. Of special interest to the English teacher are guidelines for materials selection, ways of using the language-experience approach, discussions of bilingual reading, exceptional children, and dialects in the classroom. Gives an example of an English concept-guide for Romeo and Juliet.

Early, M. "Changing Content in English Curriculum: Reading," J.R. Squire, ed., *The Teaching of English* (1977): 189-96.

Details positive change in attitudes toward teaching reading skills in the English classroom. Describes a variety of possible roles for English teachers in developing reading skills.

Eeds, M. and W. A. Cockrum. "Teaching Word Meanings by Expanding Schemata vs. Dictionary Work vs. Reading in Context," *Journal of Reading 28* (1985): 492-97.

Fifth-grade high and low achievers were assigned randomly to three treatment groups: a group in which teachers aided students in relating 85 target vocabulary words in a novel to their own background knowledge; a group who looked up words and wrote definitions; and a control group who read the words in context. Both immediate testing and delayed testing showed a significant main effect for the schema-based or prior-knowledge vocabulary instruction.

Elkins, D. *Teaching Literature: Designing for Cognitive Development*. Columbus, Ohio: Charles E. Merrill, 1976.
Illustrates several informal tests to evaluate students' reading abilities. Approaches reading difficulties of students in two ways: making the classroom a library with materials available for different reading levels; and providing instruction such as text glossing, previewing, setting purposes, and reading the opening aloud.

Enscion, B., M. Hubler, T. W. Bean, C. C. Smith, and J. V. McKenzie. "Increasing Critical Reading in Junior High Classrooms," *Journal of Reading 30* (1987): 430-39.
Defines critical reading and thinking along with providing three content-area reading strategies for both English and social studies: anticipation-reaction guides, text previews, and three-level study guides based on Raphael's taxonomy. Features examples for applying these strategies in a low-to-average English class.

Estes, T. H. and J. L. Vaughn, Jr. *Reading and Learning in the Content Classroom*. Boston: Allyn & Bacon, 1978.
Provides general information on the role of instruction and strategies for diagnosing students' reading skills, study skills, and vocabulary. Presents a sample English unit on writing. Includes sample reading guides on sequence, cause-and-effect, and different comprehension levels, with a brief discussion of using a structured overview of concepts.

Frager, A. M. "An 'Intelligence' Approach of Vocabulary Teaching," *Journal of Reading 28* (1984): 160-64.
Illustrates development of vocabulary meaning and relationships by the structured overview, categorization, and seizing-the-moment talk-through, along with the subjective approach to vocabulary developed by Manzo.

Gipe, J. P. "Use of Relevant Context Helps Kids Learn New Word Meanings," *Reading Teacher 33* (1980): 398-402.
Reports the effects of four methods of vocabulary development (association, categories, context, and dictionary methods). Finds the context method significantly better for both good and poor readers.

Heitzmann, W. R. *The Newspaper in the Classroom: What Research Says to the Teacher*. Washington, D.C.: National Education Association, 1979, 1986.

Herber, H. L. *Teaching Reading in the Content Area*, second edition. Englewood Cliffs, New Jersey: Prentice-Hall, 1978.

> Develops a philosophy of content-area reading; proposes a three-level guide to aid comprehension (literal, interpretation, and application). Emphasizes and illustrates patterns and relationships in different content areas.

Ignoffo, M. F. "The Thread of Thought: Analogies As a Vocabulary Building Method," *Journal of Reading 23* (1980): 519-21.

> Viewing analogies as an abbreviated form of sentence completion in which the reader supplies part of the context, the author provides examples of classroom use of analogies to build English vocabulary. Lists and illustrates different logical structures of analogies.

Johnson, D. D. and B. V. Johnson. "Highlighting Vocabulary in Inferential Comprehension Instruction," *Journal of Reading 29* (1986): 622-25.

> Discusses ten types of inferences made to comprehend material and illustrate how attention to vocabulary in text allows inferencing based on prior knowledge and elaboration of conceptual schemes. Strongly recommends instruction in inferencing.

Kahn, M. "Two Birds with One Stone or How to Teach Content to Reluctant and Poor Readers," *English Journal 71* (1982): 40-41.

> Details student involvement strategies such as games, quizzes, and play-acting to review content, build vocabulary, encourage wide and pleasurable reading, and develop critical thinking skills.

Kameenui, E. J., D. W. Carnine, and R. Freschi. "Effects of Text Construction and Instructional Procedures for Teaching Word Meanings on Comprehension and Recall," *Reading Research Quarterly 17* (1982): 367-99.

> Reports that in two experiments on comprehension, substituting easy vocabulary words for difficult ones made the text significantly easier to understand, and instruction on difficult vocabulary facilitated comprehension.

Lanberg, W. J. "Helping Reluctant Readers Help Themselves: Interest Inventories," *English Journal 66* (1977): 40-44.

> Presents several types of interest inventories and describes how they can be used to increase student reading both in and outside of English class.

LaRocque, G. E. "Developing Special Skills for Reading Genres," *Reading Improvement 14* (1977): 102-06.

LaRocque, G. E. "We Weren't Born Literate: Reading the Genre," paper presented at the Plains Regional Conference of the International Reading Association. St. Louis, Missouri, February 1975. [ED 103 833]

> Discusses in some detail comprehension problems for different literary genres such as poetry, drama, short stories, essays, novels, and biographies. Discusses ways of enabling students to surmount difficulties of form.

Lee, J. "Increasing Comprehension through the Use of Context Clue Categories," *Journal of Reading 22* (1978): 259-61.

> Details the use of several types of context clues that a teacher may use to increase comprehension: a teacher may develop exercises teaching the use of one particular type of clue using content materials; material with deletions can be presented, and students can pose possible substitutions; one type of word such as nouns or verbs may be deleted to assess how students use syntactic clues of English.

Lehr, F. "Promoting Vocabulary Development," *Journal of Reading*
27 (1984): 656-59.
Describes several strategies that the teacher can use to build
vocabulary beyond the direct instruction of word lists, such as
categorization and humor.

LeSourd, S. J. "Using an Advance Organizer to Set the Schema
for a Multicultural Lesson," *Journal of Reading 32* (1988):
12-18.
Argues for advance organizers for narratives to present cultural information that functions as superordinate ideas to structure comprehension.

Levinson, S. "Teaching Reading and Writing to Limited and
Non-English Speakers in Secondary Schools," *English Journal*
68 (1979): 34-42.
Describes the rationale for using language experience for
transitional English speakers: using art, experience, and discussion, the teacher can give them opportunities to produce highly
meaningful reading material with the vocabulary they know.

Lindquist, A. A. "Applying Bloom's Taxonomy in Writing Reading
Guides," *Journal of Reading 25* (1982): 768-74.
Introduces the author's general reading guides for high-school
classes on five general kinds of literature: the short story, essay,
novel, drama, and poetry. The guides followed a pattern of Before
You Read, As You Read, and After You Read, using questions from
Bloom's taxonomy and major terms, such as plot and theme. In-
cludes sample reading guide (for the novel).

Lubell, M. and B. Townsend. "A Strategy for Teaching Complex
Prose Structures," *Journal of Reading 33* (1989): 102-06.
Identifies three major syntactical difficulties for inexperienced
readers of narrative prose (conditional, periodic, and complex modification). Points out how syntactic difficulty can impede student
understanding even in the absence of vocabulary difficulty and how
students can learn to understand the relationships of structures in
literature.

Lucking, R. A. "A Study of the Effects of Hierarchically-Ordered Questioning Techniques on Adolescents' Responses to Short Stories," *Research in the Teaching of English 10* (1976): 269-76.

Reports the effects of hierarchically ordered comprehension questions based on the Bloom-Clegg taxonomy; finds significantly more interpretation by students and more positive student attitudes after this treatment.

Lutz, Elaine. "ERIC/RCS: Using Folk Literature in Your Reading Program," *Journal of Reading 30* (1986): 76-78.

Defines folk literature, lists a number of reading and writing activities using folk literature, and provides a list of resources.

McAuliffe, S. and R. Brancard. "An Experience-Based Approach to Evaluating Literature," *Journal of Reading 25* (1982): 501-04.

Reports use of Anderson's profundity scale (physical, mental, moral, psychological, and philosophical planes) with small groups of students who chose a focus for examining literature based on their interests (facts, reporting, anthropology, psychology, philosophy, etc.).

McDaniel, M. A., M. Pressley, and P. K. Dunay. "Long-term Retention of Vocabulary after Keyword and Context Learning," *Journal of Educational Psychology 79* (1979): 87-89.

Reports an experiment with approximately 40 students randomly assigned to either a keyword or context condition to learn 30 obscure English words. Keyword students learned the vocabulary at a significantly faster rate, but retention at one week was not significantly different between the two groups.

McKenna, M. C. "A Modified Maze Approach to Teaching Poetry," *Journal of Reading 24* (1981): 391-94.

Describes the maze procedure, and illustrates how the maze technique can be used to teach metrics, assonance, onomatopoeia, metaphor, simile, personification, rhyme, sensory appeal, and diction.

Moore, D. W. and S. A. Moore. "Reading Literature Independently," *Journal of Reading 30* (1987): 596-600.

Classifies the numerous possible instructional goals into three areas: skills, contents, and experiences. Proposes self-questioning by students in both content and psychological frameworks that stimulate extensive thinking within structures and divergent responses. Applies to any piece of literature.

Moore, J. C. *Guidelines for Secondary SSR.* Washington: Department of Health, Education, and Welfare, 1980. [ED 195 955]

Provides guidelines for effective use of sustained silent reading in the secondary classroom. Includes a list of possible materials for reading and discussion of the English classroom and in other content areas.

Nelson, G. L. "Culture's Role in Reading Comprehension: A Schema Theoretical Approach," *Journal of Reading 30* (1987): 424-29.

Measures recall by adult Egyptian students of four pairs of matched, culturally-based stories; student performance was significantly higher for Egyptian-based readings but there was no interaction between passage preference and recall. Concludes that culturally relevant information was necessary for recall with understanding.

O'Brien, D. and S. Schwarzberg. "A Strategy for Improving Teenagers' Understanding and Appreciation of Poetry." *Journal of Reading 30* (1977): 381-86.

Proposes using reading and reaction guides for poetry. Includes sample guide for a poem and directions for classroom use.

O'Shea, L. J., P. T. Sindelar, and D. J. O'Shea. "The Effects of Repeated Readings and Additional Cues on Reading Fluency and Comprehension," *Journal of Reading Behavior 17* (1985): 129-40.

Reports on 30 third-graders who read separate passages one, three, or seven times following cues to attend to either reading rate or meaning. Readers cued to fluency read faster but comprehended less than those cued to comprehension.

Pressley, M., J. R. Levin, and G. E. Miller. "How Does the Keyword Method Affect Vocabulary, Comprehension and Usage?" *Reading Research Quarterly 16* (1981): 213-26.

Reports the results of four related studies in which the experimental group was taught a strategy of taking the familiar part of a new word, such as "cat" from "catkin," and forming an image merging the familiar meaning with the obscure meaning. Indicates significant differences between control subjects and experimental subjects when subjects were tested in a variety of ways in the four studies.

Prince, A. T. and D. S. Mancus. "Enriching Comprehension: A Schema-Altered Basal Reading Lesson," *Reading Research and Instruction 27* (1987): 45-54.

Reports that for students in grades one through five, who were matched by reading level, age, and sex, comprehension was significantly higher for the group taught with an altered format. Within each level, one group was taught three basal stories in a traditional format while the other group was taught in the altered format: enrichment activities were presented at the beginning of the lesson instead of at the end.

Purves, A. C. and V. Rippere. *Elements of Writing about a Literary Work: A Study of Response to Literature*. Champaign, Illinois: National Council of Teachers of English, 1968.

Classifies the elements of writing about literature. Suggests four basic categories: engagement-involvement, perception, interpretation, and evaluation. Suggests that these categories form a framework for response to literature. Provides a scheme for evaluating students' essays.

Readence, J. E., T. W. Bean, and R. S. Baldwin. *Content Area Reading: An Integrated Approach*. Dubuque, Iowa: Kendall/ Hunt, 1989.

Recommends that a directed reading-thinking activity be used with secondary students in all content areas. Emphasizes predicting, setting purposes for reading, self-questioning, discussion, and enrichment activities. Provides examples.

Readence, J. E. and D. Moore. "Responding to Literature: An Alternative to Questioning," *Journal of Reading 23* (1979): 107-11.

    Proposes an alternative to study-guide questions for junior- and senior-high-school English teachers to provide students with structures to evaluate concepts while reading literature. Proposes a procedure for teaching students how to use Harris's six transactional analysis structures to process literature meaningfully as they read.

Readence, J. E. and L. W. Searfoss. "Teaching Strategies for Vocabulary Development," *English Journal 69* (1980): 43-46.

    Includes several games for the English classroom to facilitate categorical development of vocabulary words. Suggests applying the categorization of vocabulary to comprehension of literature by guiding ways of thinking about characters.

Readence, J. E. and L. W. Searfoss. *Reading in the Content Area of Language Arts*. Montgomery: Alabama State Department of Education, 1975. [ED 198 572]

    Illustrates how reading instruction can be combined with other aspects of language arts. Presents vocabulary, comprehension, and study skills with sample activities in a handbook for the language-arts teacher.

Recht, D. E. and L. Leslie. "Effects of Prior Knowledge on Good and Poor Readers' Memory of Text," *Journal of Educational Psychology 80* (1988): 16-20.

    Reports a study of 64 junior-high-school students who read an account of a half-inning of baseball, and then summarized the game and sorted passage ideas for importance. Concludes from verbal and nonverbal assessments that prior knowledge had an effect. Finds no interaction between prior knowledge and ability.

Reed, K. "Assessing Affective Responses to Reading: A Multidimensional Model," *Reading World 19* (1979): 149-56.

    Discusses advantages and disadvantages of a variety of reactive and nonreactive methods of assessment. Outlines a multi-measurement model for assessing student attitudes toward reading.

Roberts, D. E. "The Two-ended Candle," *English Journal* 67 (1978): 54-56.

Discusses briefly fundamental questions about the relationship between the English teacher and secondary reading instruction. States that English teachers can and should work with reading teachers to develop reading skills.

Roberts, T. A. "Development of Pre-instruction versus Experience: Effects on Factual and Inferential Comprehension," *Reading Psychology* 9 (1988): 141-56.

Reports a test of comprehension in fifth- and ninth-grade students with and without club soccer experience who read a narrative about a soccer game after receiving soccer or non-soccer prereading instruction. Demonstrates that knowledge is more powerful than prereading instructions in facilitating comprehension for older students, but that younger students' experience is externally activated by relevant prereading instruction.

Robinson, H. A. *Teaching Reading and Study Strategies: The Content Areas,* second edition. Boston: Allyn & Bacon, 1978.

Discusses the specific strategies students must develop to comprehend various genres. Proposes a traditional analysis framework for discussion (exposition and argument/narration and description). The analysis of literature using a profundity scale may be of interest to the classroom teacher as a way to direct analysis at different comprehension levels. Includes a sample of adapting materials and a sample concept guide.

Roe, B. D., B. D. Stood, and P. C. Burns. *Reading Instruction in Secondary Schools.* Chicago: Rand McNally, 1978.

Provides general comprehension and vocabulary building information for the content areas, and a special section for the language-arts teacher. Includes a sample literature lesson.

Rygiel, M. A. "Preparing Students to Read," *English Journal 71* (1982): 42-44.

> Provides an example of a directed reading activity of a difficult poem, based on some knowledge of physics. Could be used as a model in English for three aspects: preparation, guidance, and extension of meaning.

Sager, M. "Exploiting the Reading-Writing Connection to Engage Students in Text," *Journal of Reading 33* (1989): 40-43.

> Proposes using study guides as a base to move to an active engagement with text. Assigns additional related readings about history, social aspects, or biographies to make each student in a small group an expert with additional knowledge to share; small groups share knowledge, vocabulary lists, and then write a similar group story to which each student writes an individual ending.

Sampson, M. R., W. J. Valmong, and R. V. Allen. "The Effects of Instructional Cloze on the Comprehension Vocabulary and Divergent Production of Third-Grade Students," *Reading Research Quarterly 17* (1982): 389-99.

> Reports that substituting instructional cloze materials and lessons in reading centers for 15 weeks resulted in significantly better comprehension and divergent production for an experimental group of third-grade students, but that no significant difference was found in vocabulary development.

Singer, H. and D. Dolan. *Reading and Learning from Text.* Boston: Little, Brown, 1980.

> Uses a topical unit in English literature to illustrate single-text strategies: gloss, directed reading-thinking activity, learning-from-text guides, and multitext strategies (concept development, inquiry, and projects).

Singer, H. and D. Dolan. "Active Comprehension: Problem-Solving Schema with Question Generation for Comprehension of Complex Short Stories," *Reading Research Quarterly 17* (1982): 166-86.

> Reports on fifteen eleventh-grade students, randomly assigned to an experimental group, who were taught to construct

story-specific questions for complex short stories from schema-general questions, and a control group that answered teacher-proposed questions. Criterion-referenced tests revealed significantly greater comprehension for the experimental group.

Soltis, J. M. and S. W. Pflaum. "The Effect of Instruction in Connectives on Reading Comprehension," *Reading World 19* (1979): 179-84.

Investigates the effects of instruction in connectives on the comprehension of seventh- and eighth-grade inner-city subjects. A significant effect of instruction was found on a cloze-like connective text but not on the *Standard Test Lessons in Reading*.

Stauffer, R. G. *Teaching Reading as a Thinking Process*. New York: Harper and Row, 1969.

Presents the directed reading-thinking activity in an outstanding way.

Styles, K. and G. Cavanagh. "Language across the Curriculum: The Art of Questioning and Responding," *English Journal 69* (1980): 24-27.

Argues for developing student thinking through abstract representation of thoughts and feelings in precise language. Discusses belief that different types of thinking skills are fostered by different questioning levels; proposes a school language-arts policy to enable students to grasp logical thinking patterns by responding to questioning at different levels.

Tchudi, S. N. and S. J. Tchudi. *The English Teacher's Handbook*. Cambridge, Massachusetts: Portsmouth, New Hampshire, 1991.

Emphasizes individualization and variety in the chapter on reading. Details reading general or genre-related skills, diagnosis, grouping, and design of units. Suggests many activities and possible resources in reading for the English teacher.

Theofield, M. B. "ESSO Self-Concept and Basic Reading in a Secondary School Program," paper presented at the annual convention of the International Reading Association. New York, May 1975. [ED 110 951]

Describes an integrated English/social-studies curriculum for secondary students with learning problems. Details the integration of reading and study skills, coping skills, special education, and the building of self-concept in the English and social studies content areas, using personal journals as a basis for composition correction, language experience, and private communication with the teacher.

Thomas, D. G. and J. E. Readence. "Effects of Differential Vocabulary Instruction and Lesson Frameworks on the Reading Comprehension of Primary Children," *Reading Research and Instruction* 27 (1988): 1-12.

Compares traditional basal reader vocabulary instruction with two other frameworks: a) reconciled reading lesson (RRL) and b) list-group-label. The dependent measure was comprehension; the subjects were 66 second-graders. The RRL involved using the basal enrichment activities before reading rather than after. Students in the RRL group outperformed the other two groups on comprehension tests.

Thomas, E. L. and H. A. Robinson. *Improving Reading in Every Class*, third edition. Boston: Allyn & Bacon, 1982.

Presents general strategies for building comprehension and vocabulary, and specific activities that the English teacher may use to build readiness, provide advance organizers, and overcome initial reading difficulties. Includes a sample reading guide for comprehension and vocabulary building games and activities.

Weisberg, R. A. "A Comparison of Good and Poor Readers' Ability to Comprehend Explicit and Implicit Information in Short Stories Based on Two Modes of Presentation," *Research in the Teaching of English* 13 (1979): 337-51.

Investigates fourth-grade readers' comprehension of six short stories presented through visual and auditory modes and tested through free and probed recall. Probes three types of inferencing.

White, R. H. "Reading Skills in the English Class," *The Clearing House 51* (1977): 32-35.

Outlines a plan for integrating and managing the development of reading skills in English. Suggests a program of free reading, interest-centered projects, teacher-directed units, and planned development of language skills. Contains several charts to facilitate planning and management of small and large groups.

2
Reading in Foreign Language Study

Michele M. Tellep
The Pennsylvania State University

John E. Carlson
Virginia Wesleyan College

Reading in Foreign Language Study

The popularity of foreign language study is increasing. The President's Commission on Foreign Languages and International Studies may deserve some credit for public awareness of the importance of the field, but the commission itself merely reflects the United States' increasing diversity, both ethnically and linguistically. More and more Americans need and want to communicate in languages other than English.

With this need for students to develop the ability to communicate in other languages, foreign-language instruction is changing to meet these needs. This chapter is about outstanding changes based on current research that may help educators both to teach reading skills in the target language and to develop programs to increase proficiency.

Trends and Patterns in Teaching Foreign Languages

The current trend in the teaching of foreign languages is towards expanding the student's language and thinking skills. Less emphasis on decoding or word-by-word reading has given way to more emphasis on the global comprehension of reading passages.

This global understanding of reading passages is reinforced through social interaction in classroom activities. Students gain verbal practice by retelling stories in either their native language or the target language using the new language's patterns that they have learned. Reading a passage becomes an active, rather than a passive, exercise.

Martin Levine and George Haus noted the effect of relevant background knowledge on reading comprehension in foreign languages.[1] Results of their study indicate that background knowledge is a significant factor in reading comprehension. Background knowledge may be more important to the global comprehension of passages than is language level.

Because of the lessened emphasis on decoding and word-by-word translation, oral reading has lost the popularity it once held in foreign-language classes. Unless the student is already orally proficient in the target language, the ability to sound out words correctly is deemed not especially helpful in the comprehension process.[2] Researchers relate that the once-popular grammar-translation and audio-lingual methods of instruction have lost their impact in classrooms where language proficiency is the goal. In the proficiency-oriented curriculum, students learn to use four skills—speaking, reading, writing, and listening—to communicate in an "authentic" context. Accuracy of grammar and pronunciation, though important, is not the primary goal of instruction at the start.

Audiotapes, once the mainstay of audio-lingual instruction, now help students understand longer reading passages in the target language. Students listen to stories on tapes while following along in the book. These activities, together with computers for drill and practice, can help educators give the immediate feedback necessary to learners studying a foreign language.[3]

Another trend influencing the field is the growing expansion of foreign-language programs in elementary schools. There are sound reasons for beginning second-language study early, one being that younger students are not at all intimidated about imitating strange sounds. FLES (Foreign Language in the Elementary School) programs, taught totally or partially in the foreign language, give students limited listening, speaking, reading, and writing skills, along with some cultural awareness.

FLEX (Foreign Language EXperience) programs, usually taught in English, introduce English-speaking students to other languages, focusing on cultural awareness and limited language skills.

Immersion programs, generally the most extensive and intense styles of foreign language education, involve teaching all or part of the curriculum in the other language. These programs provide the most opportunity for fluency in the foreign language. Repeated exposure to meaningful language is necessary for maximal second-language acquisition.[4]

The trend in some schools has also been to provide a diverse selection in the languages offered. A number of the less commonly taught (LCT) languages have appeared in districts as a means of promoting an expansion of course offerings.

Barbara Lomas Rusterholz indicated the need for foreign languages to be included as part of the business curriculum.[5] One has a considerable edge on one's competitors if one can communicate in the language of the client. Graduates with foreign-language ability also can offer employers an understanding of the cultural context in which business transactions take place.

Many leaders in the field caution that much needs to be done to make programs less diverse and more comprehensive. Most language programs are neither long enough nor thorough enough to make the student proficient. Instruction requires ample time to encourage students to do something with the language, not just know about it.

Skills and Strategies for Reading

June Phillips noted that the successful reading of any passage depends upon a combination of linguistic knowledge, cognitive skill, and general experience and knowledge of the world. An important step that teachers can take to improve reading in the second language is to use a student's background knowledge of the topic. Prior knowledge is critical in the understanding of passages.[6] The lack of a relevant schema, a framework into which to put the information being read, inhibits comprehension.[7]

Another critical component of reading comprehension in foreign languages is the student's skill in playing the contextual guessing game. Students need to be encouraged to estimate the meaning of a word from contextual clues.[8] They learn new words best in semantically related groups that are also somehow related to words and information that they already know.[9]

Encouraging students to anticipate and predict will help them read actively for meaning.[10] Owen F. Boyle and Suzanne F. Peregoy suggested the use of the directed-reading-thinking activity (DRTA) to provide a scaffold like the ones used by experienced readers so that the language learner can ask questions of a text and predict what will happen next.[11]

Questioning and predicting skills were described by Phillips. Others supported the use of questioning and predicting skills in a five-stage process.[12] The five stages are prereading, skimming and scanning, decoding, comprehension, and transfer of integrating skills. This process is adaptable for teacher-directed classroom instruction or individualized reading instruction. It has potential for computer-aided instruction.

In the first stage, prereading, the goal is to make the conditions of learning such that the reader has the best possible chance of advancing understanding. The emphasis is on the interaction of the reader's mind with the written text.[13] In this first stage, background knowledge becomes the basis for understanding—a basis that will continue to be essential in subsequent stages. Guy Arcuri promoted the use of a relevant writing activity during prereading to ensure more efficient comprehension in subsequent stages.[14]

Skimming and scanning are the two steps of the second stage. The teacher first asks the students to skim for the gist of the passage. Rightness or wrongness is not an issue; the exercise is meant to force eyes over the text a first time. Then the students are asked to scan the material for specific information pertinent to their understanding of the passage. Skimming and scanning facilitate the contextual guessing process and help the student acquire a global view of the passage's meaning. Skillful readers do some scanning while attempting to skim.

Decoding is essential for intensive reading and locating specific information. The goal of this third stage is to reduce the amount of effort required for decoding to a minimum. When students begin dealing with larger chunks of reading material, they will begin to recognize that if they understand larger meaningful phrases of a text, they will not have to work so hard at word-for-word translation.

In the comprehension stage, a range of reading skills is assessed. Are inferencing and evaluation occurring? It is essential to convince the reader to use information given in the passage and to infer meaning by reading between the lines and from the reader's background of experiences. Comprehension checks take many different forms in real-world reading. The classroom can reflect this variety as well. Extensive research done with the cloze procedure has identified it as a valuable device to improve and check comprehension in this fourth stage.[15]

In the final stage, the transfer of integrating skills, the focus changes from the passage to the process of reading. This is the time to use exercises whose sole intent is enhancing reading skills. During these reading activities, learners must develop cognitive strategies that will help them apply their comprehension skills to make a transfer to future selections in the foreign language. Practice in recognizing word-family patterns, using marginal glosses and guides, locating main ideas, outlining supporting details, correcting wrong guesses about the meanings of words, and making inferences, enable students to become better readers in their second language. [16]

Phillips encouraged educators to understand that second-language learning is complex; it requires processing information with language skills that are still developing and that may not be firmly established in the learner's mind. [17] An understanding of these five stages may support teaching strategies that encourage active reading. Active reading requires using cognitive strategies that learners have developed at various levels in their native language. The transfer of these cognitive strategies is needed for them to become better readers of a second language.[18]

Textbooks and Technology

Texts and other materials need to be adapted to the trend toward a proficiency-based program. Research has shown the value of using authentic materials to give students a basis in the culture. According to theory, students acquire a language when they understand messages in that language. Reading for meaning is a way of directly increasing second-language proficiency. Using texts written in the target language gives the student the opportunity to engage in an authentic act of reading for meaning.[19]

Research has also shown that readability (text difficulty measured by syntactic complexity and word difficulty) plays an important part in reading comprehension.[20] A text that registers above the frustration level of the student destroys motivation in the student to study the language further. Ruth A. Hough and Joanne R. Nurss suggested using difficult texts in story-reading activities.[21]

All children find story reading with adults pleasurable. Story reading with related follow-up activities helps clarify meaning; it sustains attention while providing additional context. Audiotapes and computers have great potential in the foreign-language classroom. Audiotapes can let students listen while they read longer passages. Tapes model authentic pronunciation and give students an opportunity to deal with the spoken word. Computers provide the individual feedback that is most beneficial during the decoding and intensive reading stages. Computers confirm guesses or redirect the student to accurate information. Because one must be challenged upward if higher-level skills are to be achieved, the issues of proficiency scales and reading guidelines need to be addressed in future research. Textbooks scaled down to the students' proficiency levels may or may not satisfy the needs of the foreign-language classroom.

The issue of less commonly taught (LCT) languages is a growing concern, especially because of the unavailability of materials. Teacher training in new reading strategies related to foreign languages needs further attention. Studies of the strategies being used in classrooms, and the results of studies on these strategies, need to be published. The following annotated list of publications related to the field of reading in the foreign-language content area is a resource for awareness of new trends, and a stimulation to generate more questions leading to further research.

Resources

The following organizations may be helpful in providing materials for strengthening foreign-language programs:

Advocates for Language Learning
P. O. Box 4964
Culver City, Ca 90231
(213) 397-2448

American Council on the Teaching of Foreign Languages
6 Executive Plaza
P. O. Box 1077
Yonkers, NY 10701
(914) 963-8830

The American Forum on Global Education
45 John Street
New York, NY 10038
(212) 732-8606

Center for Applied Linguistics/ERIC Clearinghouse on
Languages and Linguistics
1118 22nd Street, N.W.
Washington, DC 20037
(202 429-9292

Joint National Committee for Languages/
National Council for Languages and International Studies
300 I Street N.E., Suite 211
Washington, DC 20002
(202) 546-7855

Modern Language Association/Foreign Language Programs
10 Astor Place
New York, NY 10003-6981
(212) 475-9500

National Foreign Language Center
1619 Massachusetts Avenue, N.W.
Washington, DC 20036
(202) 667-8100

Notes

1. M. G. Levine and G. J. Haus, "The Effect of Background Knowledge on the Reading Comprehension of Second Language Learners," *Foreign Language Annals 18* (1985): 391-97.

2. J. K. Phillips, "Practical Implications of Recent Research in Reading," *Foreign Language Annals 17* (1984): 285-96; M. Trayer, "Applying Research in Reading to the Foreign Language Classroom," *Hispania 73* (1990): 829-32.

3. Phillips, *op. cit.*

4. S. D. Krashen, *Principles and Practices in Second Language Acquisition*, Oxford: Pergamon Press, 1982.

5. B. L. Rusterholz, "Reading Strategies for the Business Foreign Language Class," *Foreign Language Annals 20* (1987): 427-33.

6. Phillips, *loc. cit.*

7. E. J. Melendez and Robert H. Pritchard, "Applying Schema Theory to Foreign Language Reading," *Foreign Language Annals 18* (1985): 399-403.

8. J. V. Aspatore, "But I Don't Know All the Words!" *Foreign Language Annals 17* (1984): 297-99; M. Zvetina, "From Research to Pedagogy: What Do L2 Reading Studies Suggest?" *Foreign Language Annals 20* (1987): 233-38.

9. S. A. Hague, "Vocabulary Instruction: What L1 Can Learn from L1," *Foreign Language Annals 20* (1987): 217-25.

10. Melendez and Pritchard, *op. cit.*

11. O. F. Boyle and S.F. Peregoy, "Literacy Scaffolds: Strategies for First- and Second-Language Readers and Writers," *The Reading Teacher 44* (1990): 194-200.

12. Levine and Haus, *op. cit.:* 391-97; Alice C. Omaggio, "Making Reading Comprehensible," *Foreign Language Annals 17* (1984): 305-08; Renate A. Schulz, "Second Language Reading Research: From Theory to Practice," *Foreign Language Annals 17* (1984): 309-12; E.W. Tetrault, "In Support of a Natural Order in Second Language Reading," *Foreign Language Annals 17* (1984): 313-15.

13. M. A. Barnett, "Teaching Reading Strategies: How Methodology Affects Language Course Articulation," *Foreign Language Annals 21* (1988): 109-16.

14. G. Arcuri, "Pre-reading and Pre-writing Activities to Prepare and Motivate Foreign Language Students to Read Short Stories," *Hispania 73* (1990): 262-266.

15. J. Caufield and W.C. Smith, "The Reduced Redundancy Test and the Cloze Procedure as Measures of Global Language Proficiency," *Modern Language Journal 65* (1981): 59-66; R. Meyer and Emery Tetrault, "Open Your Clozed Minds: Using Cloze Exercises to Teach Foreign Language Reading," *Foreign Language Annals 19* (1986): 409-14; Omaggio, *op. cit.*

16. J. N. Davis, "Facilitating Effects of Marginal Glosses on Foreign Language Reading," *Modern Language Journal 73* (1989): 41-48.

17. Phillips, *op. cit.*

18. H. Z. Loew, "Developing Strategic Reading Skills," *Foreign Language Annals 17* (1984): 301-03.

19. A. E. Babcock, "Teaching Reading: Asking the Right Questions," *Foreign Language Annals 18* (1985): 385-87; Tretault, *op. cit.*

20. R. A. Schulz, "A Second Language Reading Research: From Theory to Practice," *Foreign Language Annals 17* (1984): 309-12.

21. R.A. Hough, J.R. Nurss, and D.S. Enright, "Story Reading with Limited English Speaking Children in the Regular Classroom," *The Reading Teacher 39* (1986): 510-14.

Annotated Bibliography

Arcuri, Guy. "Pre-reading and Pre-writing Activities to Prepare and Motivate Foreign Language Students to Read Short Stories," *Hispania 73* (1990): 262-66.

    Proposes the following procedure for short-story reading comprehension steps to prepare and motivate students to read in a second language: 1) State purpose of prereading/prewriting activity. 2) Solicit from the students personal responses or reactions to prepared guiding questions. 3) Model correct speech, introduce new vocabulary, or develop complex thoughts by connecting and combining ideas in the students' responses. 4) Choose a writing assignment with a purpose that allows the student to "invest" even more in the reading of the story. 5) State purpose for reading the short story as it relates to the writing assignment. Includes examples of activities for two short stories.

Aspatore, Jilleen V. "But I Don't Know All the Words!" *Foreign Language Annals 17* (1984): 297-99.

    Suggests exercises related to specific reading skills necessary to second-language acquisition. Emphasizes the definitions required for important words in passages and for the use of contextual clues to obtain the gist of the reading material. Makes practical suggestions with comments justified by classroom experience and application.

Babcock, Arthur E. "Teaching Reading: Asking the Right Questions," *Foreign Language Annals 18* (1985): 385-87.

    Advocates reading in foreign language classes as an important source of the comprehensible input that fosters second-language acquisition. Reexamines some widely held ideas about reading materials. Suggests choosing materials to encourage reading for meaning, the use of questioning techniques, and the use of authentic materials.

Barnett, Marva A. "Teaching Reading Strategies: How Methodology Affects Language Course Articulation," *Foreign Language Annals 21* (1988): 109-16.

    Examines whether university-level French students trained during the second semester to use effective reading strategies and skills demonstrated better reading comprehension and performed better in the third semester than did their untrained peers. The experimental reading activities were derived from recent first-language and second-language reading process theory and research; a sample text, exercises, and lesson plan appear together with teacher and student reactions to the experimental reading practice.

Boyle, Owen F. and Suzanne F. Peregoy. "Literacy Scaffolds: Strategies for First- and Second-Language Readers and Writers," *The Reading Teacher 44* (1990): 194-200.

Defines literacy scaffolds as temporary frameworks that offer students immediate access to the meaning and pleasure of print. Explains why literacy scaffolding applies to both first- and second-language learners. Offers criteria for teachers to apply in developing scaffolds. Illustrates with scaffolding activities that the authors used with elementary school children.

Caufield, Joan and William C. Smith. "The Reduced Redundancy Test and the Cloze Procedure as Measures of Global Language Proficiency," *Modern Language Journal 65* (1981): 59-66.

Demonstrates that either a cloze test or a reduced redundancy test (also called the noise test) could be used in place of the MLA total score or an interview test. Recommends the cloze procedure rather than reduced redundancy in view of the relative ease of construction of the cloze test.

Davis, James N. "Facilitating Effects of Marginal Glosses on Foreign Language Reading," *Modern Language Journal 73* (1989): 41-48.

Examines the effect of marginal glosses on improving the comprehension of foreign-language literary text. Students who received a vocabulary list and guide before or during reading recalled significantly more of the passage than those who did not.

Hague, Sally A. "Vocabulary Instruction: What L_2 Can Learn from L_1," *Foreign Language Annals 20* (1987): 217-25.

Summarizes five theories on the relationship between word knowledge and comprehension of text in first-language acquisition. Reviews recent research that demonstrated this relationship. Explores possible implications for second-language researchers and practitioners.

Hough, Ruth A., Joanne R. Nurss, and D. Scott Enright. "Story Reading with Limited English Speaking Children in the Regular Classroom," *The Reading Teacher 39* (1986): 510-14.
Reports results of research on story reading and second-language acquisition. Proposes specific strategies for using story reading to assist language-minority students in grades one through six. Illustrates specific ways in which story reading helps develop language skills for enjoyment of reading and interactive activities.

Krashen, Stephen D. *Principles and Practices in Second Language Acquisition.* Oxford: Pergamon Press, 1982.
Advocates a language teaching methodology with emphasis on second-language acquisition and learning in a natural order. This natural order is determined by the frequency with which elements actually occur in the foreign language. Provides activities.

Levine, Martin G. and George J. Haus. "The Effect of Background Knowledge on the Reading Comprehension of Second Language Learners," *Foreign Language Annals 18* (1985): 391-97.
Reports the effect of relevant background knowledge on the reading comprehension of high school students of Spanish as a foreign language. Background knowledge is a significant factor that affects reading comprehension, and it may be more important than language level in comprehension.

Loew, Helene Z. "Developing Strategic Reading Skills," *Foreign Language Annals 17* (1984): 301-303.
Argues that reading should be taught as a set of highly interdependent skills, none of which can be effectively learned and practiced in isolation. Defines strategic reading skills according to three categories: declarative, procedural, and conditional. Proposes five means of translating the related research into practice: 1) Determine reading goals and characteristics of the text. 2) Choose appropriate strategies. 3) Connect ideas in text. 4) Monitor comprehension. 5) Develop positive attitudes toward reading.

Melendez, E. Jane and Robert H. Pritchard. "Applying Schema Theory to Foreign Language Reading," *Foreign Language Annals 18* (1985): 399-403.

   Describes reading as an interactive process. The schematic information that a reader possesses for the topic of a given text is as important to adequate comprehension as the information presented on the printed page. Describes several classroom activities for use before, during, and after reading.

Meyer, Renée and Emery Tetrault. "Open Your Clozed Minds: Using Cloze Exercises to Teach Foreign Language Reading," *Foreign Language Annals 19* (1986): 409-14.

   States that various types of cloze-like exercises are effective integrative tasks that allow students to operate meaningfully on authentic foreign-language materials. Gives examples of incomplete texts for use as part of a general sequence of reading activities in class.

Meyer, Renée and Emery Tetrault. "Getting Started: Reading Techniques That Work from the Very First Day," *Foreign Language Annals 21* (1988): 423-31.

   Reflects on workshops at Department of Defense schools and other institutions, where teachers who like the idea of a proficiency-based approach argue, nevertheless, that it will not work for their languages, at least not with beginners. Sets forth a number of reading techniques and activities that demonstrate the feasibility of using real foreign-language texts and proficiency-oriented tasks at the earliest stages of a beginning course.

Omaggio, Alice C. "Making Reading Comprehensible," *Foreign Language Annals 17* (1984): 305-08.

   Discusses some of the practical issues involved in teaching second-language reading skills. Reviews and summarizes the literature.

Phillips, June K. "Practical Implications of Recent Research in Reading," *Foreign Language Annals 17* (1984): 285-96.

   Summarizes recent research findings and promotes efficient strategies for dealing with the language in reading selections and for playing the contextual guessing game skillfully. Recommends a five-stage process adaptable for teacher-directed classroom instruction, for individualized reading instruction, and possibly for computer-aided instruction. Illustrates the five stages.

Rusterholz, Barbara L. "Reading Strategies for the Business Foreign Language Class," *Foreign Language Annals 20* (1987): 427-33.

Argues that teaching students how to read newspapers and magazines in the target language can prepare them to make an important contribution to their future employers. Examines current principles of reading pedagogy, including prereading activities, schema theory, the importance of background knowledge, and postreading activities. Provides concrete examples of applications in the business foreign-language classroom.

Schulz, Renate A. "A Second Language Reading Research: From Theory to Practice," *Foreign Language Annals 17* (1984): 309-12.

Discusses the implications of reading research for second-language instruction. Gives attention to specific areas of linguistic knowledge, background knowledge, reading aloud, cloze procedure, and text selection. Emphasizes improving the teaching of reading and foreign languages.

Tetrault, Emery W. "In Support of a Natural Order in Second Language Reading," *Foreign Language Annals 17* (1984): 313-15.

Supports research trends and patterns relating to teaching foreign languages. Reviews research for the foreign-language teacher by synthesizing terminology, strategies, and background reading skills needed for language acquisition.

Trayer, M. "Applying Research in Reading to the Foreign Language Classroom," *Hispania 73* (1990): 829-32.

Provides summary of research-based reading strategies, which, when used effectively in the foreign-language classroom, can enhance reading success and generate more interest in the students. Summarizes first-language research on reading. Applies first-language research to the second-language classroom. Suggests reading strategies for use in the foreign-language classroom.

Zvetina, M. "From Research to Pedagogy: What Do L2 Reading Studies Suggest?" *Foreign Language Annals 20* (1987): 233-38.

Summarizes popular perspectives on the first-language reading process as expressed in recent articles on various aspects of both first- and second-language reading tasks. Presents pertinent studies of second-language reading. Analyzes these studies for their pedagogical implications.

3 Reading in Math

Linda A. Hoover
The Pennsylvania State University

James F. Nolan
The Pennsylvania State University

Integrating Math and Reading: Facing the Challenge

According to Joan Curry, "Mathematics is a highly condensed system of language."[1] Because reading in mathematics involves not only decoding words but also attaching literal meaning to mathematical symbols, and discerning the relationship between the two, teaching reading in the content area of mathematics is a particularly challenging task.[2]

Further complicating the integration of the two disciplines is the usual practice of teaching reading skills and processes separate from mathematics. Thus, the transfer from reading class to mathematics is difficult[3] but essential.

An especially difficult problem faced by students is that the reading level normally associated with a particular grade is often lower than the level necessary to comprehend that grade's mathematics text.[4] Even the best of readers can have difficulty making the transition from a narrative text, with its plot, characters, and setting, to a content-area expository text with a hierarchical pattern of main idea and supporting details.[5] Math texts are written in an especially terse and unimaginative style; they offer few verbal context clues to help with decoding meaning; and they lack the redundancy that makes writing easier to read.[6] Another complicating factor is the variety of eye movements required to read math. The left-to-right rule often does not apply in reading number operations, as the set of diagrams on page 65 makes graphically clear.[7]

The classic example of a reading pitfall in math class is the "word problem." Students of mathematics who have not previously developed the necessary reading skills might be able to do the arithmetic if only they could read the problem with understanding. Harry Singer and Dan Donlan cited several difficulties that students encounter in "story problems":

We read and reread mathematics...
LEFT TO RIGHT sometimes,
but other times we read

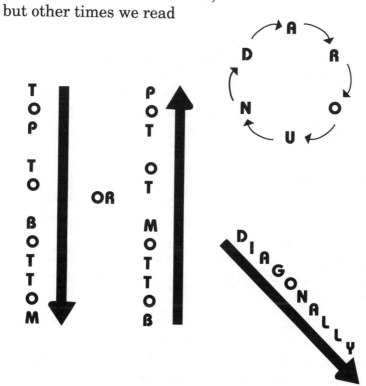

F→O→L→L→O→W→ T→H→E→ A→R→R→O→W

FORWARD and DRAWKCAB

1) synonyms rather than mathematical terms usually associated with a formula (for example, rate instead
   of *speed*)

2) information presented in the word problem in an order
   different from the order of the formula that students know

3) extraneous facts[8]

Classroom teachers can help students overcome these stumbling blocks to reading in the content area of mathematics if they
become aware of the problems, learn how to help students develop essential skills, and have their own instructional strategies to promote skill development.

Help from the Research

Empirical research concerning reading in mathematics has
concentrated in the areas of word-problem solving and vocabulary development. As early as 1970, N. Wesley Earp reported the
existence of a fairly large body of research indicating that specific
instruction in reading word problems helped pupils improve problem solving. [9]

A decade later, Deborah O'Mara estimated that approximately
35 percent of the errors on math achievement tests may actually
have been due to problems in reading.[10] Similarly, Hunter Ballew
and James Cunningham determined that 29 percent of the sixth-
grade students in their study found reading to be the main source
of their difficulty in solving word-problems.[11]

Philip Rubens studied the problem-solving abilities of two
groups of students. One group was instructed by a math teacher
who, having little background in reading, concentrated on math
skills. The other group was instructed by a reading teacher with
little math background, who concentrated on reading skills.
Those students instructed by the reading teacher were able to

solve math word-problems more accurately than the other group.[12]

Other studies have indicated that rewriting word-problems to make them easier to read and to pattern them after the oral language of students seems to be an effective strategy for facilitating problem solving.[13] For example, Anne Ferguson and Jo Fairburn told about a teacher who asked groups of students to write story-problems to match simple computational problems. Later, the teacher wrote these stories on an experience chart for the class. As the students' proficiency increased, they began working independently.[14] This approach, known as "language experience," involves the students personally, and it provides concrete connections between mathematics and the real world.[15]

S. Alan Cohen and Georgia Stover identified important factors to keep in mind while rewriting word-problems to make them easier:

- simplify vocabulary

- reduce sentence length

- add diagrams

- change the order in which the information is presented to follow the order of the formula

- remove extraneous information[16]

K. Denise Muth reported that the presence of extraneous information in word-problems reduces the accuracy of finding solutions and "can impose a formidable demand on students' limited processing capabilities."[17]

Research concerning the effects of providing specific skills instruction in the area of math vocabulary has added support to the importance of teaching reading skills in math classes. Using gain scores of the Stanford Diagnostic Test in math vocabulary and problem solving as the dependent variables, George McNinch found that even small amounts of direct and planned

teaching of vocabulary terms produced dramatic results in comprehension.[18] Aldona Skrypa concurred; she reported on studies
indicating that teaching math vocabulary leads to improved
scores in both vocabulary and problem-solving.[19] Thus, several
strong links among reading skills, knowledge of math vocabulary, and problem-solving ability exist.

Developing Essential Skills

The specific skills required to read mathematics may be
separated into a sequence of four general steps:

1) perceiving and decoding symbols

2) attaching literal meaning, or concept development

3) interpreting literal meanings in terms of mathematical
   symbols, or inferential comprehension

4) applying these interpretations to the solution of word-
   problems.[20]

The first step, perceiving and decoding symbols, requires the
ability to associate words with the corresponding symbols, both
numeric (1/2) and non-numeric (+, =); to express ideas in pictures; and to recognize words on sight.[21]

To take the second step and grasp the literal meaning of
vocabulary, students must possess the ability to sift through the
general and technical meanings of words.[22] Mathematical vocabulary includes the following:

• general vocabulary from everyday experiences

• technical words unique to a particular area of
  mathematics (e.g., sine, cosine)

• words with a meaning in mathematical language
  different from everyday usage (e.g., prime, radical)

- words that signal a mathematical process
  (e.g., multiply, divide)[23]

The specific skills required for concept or vocabulary development are phonetic analysis, structural analysis, and contextual analysis of the words found in the mathematics text.[24] Phonetic analysis, or sounding out the words from the way they are spelled, benefits only beginning readers.

Taking the next step, teaching structural analysis entails exposing students familiar to words that have been extended by common affixes, and showing them how to separate the extended words into meaningful parts. For example, "ir/rational" consists of the root word "rational" and the prefix "ir-." This method also is subject to limitations; it is successful only with words of more than one syllable in which the root retains its own meaning. Contextual analysis involves using the environment of the word to decode its meaning.[25]

The third step in reading math, interpreting the literal meanings in symbols, includes understanding the main idea;[26] understanding supporting details;[27] interpreting graphs, formulas, and equations; and recognizing the reversibility of math sentences.[28]

Fourth and finally, specific skills required for applying these interpretations to solving word-problems include analyzing the given information and identifying it as sufficient, insufficient, or extraneous;[29] choosing the correct operation through metacognitive behaviors;[30] using the appropriate sequence clues;[31] and translating from general language to mathematical terms to numeric symbols and back again to general meaning.[32] Teachers can help students develop these skills.

Implementing Instructional Strategies

General strategies especially helpful in developing the ability to read mathematics successfully are similar to those strategies used in other content areas.

- emphasizing the function and importance of special textbook sections such as the preface, glossary, table of contents, and index

- teaching students to draw appropriate conclusions from scanning pictures, illustrations, and other accompanying graphic aids

- clarifying the crucial role that punctuation plays in avoiding ambiguity (e.g., parentheses indicate which operation to perform first)[33]

Another general strategy is to teach students the specialized study skill of adjusting their reading rate to a slower, more deliberate pace than when reading literature.[34]

Integrating children's literature into content-area classrooms has become an ingredient crucial to the process of successfully transferring reading skills to mathematics class, while simultaneously introducing, reinforcing, or broadening mathematical skills and concepts. For example, John Madison and Roslynn Seidenstein integrated the reading of Madeleine L'Engle's *A Wrinkle in Time* (suggested reading level, grades 4-8) with a mathematics lesson on computation and problem-solving.

Raffaella Borasi, John Sheedy, and Marjorie Siegel tout the power of literature in learning mathematics at the secondary level. For example, they use a story entitled "Moving around the City," set in a metropolis with a regular pattern of streets, to exemplify non-Euclidean geometry. The authors explain: "In such a city, diagonals do not exist, and the rules that define distance as the length of a straight line connecting two points do not always apply.[35] By providing the context of a realistic situation rather than a textbook exercise, literature can suggest more genuine problems for students to solve, and consequently "invite them to take a more active and critical stance in their learning of mathematics."[36]

Joan Curry suggested using a directed reading activity (DRA) in mathematics class, thereby systematizing students' approach to the text through the following steps:

1) Establish a readiness phase to provide motivation and activate students' prior knowledge.

2) Develop vocabulary.

3) Set the purpose for reading through a series of springboard questions.[37]

In addition, using both visual and kinesthetic aids and allowing students to manipulate concrete objects physically have proved effective in developing reading skills for mathematics.[38]

Teachers can help students learn to recognize and decode symbols by providing practice in matching words, symbols, and mathematical expressions through flash cards, puzzles, and oral and written exercises.[39] Examples include word-find exercises that require students to circle key words, and oral exercises in which students write the corresponding symbols for words and expressions read aloud by the teacher.

Several strategies have proved effective in promoting vocabulary or concept development. Allison Brennan and William Dunlap recommended the previously mentioned phonetic, structural, and contextual analysis. Cherlyn Hall suggested using modified cloze exercises, or word-completion tasks, to reinforce context clues. Stephen Krulik recommended that students keep a notebook or "dictionary" of technical terms (*polynomial*) and general terms used in special ways in mathematics (*base*). Many educators highly recommend structured overviews, or advanced organizers, that graphically depict the relationship between new concept words and concepts previously learned.[40]

Suggestions for strategies to promote skills in interpreting literal meaning are less plentiful. The Florida report suggested that teachers routinely question students regarding the main ideas of passages that they have read and the details that support each main idea.[41] Lucille Strain commented on the value of higher-level, or interpretive, questioning, as an effective teaching strategy.[42]

To help students learn to recognize the correct direction in which to read different numerical operations, the teacher might have them draw arrows that indicate the proper order.[43] To help them learn how to interpret graphs, teachers can give students a graph on which the axes are not labeled, and then require them to label the graph.[44] Margaret Henrichs and Tom Sisson recommended that students be given oral practice in reading and interpreting formulas and equations.[45]

Strategies that help students develop math problem-solving abilities, on the other hand, are abundant. One effective strategy is the language-experience approach. Anne Ferguson and Jo Fairburn reported success with an instructional technique in which the teacher first models writing situational problems by using the students' names. Then, guided by the teacher, small groups work collaboratively to write a story-problem for a given computational problem. Finally, after modeling and guided practice, the teacher expands the activity to independent work.[46] Raffaella Borasi, John Sheedy, and Marjorie Siegel explained, "Composing a story may provide yet another opportunity to generate and elaborate mathematical ideas."[47]

Because math teachers frequently drill students in doing mathematical operations, but rarely instruct them in how to select the appropriate operation, Elaine Kresse stressed the need for metacognitive strategies (reading as a thinking process). She pointed out that students first need to visualize the problem by drawing a picture of the problem on paper or the chalkboard. This process of drawing and labeling can solidify the decision for a correct operational choice and solution. Just as computational work needs to be checked, so also do the choices that lead to it. In conjunction with the visualization process, Kresse said that she relied heavily on inference awareness, or checking one's own reasoning. Students need to check their work by questioning the process they used to solve the problem, the evidence that led them to choose that particular process, and the rationale behind their decision.[48]

Denise Muth also supported the need for metacognition which she defined as "knowledge of and regulation of any cognitive task." She advocated comprehension monitoring, a three-step process of planning, monitoring, and remediation, to ensure that the reader is meeting his or her goals. The first step, planning, involves identifying goals and selecting the appropriate strategies to attain them. Monitoring means constantly testing and rechecking to make sure one is moving towards a planned goal. Finally, remediation identifies and effectively deals with any stumbling blocks one encounters during the process.[49] Until a student becomes metacognitively aware of learning strategies, he or she will never attain independence in learning.[50]

Researchers have devised several specialized procedures, or formulas, to help teachers convey the reading skills necessary for attacking word problems. In Anthony Manzo's strategem "ReQuest," students read each sentence of the word-problem individually and question one another to clarify the concepts involved.[51] D. Ray Reutzel introduced a six-step model called "C6":

1) concept clarification
   (instruction in mathematical vocabulary)

2) context clues

3) composing
(using language experience to develop student-generated word problems)

4) chaining and classification
(sorting relevant from extraneous details and
deciding upon the proper sequence of steps)

5) calculation

6) checking[52]

Other specialized formulas include SQ3R (survey, question, read, recite, review)[53] and another variation, PQ4R (preview, question, read, reflect, recite, review).[54]

Looking Toward the Future

The evidence supports reading instruction as an integral part of teaching mathematics. Dolores Wronowski reported that the National Council of Teachers of Mathematics "urged that we capitalize on the inherent relationships between disciplines in order to provide a more effective approach to our mutual problems of providing students with the skills they must have in order to survive the computer age." Furthermore, Wronowski reasoned, this transfer of reading skills across content areas must be planned and taught if it is going to be effective.[55] In other words, the best people to provide reading instruction in math classes are the mathematics instructors themselves. Denise Muth also stressed the need to teach process and content simultaneously. Because reading and computational abilities both play important roles in students' success in mathematics, Muth urged teachers and textbook authors to design activities that integrate the two.[56]

Notes

1. J. Curry, "The Role of Reading Instruction in Mathematics," in D. Lapp, J. Flood, and N. Farren, editors, *Content Area Reading and Learning: Instructional Strategies.* Englewood Cliffs, New Jersey: Prentice-Hall, 1989.

2. C. Hall, "Reading in Secondary Mathematics: Problems, Suggestions, Sources," 1984.

3. A. D. H. Brennan and W. P. Dunlap, "What are the Prime Factors of Reading Mathematics?" *Reading Improvement* 22 (1985): 152-59.

4. A. D. H. Brennan and W. P. Dunlap, *loc. cit.*; G. H. McNinch, editor. *Reading in the Disciplines: Second Yearbook of the American Reading Forum*, 1982. [ED 225 141]

5. K. D. Muth, "What Every Middle School Teacher Should Know about the Reading Process," *Middle School Journal* 19 (1987): 6-7.

6. C. Hall, *op. cit.*; S. K. Hollander, "Reading the Special Language of Mathematics," 1975; A. V. Manzo, "The Math Student/The Math Teacher/The Math Problem," 1975; J. Munro, "Language Abilities and Math Performance," *Reading Teacher 32* (1979): 900-15; D. R. Reutzel, "A Reading Model for Teaching Arithmetic Story Problem Solving," *Reading Teacher 37* (1983); 28-35; E. N. Wesley and F. W. Tanner, "Mathematics and Language," *Arithmetic Teacher 28* (1980): 32-4.

7. Georgia State Department of Education, *Reading Mathematics*, 1975.

8. S. Singer and D. Donlan, *Reading and Learning from Text.* Boston: Little, Brown, 1980.

9. N. W. Earp, "Observations on Teaching Reading in Mathematics," *Journal of Reading 13* (1970): 529-33.

10. P. A. O'Mara, "The Process of Reading Mathematics," *Journal of Reading* 25 (1981): 22-29.

11. H. Ballew and J. W. Cunningham, "Diagnosing Strengths and Weaknesses of Sixth-Grade Students in Solving Word Problems," *Journal for Research in Mathematics Education* 13 (1982): 202-10.

12. P. Rubens, "Decoding the Calculus: Double Jeopardy in Readability," 1980.

13. S. A. Cohen and G. Stover, "Effects of Teaching Sixth-Grade Students to Modify Format Variables of Math Word Problems," *Reading Research Quarterly* 16 (1981): 175-200; P. McCabe, "The Effect upon Comprehension of Mathematics Material Repatterned on the Basis of Oral Language," 1977; D. R. Rentzel, *op. cit.*

14. A. M. Ferguson and J. Fairburn, "Language Experience for Problem Solving in Mathematics," *Reading Teacher 38* (1985): 504-07.

15. A. M. Ferguson and J. Fairburn, *op. cit.*; D. R. Rentzel, *op. cit.*

16. S. A. Cohen and G. Stover, *op. cit.*

17. K. D. Muth, "Solving Arithmetic Word Problems: Role of Reading and Computational Skills," *Journal of Educational Psychology 76* (1984): 210.

18. G. H. McNinch, *op. cit.*

19. A. Skyrpa, "Effects of Mathematical Vocabulary Training on Problem Solving Abilities of Third- and Fourth-Graders," 1979.

20. A. J. Ciani, "Mastering Word and Symbol Language in Mathematics," *School Science and Mathematics 81* (1981): 371-77; R. A. Earle, *Teaching Reading and Mathematics*. Newark, Delaware: International Reading Association,

1976; A. B. Pachtman and J. D. Riley, "Teaching the Vocabulary of Mathematics through Interaction, Exposure, and Structure," *Journal of Reading 22* (1978): 240-44; D. R. Wronowski, "The Forgotten Reading Class: Math Period," *Wisconsin State Reading Association Journal 31* (1987): 59-66.

21. A. D. H. Brennan and W. P. Dunlap, "What Are the Prime Factors of Reading Mathematics?" *Reading Improvement 22* (1985): 152-59; A. J. Ciani, *op. cit.*; R. A. Earle, *op. cit.*

22. J. Curry, *op. cit.*; L. B. Strain, *Developing Interpretive Comprehension Skills in Mathematics and Science*, 1984.

23. C. Hall, *op. cit.*; G. H. McNinch, *op. cit.*; D. L. Shepherd, *Comprehensive High School Reading Methods*, third edition. Columbus, Ohio: Merrill, 1982.

24. A. D. H. Brennan and W. P. Dunlap, *op. cit.*

25. A. D. H. Brennan and W. P. Dunlap, *op. cit.*; C. Hall, *op. cit.*; D. R. Wronowski, *op. cit.*

26. W. P. Dunlap and M. B. McKnight, "Vocabulary Translation for Conceptualizing Math Word Problems," *Reading Teacher 32* (1978): 182-89.

27. S. K. Hollander, *op. cit.*

28. Florida State Department of Education, *Reading the Language of Mathematics*, 1975; M. Henrichs and T. Sisson, "Mathematics and the Reading Process: A Practial Application of Theory," *Mathematics Teacher 73* (1980): 253-57.

29. Florida State Department of Education, *op. cit.*

30. E. C. Kresse, "Using Reading as a Thinking Process to Solve Math Story Problems," *Journal of Reading 27* (1984): 598-601; K. D. Muth, *op. cit.* (1987); D. R. Wronowski, *op. cit.*

31. M. Henrichs and T. Sisson, *op. cit.*

32. W. P. Dunlap and M. B. McKnight, *op. cit.*

33. C. Hall, *op. cit.*; D. R. Wronowski, *op. cit.*

34. J. Curry, *op. cit.*; R. A. Earle, *op. cit.*; Florida State Department of Education, *op. cit.*; C. Hall, *op. cit.*; M. Henrichs and T. Sisson, *op. cit.*; Oklahoma State Department of Education, *Improving Students' Understanding of Math Word Problems*, 1988.

35. R. Borasi, J. R. Sheedy, and M. Siegel, "The Power of Stories in Learning Mathematics," *Language Arts 67* (1990): 179.

36. *Ibid.*: 182.

37. J. Curry, *op. cit.*

38. D. R. Rentzel, *op. cit.*

39. Alabama State Department of Education, *Mathematical Supplement to a Miniguide to Reading in the Content Areas*, 1976; A. J. Ciani, *op. cit.*; Florida State Department of Education, *op. cit.*; Georgia State Department of Education, *op. cit.*; S. K. Hollander, *op. cit.*; S. Krulik, "To Read or Not to Read, That Is the Question," *Mathematics Teacher 73* (1980): 248-52.

40. Brennan and Dunlap, *op. cit.* C. Hall, *op. cit.*; S. Krulik, *loc. cit.*; M. M. Dupuis and E. N. Askov, *Content Area Reading: An Individualized Approach*. Englewood Cliffs, New Jersey: Prentice-Hall, 1982; J. D. Riley and A. B. Pachtman, "Reading Math Word Problems: Telling Them What to Do Is Not Telling Them How to Do It," *Journal of Reading 22* (1978): 240-44; L. B. Strain, *op. cit.*; J. N. Thelen, "Just Because Kids Can't Read Doesn't Mean That They Can't Learn, or Every Science and Math Teacher is Not a Teacher of Reading," *School Science and Mathematics 79* (1979): 457-63.

41. Florida State Department of Education, *op. cit.*

42. L. Strain, *op. cit.*

43. A. D. H. Brennan, and W. P. Dunlap, *op. cit.*; Georgia State Department of Education, *op. cit.*

44. Florida State Department of Education, *op. cit.*

45. M. Henrichs and T. Sisson, *op. cit.*

46. A. M. Ferguson and J. Fairburn, *op. cit.*

47. R. Borasi, J. R. Sheedy, and M. Siegel, *op. cit.*

48. E. C. Kresse, *op. cit.*

49. K. D. Muth, "Comprehension Monitoring: A Reading-Mathematics Connection," *Reading Research and Instruction 27* (1988): 60-7.

50. D. R. Wronowski, *op. cit.*

51. A. V. Manzo, *op. cit.*

52. D. R. Rentzel, *op. cit.*

53. J. Curry, *op. cit.*; H. Singer and D. Donlan, *Reading and Learning from Text.* Boston: Little, Brown, 1980.

54. A. C. Maffei, "Reading Analysis in Mathematics," *Journal of Reading 16* (1973): 325-26.

55. D. R. Wronowski, *op. cit.*

56. K. D. Muth, *op. cit.* (1984).

Annotated Bibliography

Alabama State Department of Education. *Mathematical Supplement to a Miniguide to Reading in the Content Area,* 1976. [ED 189 568]

    Discusses reading skills that should be developed concomitantly with fundamental math concepts.

Ballew, H. and J. W. Cunningham. "Diagnosing Strengths and Weaknesses of Sixth-Grade Students in Solving Word Problems," *Journal for Research in Mathematics Education 13* (1982): 202-10.

    Establishes and verifies a classification scheme for four major areas of difficulties that individual students experience when solving word problems: computational skills, problem interpretation, reading, and the ability to integrate computation with interpretation and reading into the total solution of a word-problem. Suggests that an inability to read problems is a major obstacle.

Borasi, R., J. R. Sheedy, and M. Siegel. "The Power of Stories in Learning Mathematics," *Language Arts 67* (1990): 174-89.

    Analyzes the power of a literature base in secondary mathematics classes to present genuine and relevant problem-solving experiences.

Brennan, A. D. H. and W. P. Dunlap. "What Are the Prime Factors of Reading Mathematics?" *Reading Improvement 22* (1985): 152-59.

    Applies the reading process to six broad areas in mathematics: numeric symbols, nonnumeric symbols, number operations, diagrams, graphs, and story problems.

Ciani, A. J. "Mastering Word and Symbol Language in Mathematics," *School Science and Mathematics 81* (1981): 371-77.

    Suggests a taxonomy of reading skills for math; offers strategies for developing these skills at each level.

Cohen, S. A. and G. Stover. "Effects of Teaching Sixth-Grade Students to Modify Format Variables of Math Word Problems," *Reading Research Quarterly 16* (1981): 175-200.

Reports on research in which gifted students rewrote word problems to make them easier for sixth-grade math students, and identifies the variables that make word problems difficult.

Colwell, C. and J. Pohlman. *A Reading Guide: Assisting Content Area Teachers,* 1983. [ED 228 633]

Contains ideas for lessons and sample lessons for use by content-area teachers who wish to design plans incorporating reading into mathematics. Each plan lists objectives, materials, strategies, evaluation criteria, and personal comments from teachers who have used the lesson.

Curry, J. "The Role of Reading Instruction in Mathematics," in Lapp, D., J. Flood, and N. Farren, editors, *Content Area Reading and Learning: Instructional Strategies.* Englewood Cliffs, New Jersey: Prentice-Hall, 1989.

Presents the directed reading activity (DRA) as an instructional strategy for bridging the range of reading abilities in the mathematics classroom.

Denmark, T. "Sharing Teaching Ideas: Improving Students' Comprehension of Word Problems," *Mathematics Teacher 76* (1983): 31-36.

Shares instructional exercises designed to improve students' reading comprehension of word problems.

Dunlap, W. P. and M. B. McKnight. "Vocabulary Translation for Conceptualizing Math Word Problems," *Reading Teacher 32* (1978): 182-89.

Describes a three-level translation process for helping students solve word-problems in math.

Dupuis, M. M. and E. N. Askov. *Content Area Reading: An Individualized Approach.* Englewood Cliffs, New Jersey: Prentice-Hall, 1982.

Offers suggestions for teaching specific skills, selecting and evaluating materials, developing units of instruction, and dealing with exceptional learners or learners who are culturally and/or linguistically different. Includes a cloze exercise for math teachers.

Earle, R. A. *Teaching Reading and Mathematics.* Newark, Delaware: International Reading Association, 1976.

Describes a four-step hierarchy of reading skills for math class, outlines a general procedure for attacking word problems, lists words that appear most frequently in math texts, and suggests high-interest materials for math classrooms, grades 5-12.

Earp, N. W. "Observations on Teaching Reading in Mathematics," *Journal of Reading 13* (1970): 529-33.

Reviews the research on the relationship among arithmetic and vocabulary knowledge and word-problem solving ability.

Ferguson, A. M. and J. Fairburn. "Language Experience for Problem Solving in Mathematics," *Reading Teacher 38* (1985): 504-07.

Reviews findings of a study demonstrating that language-experience techniques can help students comprehend math story-problems and successfully apply the mathematical concepts necessary for solving them.

Florida State Department of Education. *Reading the Language of Mathematics,* 1975. [ED 134 972]

Offers a comprehensive overview of reading and study skills needed for math and a bibliography of math reading materials.

Georgia State Department of Education. *Reading Mathematics,* 1975. [ED 105 407]

Discusses different types of eye movements for reading math and problems with multiple meanings and word-symbol relationships.

Hall, C. *Reading in Secondary Mathematics: Problems, Suggestions, Sources,* 1984. [ED 249 466]

    Attempts to make the secondary teacher aware of some of the difficulties encountered in reading mathematics, and offers strategies and corresponding activities to overcome these difficulties.

Henrichs, M. and T. Sisson. "Mathematics and the Reading Process: A Practical Application of Theory," *Mathematics Teacher 73* (1980): 253-57.

    Lists important reading and study skills in mathematics based on the involvement of a junior high math department in a content-area reading program.

Hollander, S. K. "Reading the Special Language of Mathematics," paper presented at the annual convention of the International Reading Association, Miami Beach, Florida, 1977.

    Discusses the difficulties inherent in reading mathematics; suggests strategies to remediate difficulties.

Kresse, E. C. "Using Reading as a Thinking Process to Solve Math Story Problems," *Journal of Reading 27* (1984): 598-601.

    Provides a reading strategy to help students of mathematics choose the correct operation to solve a story-problem by identifying verbal evidence.

Krulik, S. "To Read or Not to Read, That Is the Question," *Mathematics Teacher 73* (1980): 248-52.

    Opts for reading in math class as the answer to the question in the title; suggests strategies that teachers can use.

Madison, J. P. and R. Seidenstein. "Beyond Numbers: The Mathematics Literature Connection," 1987. [ED 296 873]

    Offers a collection of activities designed to use children's literature to introduce, reinforce, and broaden mathematics skills and concepts such as time, measurement, money, and problem solving. Includes an annotated bibliography of 49 children's books appropriate for use in primary through middle-school mathematics classrooms.

Maffei, A. C. "Reading Analysis in Mathematics," *Journal of Reading 16* (1973): 325-26.
    Discusses the application of the PQ4R study formula to the solution of word-problems in math class.

Manzo, A. V. "The Math Student/the Math Teacher/the Math Problem," paper presented at the annual meeting of the Missouri Council of Teachers of Mathematics, 1975. [ED 114 767]
    Outlines the ReQuest procedure for teaching students to solve word-problems.

McCabe, P. "The Effect upon Comprehension of Mathematics Material Repatterned on the Basis of Oral Language," paper presented at the annual convention of the International Reading Association, Miami Beach, Florida, 1977. [ED 140 275]
    Isolates the factors that make word-problems more difficult than other types of math.

McNinch, G. H., editor. *Reading in the Disciplines: Second Yearbook of the American Reading Forum*, 1982. [ED 225 141]
    Focuses particularly on vocabulary instruction in mathematics.

Munro, J. "Language Abilities and Math Performance," *Reading Teacher 32* (1979): 900-15.
    Discusses differences between general verbal statements and verbal statements in math, and proposes teaching strategies to help students overcome problems they might face in math class.

Muth, K. D. "Solving Arithmetic Word Problems: Role of Reading and Computational Skills," *Journal of Educational Psychology 76* (1984): 205-10.
    Reports on a study that indicates the relative importance of computational ability and reading ability in the solution of arithmetic word-problems.

Muth, K. D. "What Every Middle School Teacher Should Know about the Reading Process," *Middle School Journal 19* (1987): 6-7.

Describes the difficult task most students face when moving from basal readers to the expository writing found in content-area textbooks; suggests various teaching strategies to ensure a successful transition.

Muth, K. D. "Comprehension Monitoring: A Reading-Mathematics Connection," *Reading Research and Instruction 27* (1988): 60-7.

Delineates a comprehension monitoring process to integrate reading skills with computational skills.

Oklahoma State Department of Education. "Improving Students' Understanding of Math Word Problems," 1988. [ED 296 892]

Suggests a four-stage framework that students can apply to the word-problem solving process. Includes exercises for teachers, sample worksheets for students, and a bibliography on problem-solving.

O'Mara, D. A. "The Process of Reading Mathematics," *Journal of Reading 25* (1981): 22-29.

Reviews research in the areas of the language contexts of math, general reading ability, specific reading skills in math, and the readability of math materials.

Pachtman, A. B. and J. D. Riley. "Teaching the Vocabulary of Mathematics through Interaction, Exposure, and Structure," *Journal of Reading 22* (1978): 240-44.

Outlines nine specific steps necessary to develop a structured overview of math vocabulary; provides sample overviews for integers and mathematical operations.

Rentzel, D. R. "A Reading Model for Teaching Arithmetic Story Problem Solving," *Reading Teacher 37* (1983): 28-35.

Explains a six-step model for showing young children how best to handle solving story problems.

Riley, J. D. and A. B. Pachtman. "Reading Math Word Problems: Telling Them What to Do Is Not Telling Them How to Do It," *Journal of Reading 22* (1978): 240-44.

Outlines specific steps for developing a three-level reading guide to help students attack word problems.

Roe, B. D., B. D. Stoodt, and P. C. Burns. *Reading Instruction in the Secondary School.* Chicago: Rand McNally, 1978.

Explores the specific skills required to integrate reading successfully into the secondary mathematics curriculum.

Rubens, P. "Decoding the Calculus: Double Jeopardy in Readability," paper presented at the annual convention of the International Reading Association, St. Louis, Missouri, 1980. [ED 188 120]

Reports on a study in which a math teacher with very little reading background instructed one group of learners in problem-solving, and a reading teacher with little math background instructed a different, but matched group. Indicates that those learners instructed by the reading teacher became better word-problem solvers.

Shepherd, D. L. *Comprehensive High School Reading Methods,* third edition. Columbus, Ohio: Merrill, 1982.

Presents in chapter twelve an overview of reading skills required in mathematics.

Singer, H. and D. Donlan. *Reading and Learning from Text.* Boston: Little, Brown, 1980.

Presents an overview of problems frequently encountered in reading mathematics and suggests strategies and study formulas.

Skrypa, A. "Effects of Mathematical Vocabulary Training on Problem-Solving Abilities of Third and Fourth Graders," doctoral dissertation, Rutgers University, 1979. [ED 172 169]

Suggests that teaching math vocabulary can increase problem-solving ability as measured by the Stanford Diagnostic Test of mathematics achievement.

Strain, L. B. "Developing Interpretive Comprehension Skills in Mathematics and Science," 1984. [ED 253 854]

Outlines seven specific skills to assist students in developing proficiency in interpretive comprehension. Provides these strategies as a requisite for reading mathematics and science materials with the kind of literacy necessary in today's technologically advanced society.

Thelen, J. N. "Just Because Kids Can't Read Doesn't Mean That They Can't Learn, or Every Science and Math Teacher Is Not a Teacher of Reading," *School Science and Mathematics 79* (1979): 457-63.

Focuses on the use of advance organizers to promote concept development, lists steps in preparing an advance organizer, and provides examples.

Thomas, E. L. and H. A. Robinson. *Improving Reading in Every Class: A Sourcebook for Teachers*, second edition. Boston: Allyn and Bacon, 1977.

Focuses on the development of special guide sheets to help students overcome reading problems.

Wesley, E. N. and F. W. Tanner. "Mathematics and Language," *Arithmetic Teacher 28* (1980): 32-4.

Discusses three elements related to reading in math: language, vocabulary, and readability.

Wronowski, D. R. "The Forgotten Reading Class: Math Period," *Wisconsin State Reading Association Journal 31* (1987): 59-66.

Points out the importance of good reading skills for success in mathematics class, and stresses the usefulness of transferring reading skills across the curriculum.

4
Reading in the Arts

Darla K. Wilshire
The Pennsylvania State University
Altoona Area School District, Pennsylvania

Bernard J. Badiali
Miami University,
Oxford, Ohio

Symphony of Creativity

Music, drama, creative writing, and the visual arts bring the artistic expression of people from different time periods and different countries into the classroom in a new way; these experiences can then provide both a deeper understanding of the creative form and an opportunity for students to respond artistically. The arts allow students great latitude for self-expression and self-interpretation—latitude sometimes lacking in forms of reading that require a more structured response.

The Human Connection

A closer look at the musical, dramatic, and visual arts reveals connections between the human spirit, creativity, and voice or language.

Reading is fundamental to music. Reading musical notation, technical directions, and the words of songs is essential to musical production; moreover, reading provides background information on musical forms and styles.[1] Music and reading go together because language naturally has rhythm and melody; music is an extension of language.[2]

In some ways, reading is even more essential to the field of drama. Students can enjoy readers' theater, which "stretches children beyond their own ideas into the words and ideas of others."[3]

Christine San José recommends story drama, a type of readers' theater that is based on a short narrative form. Students read the narrative and decide who is telling the story. The text provides the readers' lines; either one student or a group of students narrates the story. Mime can help as each reader reacts to the unfolding events. Working closely from texts, the students construct in their own minds what they think was in the mind of the writers.[4] The teacher can then help students connect their drama to other art forms such as writing.

A first step in teaching creative writing may be to encourage students to read to discover the meaning of the literature and the author's use of language to accomplish literary purposes. What is the poem or story saying, and how is it saying it?[5] After reading a poem or story as a model, students may then write and read their own works. They may also draw pictures to illustrate their written works, thus making a connection to the world of visual art.

The combination of art and reading provides an aesthetic experience as well as the opportunity of combining a study of great art with reading activities. One must ponder the words on the page just as one must ponder the colors, shapes, and subjects of the paintings and comprehend what one sees in context and in light of one's own feelings and knowledge. Thus, reading can be the connection between the arts.

Research in the Field

Musical Notes

The connection between the arts and reading skills has been little delineated, and the basis of empirical research is small.

Colleen Mullikin and William Henk explored the use of music as a background for reading. They found that what readers hear does indeed make a difference. Readers exposed to classical music retained more information than did readers who listened to no music or to rock music.[6]

Lois Hirst and Twila O'Such found that students gained more than a year in reading achievement by using commercial jingles to engage in skill-oriented activities with words.[7] Other researchers who have related music and reading, such as Bill Harp, suggested that using songs correlated to teach reading is consistent with the nature and purpose of language.[8] Charles Duke and others concluded that music education can reinforce basic reading skills.[9]

Rita Martin advocated using folk music as a language experience. The repetition of words in folk songs increased students' vocabularies when they used the words in a specific context. Because folk music concerns people's hopes, dreams, and experiences, "folk songs provide the motivation that involves children in affective concerns as well as language processes."[10]

Gail Cohen Taylor recommended the use of music as a motivational aid to the teaching of reading.[11] In addition to motivating students, beginning music instruction may have positive effects on attitude.[12] Reading music was found to involve a phenomenon similar to the eye/voice span in reading language.[13] Ruth Zinar obtained positive correlations between reading and music.[14] Other researchers, however, have maintained that there is little evidence to support using music to teach reading.[15]

Director's Notes

The Association for Supervision and Curriculum Development supported the use of drama in Resolution 9 of their *Resolutions 1989*.[16] The association concluded that the integration of visual and performing arts fostered students' abilities to create, experience, analyze, and reorganize. The arts increased self-discipline and motivation, contributed to a positive self-image, provided an outlet for emotions, and helped develop intuitive thinking.

In the field of dramatics, oral interpretation of prose in the form of readers' theater has proven effective. Students in all grades enjoyed themselves in the process, and reading became a performing art.[17] Barbara Busching found that readers' theater made its strongest contribution to programs for weaker readers. Rereadings provided repeated exposure to new vocabulary.[18] Story drama broadened students' understanding of literature.[19]

Sandra Bidwell wrote of the factors in good reading instruction vis-à-vis drama. Student actors were encouraged to analyze their parts, using metacognition. Through reading, writing to improvise or extend the part, and speaking and listening to others as they performed, the students practiced the tenets of Whole Language. They used strategic reading skills to gather information about characters from various sources. They also practiced reading skills such as skimming and using headings. The process enhanced both comprehension and fluency.[20]

Advocating giving students the means to take control of their own thinking and language, Cecily O'Neill wrote of the dramatic play as a basic activity for the learning of language. She saw the teacher as an artist rather than as a task setter, and she advocated an interactive, dynamic environment in which language would be not only spoken but also written.[21]

Writer's Notes

Creative writing, although part of the language-arts curriculum, finds expression in the fine arts. Teachers frequently choose poetry because student poems lend themselves to the development of comprehension skills in reading and writing as well as skills in the art form. Students are naturally motivated to write and read their own compositions and those of others, and to understand poetry in its many forms.[22]

Artist's Sketches

Edward Rowell states that "just as a book about art or an intriguing illustration in a book can sometimes awaken a student's interest in art, so can an interest in art often awaken and stimulate a child's interest in reading." [23] Visual images may be described by new words, and discussing surface meanings and literal interpretations of paintings will enrich students' understanding of the paintings and of what is written about them. Reading about the times and lives of great painters is a great motivator to art appreciation; a student's desire to know the what, who, when, why and how of a painting is a great motivator to reading about art. Many great artists have painted pictures of humans reading.[24] A classroom study of these paintings might help integrate art and writing.

Student Notes

Reading and writing are integral parts of the arts and an integral part of the student's world. When students take an active part in art, music, film, writing, or drama, they exercise their verbal skills by using new vocabulary and new terminology and by analyzing, interpreting, and synthesizing the world around them. They may write poems or plays, participate in a readers' theater, compose songs and lyrics, or make a film.

Both reading and the arts depend on the ability to perceive and verbalize likenesses and differences in sounds, shapes, textures, meanings, and symbols. Reading and the arts also depend on understanding context as well as on responding to a work. Recognizing the purpose and message of the composer, author, or artist and drawing inferences from a work of art, are skills critical to understanding the object.

Tools of the Trade

From the Conductor's Baton

Bill Harp used reading, music, and movement to extend comprehension in the songs sung by students. To increase their vocabulary, students made song charts and booklets, and they located similar words (homonyms) and similar sounds.[25] Mardi Gork used rhythmic patterns found in speech and in nature, and in music, chants, and cheers to help students understand rhythm. She also used selections from literature with a rhythmic sound pattern.[26] William Palmer used a rehearsed-reading strategy, in which students rewrite selected passages, adapt them for reading, rehearse them, and then read them to the class.[27]

Charles Duke combined journal writing with music, asking students to compare and contrast their own reactions to music with those of other students who hear the same music. Students read these summaries to give the teacher insight into their growth as readers, writers, listeners, and musicians.[28]

Duke also suggested a directed reading activity (DRA), that included a prereading activity, prompted reading, and a post-reading lesson.[29] Students fill in worksheets while they listen to an unknown piece of music; they place their impressions in columns. Students form judgments of musical pieces; they are encouraged to read about the music they have chosen and to revise their judgments freely. The teacher provides guide questions for the students to consider while reading. During postreading, students are invited to respond to what they have read.

Alan Frager and Loren Thompson used anticipation guides to elicit responses from students on music, and study guides to enhance their comprehension of texts. Structured overviews of musical terms show interrelationships among the key terms of a study unit, and the overviews stimulate their development of musical vocabulary. [30]

Lillian Johnson used disco, rock, country, and gospel music as a means of integrating reading into her music classroom. Her seventh-grade students found words to songs, transcribed them, and used vocabulary from them; the assignments included alphabetizing, defining, syllabicating, and writing the words in sentences. They did choral readings of the musical pieces and developed synonyms and antonyms for more difficult words.[31]

Musical cloze, a teaching strategy provided by John Mateja to increase language abilities, allows students to participate in a variety of cloze formats within the context of songs. The teacher selects a song that fits the learner's characteristics and the theme of a given unit. Then the teacher deletes from the song's text a part of speech, a phrase, a relation, or an idea. The goal for the students is to fill in the blank with an appropriate word or thought.[32]

Rita Martin used folk songs to increase student vocabulary; motivation to read is also increased when students sing, listen to, and read about folktales.[33]

From the Director's Chair

For readers' theater, Busching recommended a highly engaging script to motivate readers; vocabulary growth and connotative meaning can be gleaned from a well-written story as well as by repeated exposure to new words in rereading. The process stimulates students to use word-attack strategies. [34]

Robert McCracken and Marlene McCracken suggested that children learn language by hearing it, seeing it in print, and working with bits of it. Chanting and song provide opportunities to introduce rhythm, rhyme, and literal meaning in addition to new vocabulary. Poetry also provides children with a means of expression. Jose Garcia Villa, a poet, recommended that children be exposed to good poetry and encouraged to respond to it in poetic form. For young children, the magic of poetry should be emphasized; older children can study the form. [35]

Epilogue or Finale

Although empirical studies in support of the connection between the arts and reading are few, many educators reason that the two are interrelated. Reading literature requires comprehension at many levels, like listening to music, watching theatrical performances, and viewing art. Terminologies used in the arts are specific and unique, yet they are interrelated in terms of tone, theme, color, and contrast. They also provide ample opportunity for vocabulary development. Cloze activities, directed reading activities, semantic mapping and tree diagrams, and writing are specific strategies that teachers have used effectively to link the arts to reading and to writing.

Notes

1. A. Frager and L. Thompson, "Reading Instruction and Music Education: Getting in Tune," *Journal of Reading 27* (1983): 202-06.

2. B. Harp, "Why Are Your Kids Singing during Reading Time?" *Reading Teacher 41* (1988): 454-56; R. McCracken and M. McCracken, "Chance, Charts, and 'chievement," in J. Cowen, editor, *Teaching Reading through the Arts* (Newark, Delaware: International Reading Association, 1983).

3. B. Busching, "Readers' Theatre: An Education for Language and Life," *Language Arts 58* (1981): 330-37.

4. C. San Jose, "Story Drama in the Content Areas," *Language Arts 65* (1988): 26-32.

5. J. Cowen, "Conversations with Poet José Garcia Villa on Teaching Poetry to Children," in J. Cowen, *op. cit.*

6. C. Mullikin and W. Henk, "Using Music as a Background for Reading: An Exploratory Study," *Journal of Reading 28* (1987): 353-58.

7. L. Hirst and T. O'Such, "Using Musical Television Commercials to Teach Reading," *Teaching Exceptional Children 11* (1979): 80-81.

8. B. Harp, *op. cit.*

9. C. Duke, "Integrating Reading, Writing, and Thinking Skills into the Music Class," *Journal of Reading 31* (1987): 152-56.

10. R. Martin, "Folk Songs as a Language Experience," *Language Arts 58* (1981): 326-29.

11. G. Cohen Taylor, "Music in Language Arts Instruction," *Language Arts 58* (1981): 363-67.

12. D. Wooderson, "The Effects of Special Music Activities on Elementary Language Arts," *PMEA Bulletin of Research in Music Education 9* (1978): 30-32.

13. J. Sloboda, "Phrase Units as Determinants of Visual Processing in Music Reading," *British Journal of Psychology 68* (1977): 117-24.

14. R. Zinar, "Reading Language and Reading Music: Is There a Connection?" *Music Educator's Journal 3* (October 1976): 70-76.

15. P. Groff, "Reading Music Affects Reading Language? Says Who?" *Music Educator's Journal 1* (1977): 37-41.

16. Association for Supervision and Curriculum Development, *Resolutions 1989* (Alexandria, Virginia, 1989.)

17. M. Stuart Taylor, "Readers' Theatre in the Classroom," in J. Cowen, *op. cit.*

18. B. Busching, "Readers' Theatre: An Education for Language and Life," *Language Arts 58* (1981): 335.

19. C. San Jose, "Story Drama in the Content Area," *Language Arts 65* (1988): 28.

20. S. Bidwell, "Using Drama to Increase Motivation, Comprehension, and Fluency," *Journal of Reading 34* (September 1990): 38-41.

21. C. O'Neill, "Dialogue and Drama: The Transformation of Events, Ideas, and Teachers," *Language Arts 66* (September, 1989): 528-39.

22. K. March, "Poetry: The Child's Way to the Real World," in J. Cowen, *op. cit.*

23. E. Rowell "Developing Reading Skills through the Study of Great Art," in J. Cowen, *op. cit.*

24. *Ibid.*

25. B. Harp, *op. cit.:* 454.

26. M. Gork, "Subject Strategies: A Musical Game Plan," *Instructor 97* (1987): 80.

27. W. Palmer, "Subject Strategies: Try Rehearsed Reading," *Instructor 97* (1987): 75.

28. C. Duke, "Integrating Reading, Writing, and Thinking Skills into the Music Class," *Journal of Reading 31* (1987): 157.

29. S. Roe, B. Stoodt, and P. Burns, *Secondary School Reading Instruction: The Content Areas,* second edition. Boston: Houghton Mifflin Company, 1983.

30. A. Frager and L. Thompson, "Reading Instruction and Music Education: Getting in Tune," *Journal of Reading 27* (1983): 205.

31. L. Johnson, "Open to Suggestion. Learning to Read and Write through Modern Music," *Journal of Reading 25* (1982): 596-97.

32. J. Mateja, "Musical Cloze: Background, Purpose and Sample," *Reading Teacher 35* (1982): 444-48.

33. R. Martin, *op. cit.:* 328.

34. B. Busching, *op. cit.:* 333.

35. M. McCracken and R. McCracken, "Teaching Reading through Children's Books, Poetry, and Song," paper presented at the Reading/Language Arts Conference, Lawrenceville, New Jersey, May 1980.

36. E. Rowell, *op. cit.*

Annotated Bibliography

Association for Supervision and Curriculum Development. *Resolutions 1989*. Alexandria, Virginia, 1989.

>   Offers resolutions for student curricula. Resolution 9 states the Association's position on the integration of visual and performing arts into the curriculum.

Bidwell, Sandra. "Using Drama to Increase Motivation, Comprehension, and Fluency," *Journal of Reading 34* (September 1990): 38-41.

>   Recommends the use of drama activities to motivate students in all grades. Cites research for the connection between fluency and motivation, and offers suggestions for the classroom.

Busching, Barbara. "Readers' Theatre: An Education for Language and Life," *Language Arts 58* (1981): 330-37.

>   Provides information on the instructional potential of readers' theater and how to organize and stage it.

Cowen, John. "Conversations with Poet José Garcia Villa on Teaching Poetry to Children," in J. Cowen, editor, *Teaching Reading through the Arts*. Newark, Delaware: International Reading Association, 1983.

>   Discusses the magic and form of poetry for children with the National Artist of the Philippines.

Duke, Charles. "Integrating Reading, Writing, and Thinking Skills into the Music Class," *Journal of Reading 31* (1987): 152-56.

>   Presents journal writing and a directed reading activity (DRA) for the classroom. Provides a DRA lesson for teachers to follow. Gives extension activities.

Frager, Alan and Loren Thompson. "Reading Instruction and Music Education: Getting in Tune," *Journal of Reading 27* (1983): 202-06.

>   Presents five content-area reading strategies for teaching music; includes anticipation guides, study guides, inferential reading lessons, and vocabulary instruction.

Gork, Mardi. "Subject Strategies: A Musical Game Plan," *Instructor* 97 (1987): 80.

Suggests a musical game plan using rhythm and chants in song and in literature. Gives ideas for music integration into social studies, science, and math. Provides a resource list of "on-key" resources.

Groff, Patrick. "Reading Music Affects Reading Language? Says Who?" *Music Educator's Journal 1* (1977): 37-41.

Reviews research literature to refute the idea that music and reading are related. Says that no substantial evidence proves that teaching music helps language reading.

Harp, Bill. "Why Are Your Kids Singing during Reading Time?" *Reading Teacher 41* (1988): 454-56.

Suggests that reading and music go together. Provides strategies for using songs to teach reading through song books and vocabulary activities.

Hirst, Lillian and Twila O'Such. "Using Musical Television Commercials to Teach Reading," *Teaching Exceptional Children 11* (1979): 80-81.

Suggests that teachers take advantage of the time that children spend watching television by using it to remediate slow readers.

Johnson, Lillian. "Open to Suggestion. Learning to Read and Write through Modern Music," *Journal of Reading 25* (1982): 596-97.

Provides strategies for using modern music and lyrics to stimulate vocabulary development and reading in a seventh-grade classroom.

March, K. "Poetry: The Child's Way to the Real World," in J. Cowen, editor, *Teaching Reading through the Arts*. Newark, Delaware: International Reading Association, 1983.

Offers ways to motivate children to compose poetry by writing poems to see the beauty of language. Strategies given include sight vocabulary and listening skills.

Martin, Rita. "Folk Songs as a Language Experience," *Language Arts 58* (1981): 326-29.

> Discusses the use of folk songs as a learning activity to motivate readers and to increase their vocabulary. Integrates the music with language arts and the total curriculum, and addresses the affective domain of learning.

Mateja, John. "Musical Cloze: Background, Purpose and Sample," *Reading Teacher 35* (1982): 444-48.

> Provides the strategy of musical cloze reading activities including the background, purpose, and procedure of cloze reading and a sample lesson using music material.

McCracken, Robert and Marlene McCracken. "Chants, Charts, and 'chievement," in J. Cowen, editor, *Teaching Reading through the Arts.* Newark, Delaware: International Reading Association, 1983.

> Recommends the learning of language through experience, the hearing of language, seeing language in print, and working with 'bits' of it. Gives strategies for use of rhymes and chants in the classroom.

McCracken, Marlene and Robert McCracken. "Teaching Reading through Children's Books, Poetry, and Song," paper presented at the Reading/Language Arts Conference, Lawrenceville, New Jersey, May, 1980.

> Presents the use of children's literature, poetry, and music as a means to enhance reading in children. Suggests ways to incorporate these areas into the curriculum.

Mullikin, Colleen and William Henk. "Using Music as a Background for Reading: An Exploratory Study," *Journal of Reading 28* (1987): 353-58.

> Focuses on an empirical study that showed an increase in reading comprehension when music is provided for background: soft classical music allowed students to retain more than either no music or rock music. No music produced slightly better results than rock music.

O'Neill, Cecily. "Dialogue and Drama: The Transformation of Events, Ideas, and Teachers," *Language Arts 66* (September 1989): 528-39.

> Discusses classroom dialogue in the context of a drama focusing on content and on student themes and motivation. Proposes that the teacher become an artist through the use of "liminality" and the "mantle of the expert."

Palmer, William. "Subject Strategies: Try Rehearsed Reading," *Instructor 97* (1987) 75.

> Provides a strategy called "rehearsed reading" in which students adapt print, rehearse, and present the material in a reading format. Listeners' questions on the material strengthen comprehension.

Roe, Sally, Barbara Stoodt, and Paul Burns. *Secondary School Reading Instruction: The Content Areas,* second edition. Boston: Houghton Mifflin Company, 1983.

> Teaches reading instruction in a comprehensive text for all content areas. Integrates research, strategies, and classroom use.

Rowell, Edward. "Developing Reading Skills through the Study of Great Art," in J. Cowen, editor, *Teaching Reading through the Arts.* Newark, Delaware: International Reading Association, 1983.

> Describes the unique connection between art and reading skills in literal meaning, multiple meanings, synthesis of parts, and personal evaluation.

San Jose, Christine. "Story Drama in the Content Area," *Language Arts 65* (1988): 26-32.

> Shows how story drama is applicable to the classroom, and suggests ways to use story drama to improve comprehension skills and deepen the understanding of literature.

Sloboda, John. "Phrase Units as Determinants of Visual Processing in Music Reading," *British Journal of Psychology 68*
(1977): 117-24.

Shows that reading music involves a phenomenon similar to
the eye/voice span in reading.

Stuart Taylor, Mary. "Readers' Theatre in the Classroom," in J.
Cowen, editor, *Teaching Reading through the Arts*. Newark,
Delaware: International Reading Association, 1983.

Shows teachers how to transform literature works into scripts
for readers' theater. Gives practical advice on how to set up the
student performance.

Taylor, Gail Cohen. "Music in Language Arts and Instruction,"
Language Arts 58 (March 1981): 363-67.

States that music is a motivational tool for teachers to use in
the classroom. Connects language skills to music instruction and
recommends them as a remedial tool for learning-disabled children.
Offers resources for teachers.

Wooderson, D. "The Effects of Special Music Activities on Elementary Language Arts," *PMEA Bulletin of Research in
Music Education 9* (1978): 30-32.

Offers a series of research studies focusing on the relationship
between music and beginning reading achievement. Her conclusions do not support a causative relationship, although students
like the reading/music combinations.

Zinar, Ruth. "Reading Language and Reading Music. Is There a
Connection?" *Music Educator's Journal 3* (October 1976):
70-76.

Reviews the research to find a positive correlation between
reading music and reading language. Music acts as a motivational
tool and a means through which reading-related skills are acquired.

5

Reading in Health Education

Gail Alberini-Emmett
Huntingdon Area School District, Pennsylvania

Maria Plischke
The Huntington Learning Center
Newark, Delaware

Introduction

According to George Will, discipline problems in public schools have changed drastically during the past forty years, making the job of the educator not only more challenging but also sometimes dangerous. In the 1940s a survey listed the top seven discipline problems:

1. Talking

2. Chewing gum

3. Making noise

4. Running in the halls

5. Getting out of turn in line

6. Wearing improper clothing

7. Not putting paper in wastebaskets

A 1980s survey listed a rather different set of discipline problems:

1. Drug abuse

2. Alcohol abuse

3. Pregnancy

4. Suicide

5. Rape

6. Robbery

7. Assault

(Arson, Gang Warfare, and Sexually Transmitted Disease were "also rans.")[1]

As we peruse the most recent list, it seems clear that the new role of "health educators" was born of necessity. Many of the discipline problem areas on the list fall into our current health education curricula.

No longer is it sufficient for the physical education teacher or science instructor to give a brief lesson on first aid, physical hygiene, or menstruation. Health educators are trying to impart knowledge that will save lives.

Because health education is a new field, little "hard" research has been replicated, especially in the area of content reading. However, general content-area reading practices can easily be applied to this specific field. We hope teachers will be able to implement some of these practices in the classroom after reading this chapter.

The New Health Educator and Reading

The role of the health educator as a source of information and help—separate and apart from the nurse, the physical-education teacher, and science instructor—is a recently developed but vital one. The complex work of the health educator now reaches far beyond teaching units on nutrition, dental care, and human reproduction into high-stakes areas such as stress management, suicide prevention, sexually transmitted diseases, and aging. The goal of health educators includes both transmitting factual knowledge and nurturing young people so that they will become responsible for their own physical and mental well-being.

A newborn infant demonstrates an instinctive fear of falling. Later, the child acquires basic skills such as walking, both by trial and error and by emulating the behavior of adults. Both children and adults, however, learn certain lessons through direct experience and unpleasant surprises such as the recognition of third-degree burns and the effects on the human body of ingesting toxic substances!

Crucial to the vicarious acquisition of human experience is the ability to read—not only fiction with its personalized story line but also nonfiction, which can provide a tool for the prevention of illness. The more comfortable a health educator becomes with teaching reading, the easier it becomes for both the students and the teacher to succeed at exchanging knowledge.

Because our schools tend to separate the education of the body from the education of the mind, students also separate their accomplishments in the gymnasium from their academic achievement. Too often, their teachers fail to model the connection. Too often, the physical educator does not model reading for the students, as if exempt from the silent sustained reading that is required daily throughout many schools. As special role models to many sports-loving students, P. E. teachers are in a unique position either to stimulate interest in reading or to downplay its importance. "When physical and health educators emphasize the need to read, underscore literacy or academic achievement as well as athletic performance or fitness, and read and write themselves, young people are drawn to these endeavors."[2]

For a health teacher in an elementary school whose first-grade student has just suffered the loss of a beloved pet, or a secondary-school health teacher whose freshman students are coping with the suicide of a peer, reading can be a useful tool for teaching and learning how to face the painful aspects of life. Nonfiction can take us through the steps of grieving and help us realize that feelings of rage, denial, and sadness are normal and to be expected. So can fiction. Teachers may want to encourage students to read or listen to fiction that allows them to identify with a character who has suffered a loss. Junior-high students often confess that they cry when reading *Where the Red Fern Grows* or *A Day No Pigs Would Die*; books like these bring home the coping skills of the characters who appear to be so much like their youthful readers.

The health educator who strives to incorporate instructional reading in the content area may find the jargon of the reading experts—literary processes, metacognitive strategies, strategic learners, cooperative learning groups, prior knowledge, schema, and graphic organizers—overwhelming. Throughout this chapter we endeavor to explain such terms, and we gear their use especially to the health-education classroom.

Beyond the Textbooks

Infusing reading and writing skills into any content area improves academic achievement. Although this principle is well-known, instructional practices in the content-area classroom, nevertheless, often consist of mere lecture with a question-and-answer format or having students work independently at their desks. Many teachers assume that content learning relies heavily on the textbook as a source of information. According to B. Davey, however, "Both elementary and secondary teachers reported using textbooks primarily to supplement instruction rather than as a basis for lectures or content learning." She also observed a problem stemming from elementary and secondary teachers' use of oral reading from textbooks in class and from students' answering the questions at the end of the chapter. "Since these strategies can result in a passive, uninspired response to specific text information, teachers at all levels should be encouraged to engage students in reading activities which foster higher level thinking and more active reasoning."[3]

It is possible to infuse into the health curriculum measurable communication skills that result in students' growth in reading and language. A project in Los Angeles in 1983 included modules on Personal Health, Nutrition and Food Choices, and Communicable and Chronic Diseases. "Each module addressed a health topic as well as the following reading/language skills: word meanings, complete sentences, paragraphs, sequence, main topic, topic sentences, drawing conclusions, cause and effect, and fact and opinion."[4]

It is generally accepted that parents parent the way they were parented, and that teachers teach the way they were taught. Teachers can overcome existing poor instructional practices and implement new, more positive ones if they remain flexible and are sincerely interested in successful accomplishment for their students.

Cooperative Learning

Research shows that "better results are gained with cooperative learning strategies than with competitive and independent organizational plans."[5] It's certainly worth a try!

A simple beginning is to ask two or three students reading their health glossaries to work together to find definitions of assigned terms. When students work together to make crossword puzzles of these words for other students to complete, they have great fun and learn a lot.

It is more important to teach cooperation than it is to worry about a student's cheating when working on a task independently. Networking is becoming increasingly necessary for the corporate and technological world, and students must practice these skills of working together. Students on the playing field learn to succeed individually through team effort; similarly we can foster group responsibility and achievement in reading, writing, and understanding. "Reading strategy groups, when organized according to the principles of cooperative learning, enhance learning by providing the opportunity for all students to make decisions and participate actively."[6] Group grades may be based on participation, test scores, strategies used, and the quality of the final product.

For a group to work together effectively, however, *each* member of the group must be familiar with various strategies useful for tackling the whole project.

Metacognition and Health

An analysis of 20 studies showed that "the average effect of metacognitive instruction on reading comprehension is substantial."[7] Metacognitive instruction means teaching students to reflect on their own learning strategies so that they can determine how best to tackle the task at hand. Metacognitive "strategies need to be directly taught and modeled within the content of each subject area if students are to learn to use them successfully. Effective instruction teaches students what the strategy is, why it is appropriate, how to apply it, and when and where to use it."[8]

We cannot afford to assume that students already know these strategies or that they no longer need to have them reinforced. If the health teacher provides opportunities for students to implement techniques introduced in the reading classroom, students may begin to see knowledge as an integrated whole rather than as isolated pieces of a puzzle.

Health and Vocabulary

Another area of challenge for the health teacher is vocabulary learning: "The expository reading and writing that is required in intermediate-grade science, social studies, mathematics, and health presents sentence structures and specialized vocabulary that are foreign to the narrative reading of earlier grades."[9] Memorizing isolated words results in poor retention, especially because students are generally expected to master long lists of words weekly in each content area. Helping students deal with the challenges of content texts as they read will teach them the skills they need to become independent learners.

Many students receive their first serious look at health issues and the impact of science and technology on human beings through content-area textbooks. Unfortunately, omitting personal interest stories from textbooks generally makes them dry and lifeless. Brozo and Tomlinson contended that "children's literature used skillfully in tandem with texts makes the content curriculum more palatable, comprehensible, and memorable and that use of literature is likely to promote students' interest in and involvement with content material and thereby increase their learning."[10] Providing high-quality literature to complement concepts being addressed in the health classroom is not difficult.

Questioning strategy also has an impact on student motivation and learning. In the standard procedure, students generally read the text, and the teacher asks comprehension questions. The questions are usually either literal (recall), interpretive (understanding what is implied), or evaluative (making judgments).

The drawback of this procedure is that these follow-up questions usually function more as an oral examination. Students read in anticipation of the teacher's questions rather than to resolve the students' own questions. "A better approach to comprehension requires students to *use* information from the text to make logical predictions about outcomes. Students who do this kind of reading and discussing are actually engaged in problem solving."[11]

Learning Vocabulary

Health educators certainly recognize the importance of vocabulary for the comprehension of reading materials. What many may not realize is that learning content vocabulary is different from general vocabulary. "Many content area teachers have not been exposed to recent research findings that verify the importance of vocabulary in reading comprehension, that confirm the effectiveness of direct instruction, and that suggest the value of an expansion and refinement model of vocabulary instruction within a conceptual framework."[12]

Some educators have sought shorter, watered-down versions of text for their less-able students in an effort to enable them to enjoy greater success. The result is to short-change students who particularly need to learn the new, specialized vocabulary.

"Eliminating difficult or multi-syllabic words defeats the purpose of the content-area textbook. The words that are most likely to cause a high readability score are the technical vocabulary, the special meaning words of the content."[13]

Help Them Read Their Way to Better Health

Choosing Books

To incorporate reading techniques as part of the health curriculum, the teacher must carefully select health education literature appropriate for the capabilities of the intended readers. Generally, we find a wide range of student reading abilities within any given classroom, and readability formulas are at best a general guide to determining the usefulness of a book in a particular classroom.

"The construction and/or selection of health literature should be made in such a fashion that the poorest readers within the target population are capable of reading the literature effectively. The better reader can easily read 'down' but the poorer reader will have difficulty reading 'up'."[14]

Health educators must become actively involved with the selection of textbooks; they must not rely on a committee or publisher to tell them whether a book is suitable for their purposes and their particular students. For health education to be effective, students must understand what they are reading; therefore, it makes good sense to use more than one health text within the classroom to meet the reading needs of the student adequately.

There is more to selecting a textbook than determining its readability level or deciding whether its illustrations are colorful enough. Many teachers have never been trained to evaluate materials for classroom use.

Readability formulas neglect characteristics of readers themselves that affect comprehension: attention span, individual learning styles, and cultural background. They also fail to take into account other characteristics of text that are important to learning. Armbruster and Anderson concluded that "based on a fairly extensive body of research, it appears that structure influences the amount as well as the kind of knowledge acquired from reading."[15] Logically, the better structured a text is, the more likely the reader is to remember the information. This is especially important for books with a scientific base because they are often overloaded with too many concepts per page.

Suggestions for Evaluating Textbooks

1. Know your target audience.

2. Check the approximate reading level of the material.

3. Look for informative headings and subheadings.

4. Check the format for organization (layout, marginal notations, graphic aids, boldface, underlining).

5. Look for signal words and phrases such as "in contrast" or "first" and "second."

6. Find explicit connectives such as "because."

7. Look for logical, chronological sequence.

8. Notice graphic aids related to text (photographs, diagrams, charts, and tables that match the text).

9. Read topic sentences in paragraphs.

10. Look at preview and summary statements.

In addition to reading ability, a student brings schema (prior knowledge) to the printed word. In the interaction that takes place between this foundation and new concepts, learning takes place. For example, junior-high students may not understand at first how alienated a teenager may feel after a leg amputation, but most do have experience with hospitalization and the fear of losing any body part. We can build on this life experience before introducing a novel such as *Izzy, Wizzy, Nilly* which will allow them to identify with a young person who has to deal with such a loss.

Stimulating Interest

A teacher's prime responsibility is to motivate interest. It just does not work well to assign a chapter and assume that the students will be automatically interested in the content. Cultural and individual differences play a big part. A book such as *Deenie* may not be appropriate for all students, but might be very helpful to an individual youngster with scoliosis.

A book may have meaning and purpose for the teacher, but does it have meaning for the student? A teacher can challenge students and stimulate their interest by using the following techniques:

- Use analogies. Analogies stimulate interest by causing students to look at their past experiences and knowledge in new ways.

- Relate personal anecdotes. Students are normally curious about the personal lives of their teachers; teachers can capitalize on this curiosity by sharing their own experiences that illustrate, and are relevant to, the passages being read.

- Disrupt readers' expectations. Students may become bored and uninterested in learning unless they are challenged to reach beyond the comfort areas of knowledge and thought.

- Challenge students to resolve a paradox. Students can be directed to their textbook to find information that they will need to resolve the paradox and return to a state of equilibrium.

- Introduce novel and conflicting information or situations. Teachers can ensure students' interest in

new information by focusing their attention more
keenly on conflicting ideas within the new information.[16]

Another method of stimulating student interest is to construct an anticipation-reaction guide consisting of five teacher-prepared statements related to the material about to be studied. To prepare the statements, first identify the major concepts and issues in the reading selection, and then prompt discussion of likely experiences and/or beliefs of the students that might be challenged or supported by the information. A useful statement has more than one correct answer. Students become more interested in the text when we help them link it to events in their own lives. After discussing their reasons for their "before reading" responses in pairs or small groups, the students read to determine the author's point of view, and to clarify their own previously held beliefs.

Example of an anticipation-reaction guide:

AIDS

Directions: Read each statement below. If you agree, check the "Before Reading" blank. If you do not agree, do not put a check in the blank. Directions for the "Author's Ideas" column are given later.

Before Reading		Author's Ideas
_____	AIDS is mainly a homosexual problem.	_____
_____	People in rural areas need not worry about AIDS.	_____
_____	The communicable period of AIDS is unknown.	_____
_____	Children with AIDS have a right to go to school.	_____
_____	Scientists are on the brink of a cure for AIDS.	_____

After reading the selection, put a check in the right hand column if the author agreed with the statement. Compare the checks in each column and determine whether or not your opinions have changed because of what you have read.

Using Fiction

Make a wide variety of materials available for students to employ, once a purpose for reading has been set. "Children's literature can serve as a valuable supplement to classroom materials and activities chosen to stimulate discussion and promote learning about health topics and issues," but "only those books that entertain and inform the health educator deserve to be shared with children, since successful experiences with books depend, in part, on the teacher's enthusiasm and interest."[17]

Before selecting literature to complement a health unit, consider the following steps:

1. Identify salient concepts.

2. Identify appropriate trade books to help teach concepts. (Use annotated subject-guide indices).

3. Introduce books by reading orally.

4. Follow-up (writing, drama, interviewing).[18]

A junior-high pilot project in Iowa focused on teenage novels to complement a substance-abuse unit. "While the reading students were studying their novels, they were also taking part in the regular substance use and abuse unit that is a part of the district's science/health curriculum." Students could choose from the following novels:

Dinky Hocker Shoots Smack
by M. E. Kerr

That Was Then, This is Now
by S. E. Hinton

My Name is Davy, I'm an Alcoholic
by Anne Snyder

The Late Great Me
by Sandra Scoppetone

The Boy Who Drank Too Much
by Shep Greene

Does This School Have Capital Punishment?
by Nat Hentoff

Sarah T. Portrait of a Teenage Alcoholic
by Robin Wagner

A Hero Ain't Nothin' But a Sandwich
by Alice Childress[19]

Discussing novels and the concepts presented in them in relation to real life helps students select books and extract meaning.

> They are coming to understand that reading is the making of meaning and that, if they fail, it is possibly because they have gaps in what they are bringing to the text. It isn't just that "this book is stupid." They're developing confidence to abandon a book in which they do not make meaning, for they're learning that there is a world full of books from which to choose. They're discovering that if the gap in their knowledge prevents them from making meaning this year, they may have that knowledge in a year or so. They will know that there is no such thing as *the* meaning, and there is not some magical power of interpretation given by the literature gods to teachers only. They are learning the joy of exchanging interpretations, of expressing them in writing and speaking, or respecting what they have to say as well as what others may offer.[20]

Literature as a companion to health-education units offers vicarious experiences to students in a risk-free way.

Amateur Authors

Another interesting method of motivating students to learn about a particular concept is to have them write a book. They might begin with ordinary stories and then move on to content-area materials. A junior high school in Massachusetts experienced success with students who read below-level by taking the following steps:

- Prewriting—study textbooks and determine requirements.

- Choose Topics—assess prior knowledge by brainstorming words, concepts, and questions related to the topic.

- Research and Note Taking—review literature and develop a bibliography (review note-taking and library skills, copyright laws, use of quotations).

- Write—outline information to determine boldfaced headings, sequence of information, and specific fact; write text.

- Word Processing—revise and organize.

- Structural Components—pictures, charts, maps, book cover.

- Biography—write information about the author, compose a dedication.

- Publication—print chapters as they are finished.[21]

This type of project can offer a wonderful opportunity for students to work in pairs or small groups, sharing their skills and making up for one another's weaknesses. Students could write about topics meaningful to them: preventing communicable diseases through immunization, how to prevent dental problems, the danger of steroid use, and many others.

Cooperative Learning

Grown-up educators easily forget what it was like to be a student, as I was recently reminded when I took a summer course. The professor handed us one sheet of typed material with many blanks, and instructed us to read the material and fill in the blanks to the best of our ability (cloze procedure). Even though this was supposedly a non-graded, non-threatening assignment, I was frustrated and apprehensive when I felt that I could not supply the right word in a blank. How much more threatening this sort of experience must be for the young person who may very well be getting a grade for the effort, and who is eager to please the teacher and do what is required!

After briefly working on the page full of blanks independently, we were allowed to work in pairs; my adrenalin level went down, and my heartbeat returned to normal. Sharing knowledge allowed us to fill in many more blanks. It is one thing to know intellectually that working in groups is positive and productive; it is another to experience it personally.

Heterogeneous learning groups are usually composed of four to six students who vary in ability, sex, ethnicity, and handicaps. The benefits of cooperative learning include both improved achievement and improved self-esteem.

Reading Strategies

For students to work in groups, they need direct instruction in appropriate strategies. Students may then be grouped according to the strategy that they have chosen. Most comprehensive strategies for reading incorporate prereading, reading, and postreading activities. Marjorie Montague and Michael Tanner explained: "Pre-reading strategies focus on creating awareness and activating content knowledge that the learner brings to the learning situation, setting a purpose for reading, analyzing the text structure, and developing vocabulary.

"Strategies used during reading include note-taking, summarizing, answering adjunct questions that are textually explicit, and monitoring one's success.

"Post-reading strategies usually assist readers in reorganizing, integrating and reviewing textual material in preparation for a test."[22]

A number of comprehensive strategies help students read and understand subject-area texts. They include SQ3R (Survey, Question, Read, Recite, Review), DRTA (Directed Reading and Thinking Activity), and Multipass (Survey, Size-up, Sort-Out).

Direct instruction of a strategy by the teacher involves the following steps:

1. describing the purpose of the strategy

2. modeling the strategy by using a passage from the text

3. engaging students in practicing the strategy

4. having students use the strategy to review the text before a quiz

The greater the variety of metacognitive strategies with which students enter the health-education classroom, the better. It is well worth the time it takes to teach a few strategies so that students can grasp the material we want them to learn.

One technique is call GRASP (the Guided Reading and Summarizing Procedure). Summarizing a text is basic to sophisticated understanding: "In a content-area class...the method can be explained as an important tool for dealing with the content as well as a way of demonstrating knowledge about the subject." [23]

Summarizing

Emphasize that the steps taken to summarize a text in class closely resemble the steps that the students use when writing a summary on their own:

- reading for information

- organizing the information

- presenting it in their own words

Generally, practice in summarizing works best on a text selection of about 500 words for middle-school students, and 1,000 words for secondary-school students. First, direct the students to read to remember all they can. Second, ask them to tell all they remember while you list their responses on the chalkboard. Third, propose quick rereading to round out details and correct mistakes.

Next, the mass of information must be organized. To begin, help the students identify the text's major topics and write labels for these topics down the left side of a sheet of paper. Then have them think how the information is related to their labels, and outline that connection to the right of each label. Finally, they can write their summaries. Tell them to include only important information, and to compress information whenever possible. Sometimes they may need to add information for the sake of coherence.

"Together the teacher and students proceed through the remembered information group by group, converting each group to a sentence. Each sentence is discussed and revised before the student's eyes. At the end of the exercise, the class will have produced a paragraph that summarizes the reading in about as many sentences as there are groups of remembered information. A rough summary paragraph originated by students themselves is preferable to a verbatim copy of source material."[24]

Another approach is to teach students how to develop a summary in one sentence. The summary must identify the topic, and then tell what is most important. Regardless of the technique used to teach summarization, students will stand the best chance of achieving independence in the use of this, or any other, technique if it has meaning for them. "The goal of teaching for independence in reading comprehension is for students to develop ownership of a variety of text processing and text reorganization strategies and to determine how and when to use them."[25]

Gleaning Meaning

When scientific words are not definable from context, and the student does not bring enough prior knowledge to the text to be able to construct meaning for an unfamiliar word, then how is the reader to get meaning from the text?

Intensive direct teaching in the health education classroom is the key. Students will not perceive the relationship between the text and the word if they simply memorize a list of technical terms in isolation. They need strategies for combining new text information with their prior knowledge.

One strategy is to study the context in which the new word occurs. When the clues provided are too vague to specify particular meaning, analysis of word structure may prove helpful (e.g., prefix, stem, suffix). Example: "Hypothermia"—*hypo* means "below" or "less than"; *thermia* means "heat."

Another method, called CD or "concept of definition" instruction, provides a framework for organizing conceptual information according to three types of relationships: categories, properties, and illustrations.

To help students internalize the structure, the teacher has them write their names on sheets of paper and then decide on categories, properties, and illustrations that fit themselves.

After the teacher has modeled the process as a means to arriving at a definition of new vocabulary words, students can work in pairs or groups, and discuss their decisions. Playing with CD helps students own the strategy. "For example, at the beginning of the week the teacher might post 10 concept maps on a bulletin board with only the category information supplied. Gradually, over the week, the teacher adds properties, contrasting concepts, and finally examples. The students can work together or compete to identify all 10 terms."[26]

Another way of introducing vocabulary that relates new material to prior knowledge is a structured overview. To begin, the teacher presents the overview, relating new concepts to those the students have already learned.

Then, each new word in the overview is pronounced, as the teacher points out how the words are related or different.

Before assigning the reading, the teacher asks students to work together in groups to determine meanings of the words and their relationships to each other.

"Following the vocabulary activity, ask the student to read the text material to complete the structured overview and the *vocabulary guide*, and to write answers to some questions about the material." [27]

A graphic organizer (GO) is a slightly more complex structured overview. GOs can be implemented before, during, or after reading an instructional unit of text; in class with large or small groups, or assigned as homework activities.[28]

Questioning Techniques

The usual format in a content classroom involves the teacher's posing a question, and then calling on a single student for a response, while the other students remain passive (and anxious). We know that the teacher's questioning technique does influence reading outcomes. For example, doubling wait-time (waiting for a response to a question) before asking another student to supply the answer, makes questioning more effective.[29] Reader-response theory helped teachers understand the following ideas, which in turn suggested new questioning techniques:

- Meaning is not "contained" in the text, but comes from an interaction between the content and structure of the author's written message and the reader's experience and prior knowledge.

- Readers comprehend differently because every reader is culturally and individually unique.

- Examining readers' responses to text is more valid than establishing one interpretation as "correct."

Reader-response insight is as useful in interpreting expository texts as it is in the appreciation of literature; however, many teachers continue to question until some lucky student comes up with that one right answer. A better technique allows for multiple correct responses and the sharing of ideas and information. If all the answers offered are incorrect, say so; then supply the correct answer or help students find it.

If the health-education instructor wishes to vary from the all-too-familiar "read, close the text, and be called on" approach, students must sense that they have the right to share surprising or eccentric ideas without fear or condemnation.

Students need practice working in small and large groups to share their interpretations of what they have read. Rather than being threatened by the "closed book, exam-questions" approach, they must feel free to return to the text to validate their opinions during the questioning period.

One questioning format that increases student participation is the Multiple Response Technique (MRT) which engages all the students at once in the question, not just one at a time.

MRT is easy to implement: The teacher asks a question, giving the students several response options from which to choose. These answers can be displayed on the board or with an overhead projector. Students might respond with thumbs up or down, fingers, or cards marked with T, F, or a question mark.

Cue words are imperatives: "Think! Ready! Respond!" After students respond on cue, the teacher surveys their responses and decides whether it is time for closure, correction, or further discussion.

It's a good idea to start small and begin with well-controlled classes. Be sure that the students see the specific purpose for this activity. (Is it for a review, or is it to predict an outcome in place of a test?) Try varying the response format. Occasionally let your students generate their own MRT questions for a homework assignment.

MRT offers a viable means to engage students actively in demonstrating what they know about content concepts and skills. Insisting that they not respond before the cue builds in the wait-time essential for thoughtful responses. Important to a busy teacher, MRT activities do not require much preparation time or the development of elaborate materials.[30]

Another style of questioning in which wait-time is important is the teacher's persistent but non-threatening questioning when a student fails to complete a homework assignment or comes to class late. Careful questioning with plenty of time to reflect and respond can help the teacher and student backtrack to determine the cause and effect of the situation. Cause-and-effect relationships are a chain reaction in which an effect can become a cause, and can in turn generate another effect.[31]

The health education teacher is in a unique position to motivate students because of the nature of the subject matter, which revolves around the well-being of humans. Like other humans, students have a vested interest in themselves. Coming to view reading as a means to answering personal questions, and vicariously taking part in the positive and negative aspects of human experience, holds tremendous implications for students' motivation to become life-long learners.

Notes

1. G. F. Will, in *Newsweek* (January 5, 1987): 64.

2. D. Lapp, J. Flood, and D. Farrian, *Content-Area Reading and Learning: Instructional Strategies* (Englewood Cliffs, New Jersey: Prentice-Hall, 1989): 213.

3. B. Davey, "How Do Classroom Teachers Use Their Textbooks," *Journal of Reading 31* (January 1988): 344.

4. T. A. Meckler and J. D. Vogler, "Reading Improvement through Health Instruction," *Educational Leadership 42* (February 1985): 51.

5. L. Madden, "Improve Reading Attitudes of Poor Readers through Cooperative Reading Teams," *Reading Teacher 42* (December 1988): 195.

6. M. Montague and M. L. Tanner, "Reading Strategy Groups for Content Area Instruction," *Journal of Reading* 29 (May 1987): 719.

7. E. P. Haller *et al.*, "Can Comprehension Be Taught?" *Educational Researcher* 17 (December 1988): 8.

8. Reading/Language in Secondary Schools Subcommittee of IRA, "Secondary Perspectives: Developing Strategic Learners," *Journal of Reading 33* (October 1989): 62.

9. B. Harp, "How Are We Using What We Know about Literacy Processes in the Content Areas?" *Reading Teacher 42* (May 1989): 726-27.

10. W. Brozo and C. Tomlinson, "Literature: The Key to Lively Content Courses," *Reading Teacher 40* (December 1986): 288.

11. D. Nessel, "Reading Comprehension: Asking the Right Questions," *Phi Delta Kappan 68* (February 1987): 445.

12. J. Nelson-Herber, "Expanding and Refining Vocabulary in Content Areas," *Journal of Reading 29* (April 1986): 626.

13. *Op. cit.*: 628.

14. J. Robinson, III, "Criteria for the Selection and Use of Health Education Reading Materials," *Health Education 19* (August-September 1988): 33.

15. B. Armbruster and T. Anderson, "Selecting 'Considerate' Content Area Textbooks," *Remedial and Special Education- (RASE) 9* (January-February 1988): 47-52.

16. C. Mathison, "Activating Student Interest in Content-Area Reading," *Journal of Reading 33* (December 1989): 171-72.

17. A. L. Manna, "Children's Literature in the School Health Education Program," *Journal of School Health 54* (January 1984): 26.

18. W. Brozo and C. Tomlinson, "Literature: The Key to Lively Content Courses," *Reading Teacher 40* (December 1986): 288-93.

19. C. Diller and B. Glessner, "A Cross Curriculum Substance Abuse Unit," *Journal of Reading 31* (March 1988): 554.

20. L. G. Horton, "A Whole-Language Unit for Ninth-Graders," *English Journal 75* (December 1986): 57.

21. E. J. Carnes, "Teaching Content-Area Reading through NonFiction Book Writing," *Journal of Reading 31* (January 1988): 355-58.

22. M. M. and M. L. Tanner, "Reading Strategy Groups for Content Area Instruction," *Journal of Reading 30* (May 1987): 716-23.

23. D. A. Hayes, "Helping Students GRASP the Knack of Writing Summaries," *Journal of Reading 33* (November 1989): 97.

24. Montague and Tanner, *op. cit.*

25. L. B. Gambrell *et al.*, "Using Mental Imagery and Summarization to Achieve Independence in Comprehension," *Journal of Reading 30* (April 1987): 641.

26. R. M. Schwartz, "Learning to Learn Vocabulary in Content-Area Textbooks," *Journal of Reading 32* (1988): 113-17.

27. J. Nelson-Herber, *op. cit.*: 626.

28. S. V. Horton and T. C. Lovitt, "Construction and Implementation of Graphic Organizers for Academically Handicapped and Regular Secondary Students," *Academic Therapy 24* (1989): 635.

29. N. Chase and C. Hynd, "Reader Response: An Alternative Way to Teach Students to Think about Text," *Journal of Reading 31* (March 1987): 531.

30. B. Davey, "How Do Classroom Teachers Use Their Textbooks?" *Journal of Reading 31* (January 1988): 340-45.

31. H. E. Ollmann, "Cause and Effect in the Real World," *Journal of Reading 33* (December 1989): 224.

Annotated Bibliography

Abrahamson, R. and B. Carter, editors. *Books for You. A Booklist for Senior High Students*. Urbana, Illinois: NCTE Comprehensive List, 1988-89.

  Describes nearly 1,200 books (published or reprinted between 1985-1987) of high literary quality and of high interest to teenage readers. Groups in 48 alphabetically arranged categories.

Alvermann, Donna E. "The Role of the Textbook in Discussion," *Journal of Reading 29* (October 1985): 50-57.

  Reports on the various ways teachers use textbooks to make assignments for discussion; offers a checklist for teachers interested in analyzing their own use of text in discussion.

Armbruster, Bonnie and Thomas Anderson. "On Selecting 'Considerate' Content Area Textbooks," *Remedial and Special Education (RASE) 9* (January-February 1988): 47-52.

  Discusses three features of content-area textbooks that make them relatively easy to read, understand, and learn from—structure, coherence, and audience appropriateness. Describes the research basis for each feature, outlines problems with existing textbooks, and presents suggestions for evaluating textbooks.

Azencot, M. and A. Blum. "Effects of a Story-Based Strategy to Enhance Pupil's Ability and Motivation to Read Bio-Technical Texts," *Journal of Biological Education 19* (Spring 1985): 63-66.

  Reports that story-type chapters with dialogues, presented to lower secondary pupils before they read a biotechnical text, (1) increased their objective understanding of terms, biotechnical instructions, and sequences in a process; and (2) enhanced their subjective assessment of the ease and attractiveness of the biotechnical text.

Brozo, William and Carl Tomlinson. "Literature: The Key to Lively Content Courses," *Reading Teacher 40* (December 1986): 288-93.

    Suggests that children's literature used skillfully in tandem with textbooks makes the content curriculum more palatable and comprehensible.

Carnes, E. Jane. "Teaching Content Area Reading through Non-fiction Book Writing," *Journal of Reading 31* (January 1988): 354-60.

    Describes a teaching unit for junior high school content-area classes that is intended to provide students with effective strategies for reading nonfiction. The unit involves independent reading, research, and writing activities that culminate in the publication of student-written books on topics of the student's choice.

Chase, Nancy and Cynthia Hynd. "Reader Response: An Alternative Way to Teach Students to Think about Text," *Journal of Reading 30* (March 1987): 530-40.

    Describes the fundamentals of reader-response theory, focuses on the aspects most relevant to reading instruction, and presents a method of using reader response so as to improve students' ability to learn from text.

Davey, Beth. "Active Responding in Content Classrooms," *Journal of Reading 33* (October 1989): 44-46.

    Describes how Multiple Response Techniques (MRTs) can be used before, during, and after reading to help students comprehend content material better. Argues that MRTs enhance comprehension by engaging all students, focusing on students' strength, training students in reflectivity and self-monitoring, and allowing the teacher quick evaluation of learning.

Davey, Beth. "How Do Classroom Teachers Use Their Textbooks?" *Journal of Reading 31* (January 1988): 340-45.

    Provides results of a survey of how 90 elementary and secondary teachers used their content-area and English textbooks. Reports that both elementary and secondary teachers used textbooks primarily to supplement instruction, but that secondary content-area teachers could benefit from inservice education to assist in flexible use of textbooks.

Davis, J. E. editor, *et al. Your Reading: A Booklist for Junior High and Middle School.* Urbana: NCTE, 1988.

Describes 2,000 books published between 1983-1987 with annotations organized and written to capture student interest. Recommends titles from 61 categories, including reissued classics.

Dennis, Lynn, *et al. "Project READ:S: Effective Design for Content Area Reading," Journal of Reading 32* (March 1989): 520-24.

Describes Project READ:S (Reading Education Accountability Design: Secondary) designed to encourage teachers to adopt more effective techniques of presenting printed materials.

Diller, Christine and Barbara Glessner. "A Cross Curriculum Substance Abuse Unit," *Journal of Reading 31* (March 1988): 553-61.

Describes a reading/science health unit on substance abuse designed for seventh-graders. Finds a high level of interest and involvement as students become more informed about substance abuse and better prepared to make critical decisions.

Dupuis, Mary M. and F. Pit. "Reading Issues," *S-STS-Reporter 4* (April 1988): 9-10.

Discusses reading concerns in a science-technology-society program. Describes possible origins of the lack of reading abilities, and the teacher's role in facilitating the learning process.

Egle, Patricia A. "Open to Suggestion: Reading Trivia," *Journal of Reading 30* (March 1987): 548-49.

Describes how students enthusiastically wrote questions for a reading-trivia game based on a story they read silently in class, and then when they tested their own comprehension by playing the game.

Ericson, Bonnie, *et al.* "Increasing Critical Reading in Junior High Classrooms," *Journal of Reading 30* (February 1987): 430-39.

Describes three content-area reading strategies (anticipation-reaction guides, text previews, and three-level study guides) that capitalize on cooperative small-group learning and emphasize higher-order critical thinking.

Gambrell, Linda B., *et al.* "Using Mental Imagery and Summarization to Achieve Independence in Comprehension," *Journal of Reading 30* (April 1987): 638-42.

Recommends teaching both mental imagery (natural text-reorganization strategy) to students who do not spontaneously use them.

Haller, Ellen P., *et al.* "Can Comprehension Be Taught? A Quantitative Synthesis of 'Metacognitive' Studies," *Educational Researcher 17*(December 1988): 5-8.

Meta-analysis was used to assess the effects of metacognitive instruction.

Harp, Bill. "How Are We Using What We Know about Literacy Processes in the Content Areas?" *Reading Teacher 42* (May 1989): 726-27.

Examines the application of reading-process and writing-process research in content-area instruction. Provides a chart of characteristics and purposes for various writing formats, including outlining, note-taking, captions, news reports, scripts, and books of facts.

Hayes, David A. "Helping Students GRASP the Knack of Writing Summaries," *Journal of Reading 33* (November 1989): 96-101.

Describes the Guided Reading and Summarizing Procedure (GRASP), a classroom procedure for teaching students how to compose summaries of their reading.

Hinchman, Kathleen. "The Textbook and Three Content-Area Teachers," *Reading Research and Instruction 26* (Summer 1987): 247-63.

Describes a study in which three teachers' explanations of their use of textbooks differed from those derived from observations, an ambiguity that may confuse students.

Horton, Linda G. "A Whole Language Unit for Ninth-Graders,"
English Journal 75 (December 1986): 56-57.

    Outlines a student-conducted literature course that used
several classic novels (*My Antonia, The Pearl*, etc.) as the basis for
group discussion, writing, and oral performance activities—all
directed toward extracting meaning from the books selected.

Horton, S. V. and T. C. Lovitt. "Construction and Implementation
of Graphic Organizers for Academically Handicapped and
Regular Secondary Students," *Academic Therapy 24* (May
1989): 625-40.

    Describes a four-step procedure for constructing two types of
graphic organizers (hierarchial and compare/contrast) to help
students gain information from textbooks. Includes teacher- and
student-directed implementation and testing formats for each
method.

Konopak, Bonnie C. "Using Contextual Information for Word
Learning," *Journal of Reading 31* (January 1988): 334-39.

    Discusses possible limitations to the use of context for word-
learning (such as poor reading skills and text complexity). Recommends that content-area teachers be aware of these limitations and
provide specific instructions in determining word meaning from
difficult context.

Lapp, Diane, James Flood, and Diane Farnan, editors. *Content
Area Reading and Learning: Instructional Strategies*. Englewood Cliffs, New Jersey: Prentice-Hall, 1989.

    Covers a wide spectrum of issues. Raises the issue of whether
content-area reading strategies are generic or discipline-specific.
Includes chapters on teaching reading skills in specific content
areas: health, social studies, science, mathematics, literature, and
much more.

Lloyd, Carol V. and Judy N. Mitchell. "Coping with Too Many
Concepts in Science Texts," *Journal of Reading 32* (March
1989): 542-45.

    Describes a method of ranking the concepts in science texts by
three criteria: importance to the curriculum and student interest,

the development of the concept in the text, and the level of background knowledge expected of students. Argues that these ratings should guide instruction.

Lorentzen, Karen M. "The Secondary School Health Education Curriculum and Reading Ability," *Reading Improvement 19* (Winter 1982): 328-31.

Argues that health educators must learn to predict readability levels of textbooks through the use of readability formulas.

Madden, Lowell. "Improve Reading Attitudes of Poor Readers through Cooperative Reading Teams," *Reading Teacher 42* (December 1988): 194-99.

Asserts that reading groups of students at various reading levels motivates poor readers to learn by developing their positive feeling about reading. Describes several reading, language, and content-area activities for cooperative reading teams.

Manna, Anthony L. "Children's Literature in the School Health Education Program," *Journal of School Health 54* (January 1984): 24-26.

Discusses the use of children's literature to help develop an awareness of personal and public health. Suggests techniques for selecting both fictional and informational books. Includes bibliography dealing with nutrition and environmental issues.

Manolakes, George. "Comprehension: A Personal Experience in Content-Area Reading," *Reading Teacher 42* (December 1988): 200-02.

Describes how an expert from an electronics magazine challenged the author to examine problems in reading comprehension.

Mathison, Carla. "Activating Student Interest in Content Area Reading," *Journal of Reading 33* (December 1989): 170-76.

Argues that content-area instruction needs to emphasize factors that motivate the students to read their textbooks. Presents five strategies to link reader and text.

Meckler, Terry A. and James D. Vogler. "Reading Improvement through Health Instruction," *Educational Leadership 42* (February 1985): 50-51.

A project in Los Angeles that infused reading and language into the health curriculum, allows teachers to give additional reading instruction without sacrificing time or curriculum content.

Meeks, Linda and Philip Heit. *Health.* Columbus, Ohio: Merrill Publishing Co., 1990.

A junior-high textbook concerning the areas of mental health, family and social health, growth and development, nutrition and exercise, fitness, drugs, disease and disorders, personal health, safety and first aid, and community and environmental health. Includes an index and glossary.

Mites, Thomas H. "Have Them Read A Good Book: Enriching the Scientific and Technical Writing Curriculum," *Technical Writing Teacher 16* (Fall 1989): 221-32.

Lists about 200 recent science and technology books.

Monson, Dianne L., editor. *Adventuring with Books.* Urbana: NCTE, 1985.

Lists books for pre-K to grade 6.

Montague, Marjorie and Michael L. Tanner. "Reading Strategy Groups for Content-Area Instruction," *Journal of Reading 30* (May 1987): 716-23.

Reviews relevant research in reading comprehension strategies and cooperative learning methods. Describes reading strategy groups and makes practical suggestions for implementation.

Nelson-Herber, Jane. "Expanding and Refining Vocabulary in Content Areas," *Journal of Reading 29* (April 1986): 626-33.

Argues that new vocabulary words should be presented in concept clusters and related to prior knowledge to facilitate organization in memory.

Nessel, Dennis. "Reading Comprehension: Asking the Right Questions," *Phi Delta Kappan 68* (February 1987): 442-45.

Considers drawbacks of verbal questioning to text-reading comprehension on the literal, interpretive, and evaluative levels. Presents an example of how to develop thinking and comprehension through a questioning strategy focused on prediction.

Ollmann, Hilda E. "Cause and Effect in the Real World," *Journal of Reading 33* (December 1989): 224-25.

Describes a method of generating a flow chart that indicates the multiple cause-and-effect relationships in literature and content-area texts. Argues that this teaching strategy aids in the comprehension of difficult text.

Palincsar, Annemarie S. "Metacognitive Strategy Instruction," *Exceptional Children 59* (October 1986): 118-24.

Discusses metacognitive instruction procedures such as "reciprocal high teaching," in which students take the teacher's role and lead dialogue on text meaning. Considers components of successful metacognitive strategy instruction (selecting useful and teachable strategies; informing learners of purpose, transferring control from teacher to learner, and selecting appropriate materials).

Reading/Language in Secondary Schools Subcommittee of IRA. "Developing Strategic Learners (Secondary Perspectives)," *Journal of Reading 33* (October 1989): 61-63.

Argues that strategic teaching develops learners who are independent and able to use a variety of learning strategies derived from the basic cognitive processes that effective students use in content classes: activating, focusing, selecting, organizing, integrating, applying. Emphasizes that by modeling learning strategies and verbalizing their own thinking as they learn, teachers can develop strategic learners.

Richmond, J. B., *et al. Health for Life.* Glenview, Illinois: Scott, Foresman & Co., 1987.

An elementary health textbook, consisting of eight chapters, covering such subjects as feelings, food, the body, safety, medicines, fitness, and community health. Includes an index, a glossary, and study guides for each chapter.

Robinson, James, III. "Criteria for the Selection and Use of Health Education Reading Materials," *Health Education 19* (August-September 1988): 31-34.

Describes variables that tend to influence the utility of health-education literature. Stresses suiting instructional materials to the reading levels of the students and to their ability to comprehend the meaning of the printed materials. Includes a graph for estimating reading level.

Schwartz, Robert M. "Learning to Learn Vocabulary in Content-Area Textbooks," *Journal of Reading 32* (November 1988): 108-17.

Presents an instructional procedure known as "concept of definition" (CD), designed to help students integrate new text information with prior knowledge. Lists procedures to help students monitor their vocabulary development. Provides framework for CD maps.

Sharp, Sidney J. "Using Content Subject Matter with LEA in Middle School," *Journal of Reading 33* (November 1989): 108-12.

Relates the author's experiences using the Language Experience Approach (LEA) and computers to teach content-area material to middle-school remedial reading students. Lists nine goals that can be reached by conjoining LEA and content-area materials.

Simons, Sandra M. "PSRT—A Reading Comprehension Strategy," *Journal of Reading 32* (February 1989): 419-27.

Describes a reading comprehension strategy—Prepare, Structure, Read, and Think (PSRT)—designed for lessons in expository textbooks. Presents a generic guide for planning and conducting a lesson based on PSRT.

Smith, Patricia L. and Gail E. Tompkins. "Structured Notetaking: A New Strategy of Content-Area Readers," *Journal of Reading* *32* (October 1988): 46-53.

Describes a technique using expository text structures and graphic organizers as the basis for taking notes from content-area texts and, later, from lectures.

Spivey, Nancy N. and James R. King. "Readers as Writers Composing from Sources," *Reading Research Quarterly 24* (Winter 1989): 7-26.

Analyzes above- and below-average readers' informational reports that synthesize both source texts and writer-generated materials. Concludes that general reading ability and success at synthesis may be related to cognitive factors associated with comprehension, such as sensitivity to text structure.

Thomas, S.C. *Promoting Health through Children's Literature in Grades K-3: An Annotated Bibliography*. August 1990.

Appropriate bibliographic information and annotations for possible use as supplementary material in health education for children in grades K-3, and for parents and teachers to enrich and expand health promotion efforts.

Webre, Elizabeth C. "Content Area-Related Books Recommended by Children: An Annotated Bibliography Selected from 'Children's Choices 1975-1988." 1989. [ED 303 775]

A categorized, 121-item list of informational and interesting books recommended by students to be read when studying math, health, science, social studies, and the language arts.

Wedman, Judy M. and Richard Robinson. "Effects of Extended In-Service on Secondary Teachers' Use of Content Reading Instructional Strategies," *Journal of Reading 21* (Spring 1988): 65-70.

Discusses results of a study in which 50 secondary school English, math, history, and science teachers participated in a content-area reading inservice program that lasted for two academic years. Discusses how the program influenced teachers' attitudes and concerns about, and knowledge and use of, content-reading instructional strategies.

6

Reading in Physical Education

Elizabeth A. Martin
The Pennsylvania State University

Mary M. Dupuis
The Pennsylvania State University

Bernard J. Badiali
Miami University
Oxford, Ohio

Sports Read

There is a popular notion that reading and athletics are somehow incompatible. According to this view, an athlete cannot excel in the classroom as well as on the field. Some sort of terrible conflict separates the two worlds. This myth is put into jeopardy, of course, every time a new book about physical fitness makes the best-seller list, or a magazine features the life of an outstanding athlete. Sports fans read eagerly to know more about their favorite athletes or how to improve their own performance on the field or court.

The materials prepared to reinforce or teach reading skills and strategies in the physical education classroom are somewhat limited, but there is no lack of material to encourage reading. With a little time and ingenuity, teachers can introduce students to the ideals, motivation, and experiences of athletes whose skills fill the pages of today's sports section and of those whose efforts are a part of sports history. Student interest in sports remains high, and that interest can easily be channeled into specific ways to improve reading.

Research

A limited amount of research linking the teaching of reading skills and physical education is available. One study reported that eight schools in one school district participated in a program of inservice training for teaching reading and language-arts skills in a variety of content areas. Teachers compared their lesson plans during the year, and students were compared on the basis of their reading scores. Teachers who had received inservice training were observed to have better-prepared and more inclusive lesson plans than teachers who had not taken the training; and students of the teachers who had received inservice training scored higher on reading tests than did students of the other teachers.[1]

David Harris reported a study comparing reading and math abilities of elementary students with their motor performance. A high correlation among these three variables suggested that all three should be taught carefully in elementary schools. The goal of this study was to demonstrate that physical education should remain a part of the standard elementary curriculum. It also tells us that we can find ways to allow reading to help in teaching physical skills—and the reverse.[2]

For the past 50 years, research studies have been demonstrating a real and continuing relationship between success in reading and success in physical activities. Our task is to find ways to use the students' interest in physical activities to build an integrated curriculum in which each set of skills contributes to the development of the others.

Strategies and Skills

Reading is not usually thought of as a physical activity. The fact is, however, that reading is both physical and mental. Developing physical prereading skills in the elementary school can be very important to preparing students for reading. Skipping, balancing on one foot, and eye/hand coordination can be valuable to beginning readers.[3] An athlete training to compete, and a reader training to read, have much in common.[4]

Some curriculum guides suggest that individualized instruction in physical education can continue improving readiness beyond the primary grades in the form of read-and-do exercises. For example, learning stations in the gymnasium or an all-purpose room can accommodate small groups. Written instructions for a child to perform basic tasks might read as follows:

Do these exercises at your own pace.

Read *The Tumbler's Manual.*

Do a forward roll (page 10).

Do a backward roll (page 18).

Such exercises reinforce both the physical and the reading skills involved. They provide practice, and they can help teachers diagnose readiness in both areas.[5]

Berta Parrish suggested ways to reinforce the teaching of reading and language skills in the physical education classroom. Listening skills can be developed when teachers read directions aloud, in addition to presenting them in handouts or manuals. Current periodicals can help expand students' understanding of sports and athletic competition. Teachers can stimulate students' interest in reading by comparing personal achievements in the classroom or on the playing field to those of professional athletes.

Parrish identified three ways for physical education teachers to integrate reading and language-arts skills into their teaching. The first is to encourage reading for fun as well as for learning, building on the students' interest in sports and fitness. Second, it is important that lessons reinforce vocabulary and comprehension skills by giving students an opportunity to transfer these skills from reading class to physical education class requirements. Third, and most important, teachers must provide authentic opportunities for reading—all with respect for the time limits of physical education classes. A gesture as simple as having informal or recreational reading materials on the teacher's desk and referring to current personal reading, helps pique students' interest and encourages them to read.[6]

Physical education teachers might consider developing a locker-room library. Sports paperbacks or magazines hold high interest for young athletes.[7] Erma Bruce has collected many well-known poems and stories, both fiction and nonfiction, in *Sports in Literature*.[8] Aimed at secondary students, this collection stretches from classic literature, like Wordsworth's poem "Fishing," to the text of Abbott and Costello's classic dialogue "Who's on First?" The short selections fit many types of lessons.

The bibliography in Berta Parrish's 1980 publication needs to be updated, but it lists a variety of books and magazines that focus on sports.[9] All of the titles are arranged according to the different sports areas, and the books are rated according to reading difficulty. Although almost any newsmagazine or newspaper will have a sports section, this bibliography shows the range of magazine titles that focus on specific sports. A sample follows:

Acrobatics

World Acrobatics

Archery

Archery World

Bow and Arrow

Pro Archer

Archery

Archery and Fencing Guide

Backpacking

Backpacker

Backpacker Footnotes

Backpacking Journal

Parrish's section on "General Periodicals" includes topics such as coaching and women's sports, and overviews of current topics in sports and athletics.

Lance Gentile's monograph, though it requires updating, also includes extensive bibliographies. Gentile suggested a number of specific teaching strategies useful to physical education teachers. Generally, any sports news clipping can help students study vocabulary and help teachers ask comprehension questions on several levels.[10]

An excellent way for a physical education teacher to teach and reinforce vocabulary is through one-page handouts that summarize a lesson, including comprehension questions. Summaries will necessarily include the important terminology of the sport or activity and, perhaps, definitions or examples of each.

Richard Ammon and Suzanne Mittelstadt provided strategies for using newspapers as high-interest reading material for unmotivated readers.[11] Their suggestions fit well with the use of the sports and physical-fitness sections of the newspaper as reading materials in physical education classes.

F. J. J. Peters suggested that a three-level study guide is an excellent way to increase student comprehension. Following almost any reading assignment, students can answer questions on the literal, inferential, and evaluative levels. Peters included them in a senior-high health unit, but the strategy can easily be adapted to any reading used in the physical education classroom.[12] Bulletin boards, too, can interest and inform students in the gym or the physical education classroom.[13]

Page Bristow and Alan Farstrup discussed the physical education teacher's need to develop materials to fit individual students' specific reading needs. They warned that teachers often evaluate reading strategies or comprehension on the assumption that all students are prepared to read and learn from the materials written for their grade level. This assumption is not warranted in any classroom, but especially not in physical education. Teachers must be able to prepare diagnostic materials related to the reading materials being used in the classroom. Diagnostic tools include cloze procedures and informal reading inventories.[14]

Like reading, writing has not been part of the traditional physical education classroom. Spurgeon Wentzell recommended a change by encouraging physical education students to release their feelings about sports and physical activity, and share their reactions in expressive writing. He provided strategies for including writing activities in the physical education curriculum.[15]

Conclusion

Training athletes is not the only goal of the physical education classroom. All students need access to instruction in physcal activities, which often become lifetime sports. The physical education teacher needs to be involved with all the students and with their interests in lifetime activity.

At the same time, athletes need to read about techniques as well as the history of their sports. This method of "smart" training gives the athlete an advantage both on and off the field.

Reading, language, and sports complement the holistic development of everyone who has wanted to know more about a sport or wondered how to design a personal fitness program. Some students are predominantly physical, oriented to the activities of their bodies, in the very structure of their brain. They not only prefer bodily activity to reading and writing but also they must be appealed to in terms of their mental preference for physical activity if the teacher hopes ever to invite their greater attention to books and self-expression through writing. Physical education teachers who care about their students' development as well-rounded human beings will choose ways to involve reading and writing systematically in their classroom.

Notes

1. T. A. Meckler and J. D. Vogler, "Reading Improvement Using the Health Curriculum," paper presented at the annual meeting of the American Educational Research Association, Chicago, Illinois, 1985.

2. I. D. Harris, "Reading, Math, and Motor Performance," *Journal of Physical Education, Recreation, and Dance 53* (November/December, 1982): 21-22, 28.

3. Florida State Department of Education. *Physical Education and Reading: A Winning Team.* Tallahassee (1975).

4. L. M. Gentile, *Using Sports and Physical Education to Strengthen Reading Skills.* (Newark, Delaware: International Reading Association, 1980); *ibid.,* "Using Sports to Strengthen Content-Area Reading Skills," *Journal of Reading 24* (1980): 245-48.

5. Alabama State Department of Education, *How to Reinforce Reading through Health, Physical Education, and Recreation.* (Montgomery: Division of Instructional Services, 1976).

6. B. Parrish, "A Physical Education Teacher's Primer to Reading," supplemental materials for reading courses (Tempe: Arizona State University, 1980).

7. G. H. Maring and R. Ritson. "Reading Improvement in the Gymnasium," *Journal of Reading 24* (1980): 27-31; Parrish, *op. cit.*

8. E. Bruce, *Sports in Literature.* Chicago: National Textbook Co., 1991.

9. Parrish, *op. cit.*

10. Gentile, *op. cit.*

11. R. Ammon and S. Mittelstadt, "Turning on Turned-off Students: Using Newspapers with Senior High Remedial Readers," *Journal of Reading 30* (1987): 708-15.

12. F. J. J. Peters, "The 1980 Olympics: A Schoolwide TV-Reading Project," *Journal of Reading 23* (1980): 300-04.

13. G. H. Maring and Ritson, *op. cit.*

14. P. S. Bristow and A. E. Farstrup, *Reading in Health / Physical Education / Recreation Classes*. (Washington: National Education Association, 1981).

15. S. R. Wentzell, "Beyond the Physical—Expressive Writing in Physical Education," *Journal of Physical Education, Recreation, and Dance 60* (November/December, 1989): 18-20.

Annotated Bibliography

Alabama State Department of Education. *A Miniguide to Reading in the Content Area of Driver and Traffic Safety Education*. Montgomery: Division of Instructional Services, 1976.

  Designed to help the driver-education teacher understand the reading process. Gives suggestions for implementing reading instruction and for identifying the reading skills that students need to become proficient drivers. Lists specific vocabulary development activities. Also covers study skills and methods of making assignments.

Alabama State Department of Education. *How to Reinforce Reading through Health, Physical Education and Recreation*. Montgomery: Division of Instructional Services, 1976.

  Intended for use in inservice workshops for health and physical-education teachers. Contains suggestions to help these teachers integrate the teaching of reading skills into their curricula. Provides sample activities to help students extend their vocabularies and reinforce their comprehension skills. Includes a checklist of study skills, a model teaching unit for beginning volleyball, and a sample test.

Ammon, Richard and Suzanne Mittelstadt. "Turning on Turned-off Students: Using Newspapers with Senior High Remedial Readers," *Journal of Reading 30* (1987): 708-15.

  Describes strategies for using the newspaper sports features as a source of high-interest reading material in classroom reading activities.

Bristow, Page S. and Alan E. Farstrup. *Reading in Health / Physical Education / Recreation Classes*. Washington, D.C.: National Education Association, 1981. [ED 207 973]

  Includes teaching strategies and ways to develop materials to use in the classroom. Emphasizes informal diagnosis of students' reading level, and assessment of the reading level of available materials.

Bruce, Erma. *Sports in Literature*. Chicago, Illinois: National Textbook Co., 1991.

Makes available poems, stories, and nonfiction about sports, from Abbott and Costello's "Who's on First?" to Wordsworth's "Fishing," Thayer's "Casey at the Bat," Housman's "To an Athlete Dying Young," and John Updike. Includes women as athletes and family responses to athletics. Closes with John Kennedy's speech at the National Football Hall of Fame, "The Importance of Participation." Funny, touching, historic—all types of responses to sports.

Colwell, Clyde G. *et al. A Reading Guide: Assisting Content Area Teachers*. Manhattan: Kansas State University and the Manhattan Unified School District, 1983. [ED 228 633]

Provides sample lesson plans and resource lists for many subject areas. Includes physical-education word scrambles, game/activity terms, categorizing and defining terms, comprehension activities.

Florida State Department of Education, *Physical Education and Reading: A Winning Team*. Tallahassee, 1975.

Acquaints physical education teachers with the meaning of reading terms related to physical education. Identifies reading skills that can be taught or reinforced through physical education activities, provides a source for models of such activities, and assists reading teachers in relating reading skills to physical education. Suggests activities for readiness, comprehension, decoding, reference and study skills, and diagnosis. Lists sensorimotor activities under "readiness," including locating parts of the body, balancing on one foot, skipping, and coordinating eye/hand and foot/eye movements. Suggests that teachers use these activities in physical education and reading classes at all levels to help students upgrade their reading skills.

Gentile, Lance M. *Using Sports and Physical Education to Strengthen Reading Skills*. Newark, Delaware: International Reading Association, 1980.

Gives an overview of reading for coaches and physical-education teachers, samples of reading activities for their classes, and procedures for readability testing and evaluation of teaching materials. Includes a good, if dated, bibliography of readings for students in various sports.

Gentile, Lance M. "Using Sports to Strengthen Content Area Reading Skills," *Journal of Reading 24* (1980): 245-48.
Suggests using materials dealing with sports in a variety of ways in content classes to improve reading and critical thinking. Provides specific suggestions for English, mathematics, social studies, science, and health classes.

Harris, I. David. "Reading, Math, and Motor Performance," *Journal of Physical Education, Recreation, and Dance 53* (November/December 1982): 21-22, 280.
Reports on the assessment of 1,767 elementary-school students in reading and math abilities and motor performance; findings were that all three variables are significantly related. Supports earlier research showing that reading and motor skills are highly correlated.

Maring, G. H. and R. Ritson, "Reading Improvement in the Gymnasium," *Journal of Reading 24* (1980): 27-31.
Gives ten teaching strategies for combining reading skill development and physical education instruction.

Meckler, Terry Anne, and James D. Vogler, "Reading Improvement Using the Health Curriculum," paper presented at the annual meeting of the American Educational Research Association, Chicago, Illinois, 1985. [ED 254 836]
Reports on an inservice program for health teachers whose students' scores on reading tests were higher than scores of students whose teachers did not receive the training.

Parrish, Berta. "Reading Practices and Possibilities in Physical Education," *Journal of Physical Education, Recreation, and Dance 55* (March 1984): 73-77.
Reports teaching reading strategies to physical education teachers who use these techniques in their classes. Recommends locker-room libraries to stimulate reading, including books about sports techniques, sports history, athletes, and physical fitness.

Suggests vocabulary reinforcement, alternative learning strategies, and reading and writing options for nonparticipants.

Parrish, Berta. "A Sporting Proposition: Reading in the Physical Education Curriculum," *Reading World 22* (October 1982): 17-25.

Presents these three ways to integrate reading and thinking into physical education classrooms: 1) stimulate recreational reading through students' interest in sports, 2) reinforce vocabulary and comprehension skills by helping students transfer these skills into physical education, 3) provide reading opportunities through individualized instruction.

Parrish, Berta. "A Physical Education Teacher's Primer to Reading." Supplemental materials for reading courses at Arizona State University, Tempe, Arizona, 1980. [ED 225 962]

Includes specific models of reading activities for physical education classes, lesson plans, and other teaching materials.

Peters, F. J. J. "The 1980 Olympics: A Schoolwide TV-Reading Project," *Journal of Reading 23* (1980): 300-04.

Encourages teachers to use the televised broadcasts of the 1980 Olympics as material for reading and other classes. Suggests that the high interest level of the Olympics will motivate reluctant readers to consider reading about Olympic activities and athletes.

Wentzell, Spurgeon R. "Beyond the Physical—Expressive Writing in Physical Education," *Journal of Physical Education, Recreation, and Dance 60* (November/December 1989): 18-20.

Suggests using expressive writing in physical education to encourage students to share their experiences and responses to experiences in sports or other physical activity. Includes specific strategies to place writing in physical education classes; answers teachers' concerns about assessing writing and handling the paper load.

$E=MC^2$

7

Reading in Science

Brian E. Maguire
The Pennsylvania State University

Sarah D. Weidler
Buffalo State College, Buffalo, New York

Overview

A review of the literature of science reading since 1975 yields a variety of information in the areas of research, theory, and practical application. This report is divided into three sections: (1) research on learners, texts and their structure, and the reading process; (2) ideas about skills, strategies, and activities that could be used in teaching reading in the content area of science, and (3) an annotated bibliography.

Learners, Texts, and Comprehension

Many science classes in elementary, middle, and secondary schools depend upon some sort of textbook. Appropriately, much of the research on reading in the content area of science is directed towards textbooks, their structure, visual aids, vocabulary, and readability.

Several researchers have examined the text structure of science materials. Jane Catterson suggested that careful consideration of text structures in content-area textbooks can increase content-area teachers' abilities to help their students read and study textbooks.[1] In a comparative study of four science programs, Linda Meyer examined texts to determine content and general properties. In some texts, content was highlighted by the use of appropriate titles, headings, and subheadings. In other texts, it was necessary to read the entire section in order to identify the specific content. Meyer labeled texts as either "considerate" or "inconsiderate." Considerate texts contained logical structure; the titles, headings, subheadings, and underlying content were arranged in hierarchical patterns that aided comprehension. Inconsiderate texts were plagued by confusing or incorrect sentences and explanations that were not clear. Generally, inconsiderate texts lacked cohesiveness. Not surprisingly, texts with the greatest number of hands-on activities had fewer problems with inconsiderateness.[2]

Carol Lloyd examined scientific concepts presented in text-books and found that texts designed for the least-able students presented the least information and little elaboration. Although other texts presented similar amounts of information, the degree of elaboration that they provided was judged to vary.[3]

James Baumann adapted texts that were judged inconsiderate, rewrote them in a considerate fashion, and compared students' comprehension of the two kinds of texts. He restructured texts by placing the main idea of the paragraph in the first sentence of each paragraph, and the main idea of the passage in the first paragraph of each passage. Titles and subheadings were chosen to cue the content that followed. Boldface, underlined type, or italics were employed to provide additional cues. Baumann found that fifth-grade students who read the rewritten forms of the science texts performed significantly better when asked to compose statements about the main idea of the selection.[4]

That same year, Glen Powell and David Isaacson studied how above-average, average, and below-average readers comprehended science textbooks. On the basis of student performance on tests of free recall of important ideas, they concluded that able readers could identify the hierarchical structure of the text and organize the material they had read.

Powell and Isaacson offered two suggestions to science and reading teachers:

1) Help students identify main supporting ideas as well as major ideas of a paragraph or passage.

2) Teach students to use organizational skills. Outlining is one technique that might be used. Another could be syntactic webbing, or diagramming, which identifies relationships between ideas.[5]

From a survey of high-school biology teachers, Dixie Spiegel and Jill Wright identified textbook characteristics that biology teachers felt were important. Accurate and attractive formats are not the sole requirements of a textbook; organization is also a primary concern. Curiously, teachers seemed not to see the importance of overviews, summaries, questions at the beginning and the end of chapters, and project suggestions. The researchers recommended that high-school biology teachers need to learn about the significance of prereading activities and survey strategies; they should foster students' use of these reading strategies.[6]

Another factor, readability, has long been considered important in textbook selection. Wright and Spiegel stressed that textbooks that help bridge the gap between the students' present level of achievement and the requirements of new tasks, improve students' attitudes toward the topic.[7]

Jeanne Gionfriddo investigated science texts produced over a twelve-year period by one science textbook publisher. During that time span, the reading level of those texts decreased, and the students involved in the study performed significantly better when using the newer, lower-level texts.[8] S. Alan Cohen and Joan Steinberg divided vocabulary found in science textbooks into three groups: technical vocabulary, technical support vocabulary, and non-technical vocabulary. They stressed that the frequent repetition of technical vocabulary supports comprehension by letting students use context clues. Perhaps the mere presence of technical vocabulary does not make texts more difficult, if that vocabulary is presented often and in a variety of contexts.[9]

D. J. Reid and others studied the effect of pictures in text to see if they enhanced comprehension on criterion-referenced tests. They found that pictures may, indeed, help clarify concepts.[10] Roxie Covey and James Carroll concluded from their study of 132 sixth-graders that adjunct pictures facilitate comprehension for some texts. Pictures are an important factor in the comprehensibility of textbooks.[11]

But Richard Williams and Larry Yore found that when students could not extract information from visuals, they tended to ignore those visuals completely. Williams and Yore recommended that students be instructed in the use of supportive instructional strategies, and that text designers, authors, and publishers employ sound design principles in fashioning textbooks.[12]

Donna Alvermann and her colleagues investigated the relationship between a student's available prior knowledge of a topic and the comprehension of text. They read both "compatible" and "incompatible" texts in their study. Compatible text contains ideas or concepts that are supported by a learner's prior knowledge, whereas incompatible text consists of material that is inconsistent with the background knowledge of a student. The inconsistency may stem either from inaccuracies within the text or from misconceptions and errors in the learner's understanding. Alvermann proposed that when texts are incompatible, prior knowledge (whether correct or not) will override the textbook material. It is therefore important for teachers at the middle- and high-school levels to consider both the quantity and quality of the students' prior knowledge resources. Additionally, it is imperative that elementary teachers strive to help students develop accurate representations of science concepts.[13] Hands-on experiences in science can contribute immensely to helping students develop vocabulary knowledge in science. Carol Lloyd and Norma Contreras compared traditional and experiential approaches to teaching science vocabulary. In the traditional approach, students were given lists of glossary words to look up and remember. In the experiential approach, teachers used vocabulary appropriately when talking with students about the hands-on activities in which they were participating. Students in the experiential setting performed significantly better than did those taught traditionally.[14]

Other aids to comprehending science reading include study skills useful in the content areas. On the basis of research with

thirty-two seventh-graders, Candace Grimaldi showed that instruction in the use of advance organizers, headings, pictures,
and diagrams, along with reviewing the previous lesson's concepts, can enhance learning of new material.[15]

Strategies, Methods, and Skill Development in the Classroom

In describing the roles of science and reading teachers in
teaching science, several writers have stressed the importance of
encouraging students to be active learners who interact with
text. It is naive to think that all students will develop critical and
interpretive thinking and study skills on their own. Students
need meaningful experiences in which they can practice and
apply strategies, if they are to find the strategies useful.[16]

Lucille Strain recommended that developmental reading
teachers at the elementary level, and content area teachers at
the high-school level, word questions carefully to facilitate activation of appropriate prior knowledge which the student can
then relate to the current information and that teachers spend
time helping students acquire the following abilities:

- predict outcomes

- draw conclusions

- form generalizations

- perceive relationships

- identify implied sequences

- determine implied causes and effects

- construct summaries.[17]

Lamb[18] and Perry[19] similarly stressed the importance of
appropriate questioning techniques. Prior knowledge also
can be activated through the use of structured overviews,

graphic organizers, and advance organizers in which the ideas and their relationships are represented.[20] Although many content-area teachers feel compelled by time constraints to teach only content, time spent in helping students acquire necessary study skills is time well-spent. The Texas Education Agency offered suggestions on improving reading skills and strategies for questioning, note taking, and testing.[21] Susan Davis suggested using "real" content-area materials when teaching study skills. She reported that students' self-reports of study habits, and their grades in science classes, improved as a result.[22] Beverly Morrison designed a questionnaire to give content-area teachers an opportunity to review prerequisite skills necessary for vocabulary development, comprehension, and efficient study skills.[23]

Anthony Manzo presented three strategies to help students understand concepts in science-related material.[24] Elaine Kaplan and Anita Tuchman suggested five strategies to foster independent learning of content area vocabulary.[25] B. R. Shuman recommended a group approach to learning specialized vocabulary.[26]

Judith Thelen stressed the importance of prereading strategies and the use of guided materials for enhancing understanding of science texts. In her bulletin, she gave examples of two- and three-level concept guides, and made suggestions for simple study guides and study materials that students themselves can construct.[27]

Thomas Bean suggested the use of analogical study guides to enhance background knowledge and facilitate comprehension. For example, when students are learning about the brain, an analogical study guide illustrates the parts and functions of a computer with which the students are already familiar in their classroom use. In the study guide, analogies are drawn between the parts of the brain and the functions of a computer. In addition to facilitating comprehension, analogies may also serve as retrieval cues for recalling new information.[28] Lillian Putnam encouraged comprehension of main ideas through the use of study guides,[29] and C. Miceli described a junior-high school program that incorporated science vocabulary in other content areas such as math, social studies, and the language arts.

Several writers have offered suggestions for using stories and books other than textbooks to enhance and extend students' understanding of scientific concepts.

Daniel Woolsey and Frederick Burton explained the differences between efferent and aesthetic reading. In efferent reading, the reader is interested in extracting usable information from the text. For example, in the efferent reading of an entry about oceans in an encyclopedia, the reader's purpose is to acquire important information about oceans.

In aesthetic reading, the reader is interested in enjoying the text; elements such as action, emotions, and characters all contribute to the reader's enjoyment. For example, reading a narrative about the journey of a crew aboard an experimental submarine might be aesthetic reading. When aesthetic reading includes accurate information, it can enhance concepts taught in science. Woolsey and Burton suggested using a variety of books such as journals and narratives to give students aesthetic reading opportunities in science.[30]

Similarly, in an effort to increase motivation and to clarify difficult concepts, Abraham Blum used narrative stories in which technical terms are part of an attractive story.[31]

John Butzow and Carol Butzow recommended using children's books with scientific themes (whether stated or not) to enhance science lessons. They supplied sample lessons, activities, and a bibliography of children's books that contain scientific themes.[32] Patrick Kangas used analysis of trade books to help students understand the roles of animals in ecosystems.[33]

A language-experience approach to reading in science was described in an article by Carolyn Fehrenbach and others. Their examples of integrating reading and science were developed for grades 1-3, but they could easily be adapted for use at any grade level.[34]

Science Language Experience (SLE), described by Lloyd Barrow and others, is a hands-on program of investigations or experiences with manipulatives as the common starting ground for all students. Speaking, reading, listening, and writing are important components of this approach, which is designed to extend the students' experience beyond the textbook.[35]

Rita Fisher and Robert Fisher recommended using reading and writing activities to enhance students' understanding of science content. They suggested that the traditional sequence of reading—talking—doing—talking should be replaced by *doing—talking—reading—talking*. Rather than being concerned solely with recall, this alternative approach encourages hands-on experiences and understanding.[36]

C.F. Cornett successfully incorporated sustained silent reading into a ninth-grade science classroom.[37] Nicholas Criscuolo used biology as a base for developing interest in reading for sixth-graders,[38] and Ruth Keimig examined a system for integrating reading into the earth-sciences curriculum.[39]

Robert DiSibio and JoAnn Parla described in detail a program known as REAP—Reading Experiences Associated with Partners. In this approach, the teacher acts as guide, stimulator, facilitator, and questioner. Students and their partners work cooperatively to complete task cards that guide their science learning experiences.[40]

A pamphlet produced by the Ohio Academy of Science offered suggestions for developing science programs that encourage research by students. Planning and management strategies are included in the design, as are science, language, reading, writing, and thinking skills.[41] Other writers such as Christine

Diller, Barbara Glessner, Barbara Spector, and Sharon Kossack, provided sample activities and units for integrating reading and science with other areas of the curriculum.[42] These articles describe units focusing on substance abuse and using the news, but the approaches could be used to enhance other science topics as well.

Similarly, Karl Matz encouraged students to develop research strategies and imagination through an integrated approach to reading, writing, and science,[43] and Anita Hewitt and Marie Roos incorporated thematic units and children's literature to develop content-area concepts in the primary grades.[44]

In the area of testing, Steven Rakow and Thomas Gee illustrated some common reading problems found in tests that may confuse students. They offered suggestions to eliminate these problems, and they provided a checklist that should aid in the construction of reader-friendly science tests.[45]

The most important strand that threads its way through the research in reading in the content area of science is the idea that instruction must be meaningful to the learner. Activities and lessons ought to arm students with reading and study strategies that will help them understand their texts and the relationships among the concepts they are learning. Through the use of appropriate literature and activities, science can be integrated with other subject areas to enrich, elaborate, and extend students' learning in science. Science activities, even when isolated and detached, serve as springboards for learning; the science study skills of observation, classification, and record-keeping, when they become integral parts of a student's learning strategies, inform other academic areas as well.

Notes

1. J. Catterson. "Discourse Forms in Content Texts (Open to Suggestion)," *Journal of Reading 33* (1990): 556-58.

2. L. A. Meyer, *et al. Elementary Science Textbooks: Their Contents, Text Characteristics, and Comprehensibility* (Technical Report 386), 1986.

3. C. Lloyd, *How Ideas Are Elaborated in One Topic across Three Biology Textbooks*, 1990.

4. J. F. Baumann, "Effect of Restructured Content Textbook Passages on Middle Grade Students' Comprehension of Main Ideas: Making the Inconsiderate Considerate," 1984.

5. G. H. Powell and D. Isaacson, "Effects of Text Structure on Children's Recall of Science Text," 1984.

6. D. L. Spiegel and J. D. Wright, "'Biology Teachers' Preferences in Textbook Characteristics," *Journal of Reading 27* (1984): 624-28.

7. J. D. Wright and D. L. Spiege, "Teacher-to-Teacher: How Important Is Textbook Readability to Biology Teachers?" *American Biology Teacher 46* (1984): 221-25.

8. J. Gionfriddo, "The Dumbing Down of Textbooks: An Analysis of Six Textbook Editions during a Twelve Year Span," 1984.

9. S. A. Cohen and J. E. Steinberg, "Effects of Three Types of Vocabulary on Readability of Intermediate Grade Science Textbooks: An Application of Finn's Transfer Feature Theory," *Reading Research Quarterly 19* (1983): 86-101.

10. D. J. Reid, *et al.*, "The Effect of Pictures upon the Readability of a School Science Topic," *British Journal of Educational Psychology 53* (1983): 327-35.

11. R. Covey and J. Carroll, "Effects of Adjunct Pictures on Comprehension of Grade Six Science Texts under Three Levels of Text Organization," 1985.

12. R. L. Williams and L. D. Yore, "Content, Format, Gender, and Grade Level Differences in Elementary Students' Ability to Read Science Materials as Measured by the Cloze Procedure," *Journal of Research in Science Teaching 22* (1985): 81-88.

13. D. E. Alvermann, *et al.*, "Prior Knowledge Activation and the Comprehension of Compatible and Incompatible Texts," *Reading Research Quarterly 20* (1985): 420-36.

14. C. V. Lloyd and N. J. Contreras, *The Role of Experience in Learning Science Vocabulary*, 1985.

15. C. Grimaldi, "Can Improvement of Retention of the Science Content Area Be Had By the Addition of Study Skills?" 1987.

16. D. J. Kurland, "The Nature of Scientific Discussion: Reading and the Introductory Science Course," *Journal of Reading 27* (1983): 197-201; J. Guthrie, "Research: Scientific Literacy," *Journal of Reading 27* (1983): 286-88; L. B. Strain, "Developing Interpretive Comprehension Skills in Mathematics and Science," 1984; J. D. Thelen, "Improving Reading in Science," 1984.

17. L. B. Strain, "Developing Interpretive Comprehension Skills in Mathematics and Science," 1984.

18. W. G. Lamb, "Ask a Higher-level Question, Get a Higher-level Answer," *Science Teacher 43* (1976): 22-23.

19. C. M. Perry, "Questions," *American Biology Teacher 41* (1979): 360-62.

20. S. M. Karahalios, "Using Advance Organizers to Improve Comprehension of Content Textbooks," *Journal of Reading 22* (1979): 706-08.

21. Texas Education Agency, *Strategies for Improving Reading Skills in Science*, 1981.

22. S. J. Davis, "Applying Content Study Skills in Co-Listed Reading Classrooms," *Journal of Reading 33* (1990): 277-81.

23. B. Morrison, "The Identification of Reading Skills Essential for Learning in Seven Content Areas at Postelementary Levels," 1980.

24. A. V. Manzo, "Three 'Universal' Strategies in Content Area Reading and Languaging," *Journal of Reading 24* (1980): 146-49.

25. E. M. Kaplan and A. Tuchman, "Vocabulary Strategies Belong in the Hands of Learners," *Journal of Reading 24* (1980): 32-34.

26. B. R. Shuman, "Teaching Teachers to Teach Reading in Secondary School Content Classes," *Journal of Reading 22* (1978): 205-11.

27. J. D. Thelen, *Improving Reading in Science* (Newark, Delaware: International Reading Association, 1984).

28. T. W. Bean, "Analogical Study Guides: Improving Comprehension in Science," *Journal of Reading 29* (1985): 246-50.

29. L. R. Putnam, "Skills and Techniques Useful in Developing Reading Abilities in Science," 1979; C. Miceli, "Developing a Useful Model for Teaching Vocabulary Concepts in Science," *Science Teacher 42* (1975): 21.

30. D. P. Woolsey and F. R. Burton, "Blending Literary and Informational Ways of Knowing," *Language Arts 63* (1986): 273-80.

31. A. Blum, "The Rose Detective—A Strategy to Train Pupils in Reading Bio-technical Texts," *Journal of Biological Education 16* (1982): 201-04.

32. J. Butzow and C. Butzow, "Make Science Livelier with Children's Fiction," *Learning 16* (1988): 50-53.

33. P. C. Kangas, "How to Do It: A Demonstration on the Role of Animals in Ecosystems," *American Biology Teacher 52* (1990): 50-52.

34. C. R. Fehrenbach *et al.*, "LEA On the Moon." *Science and Children 23* (1986): 15-17.

35. L. H. Barrow *et al.*, "Building Bridges between Science and Reading," *Reading Teacher 38* (1984): 188-92.

36. R. J. Fisher and L. Fisher, "Reading, Writing, and Science," *Science and Children 23* (1985): 23-24.

37. C. F. Cornett, "Reading for Fun...in Science Class?" *Science Teacher 42* (1975): 58-59.

38. N. P. Criscuolo, "Centering In on Books and Life Sciences," *Teacher 94* (1977): 82-85.

39. R. T. Keimig, "System for Integrating Reading Content Areas (SIRCA): An Earth Science Application," paper presented at the annual convention of the International Reading Association, Anaheim, California, May 1976.

40. R. DiSibio and J. Parla, "Expand Children's Limits in Reading, Integrate REAP: Reading Experiences Associated with Partners," 1985.

41. Ohio Academy of Science, "Why? Student Research," 1988.

42. C. Diller and B. Glessner, "A Cross-Curriculum Substance Abuse Unit," *Journal of Reading 31* (1988): 553-61; B. Spector and S. Kossack, "Use the News," *Journal of Reading 31* (1988): 566-68.

43. K. A. Matz, "Look What Followed Me Home, Mom!" *Science and Children 27* (1990): 12-15.

44. A. M. Hewitt and M. C. Roos, "Thematic-Based Literature throughout the Curriculum," 1990.

45. S. J. Rakow and T. C. Gee, "Test Science, Not Reading," *Science Teacher 54* (1987): 28-31.

Annotated Bibliography

Alvermann, D. E., *et al.* "Prior Knowledge Activation and the Comprehension of Compatible and Incompatible Texts," *Reading Research Quarterly 20* (1985): 420-36.

> Concludes that in some instances, prior knowledge may interfere with, rather than facilitate, comprehension.

Baumann, J. F. "Effect of Restructured Content Textbook Passages on Middle Grade Students' Comprehension of Main Ideas: Making the Inconsiderate Considerate," paper presented at the National Reading Conference, St. Petersberg, Florida, 1984. [ED 255 865]

> Compares performance of fifth-grade students who used rewritten text passages that were hierarchically arranged ("considerate") with those reading "inconsiderate" texts. Children who read the rewritten forms of the text were able to compose significantly more correct main-idea statements than were the other students.

Barrow, L. H. *et al.* "Building Bridges between Science and Reading," *Reading Teacher 38* (1984): 188-192.

> Describes a K-3 program called SLE (Science Language Experience) that entails speaking, listening, reading, and writing, as well as investigating and manipulating, to extend science learning beyond the textbook.

Bean, T. W. "Analogical Study Guides: Improving Comprehension in Science," *Journal of Reading 29* (1985): 246-50.

> Explains how the use of analogical study guides can enhance background knowledge, guide reading strategies, and provide retrieval cues.

Blum, A. "The Rose Detective—A Strategy to Train Pupils in Reading Bio-technical Texts," *Journal of Biological Education 16* (1982): 201-04.

> Suggests introducing new vocabulary and technical terms within the context of attractive stories to help students overcome difficult texts and to combat lack of motivation. Provides examples.

Butzow, J. and C. Butzow. "Make Science Livelier with Children's Fiction," *Learning 16* (1988): 50-53.

Offers suggestions for using children's books with scientific themes to enhance science teaching. Includes sample lessons, activities, and a bibliography.

Catterson, J. "Discourse Forms in Content Texts (Open to Suggestion)," *Journal of Reading 33* (1990): 556-58.

Stresses that reading specialists must carefully consider text structures when encouraging content-area teachers to help their students read and study texts. Discusses text structures of mathematics, social studies, and science textbooks.

Cohen, S. A. and J. E. Steinberg. "Effects of Three Types of Vocabulary on Readability of Intermediate Grade Science Textbooks: An Application of Finn's Transfer Feature Theory," *Reading Research Quarterly 19* (1983): 86-101.

Suggests that, because technical words are repeated so often, science texts may not be so difficult to read as we may have believed.

Collins, M. "Helping Students Do Better on Tests," *American Biology Teacher 41* (1979): 239-40.

Describes a technique (self-checking key) that should prove useful to students. The key assesses a student's test-taking and study attitudes. Includes directions and the actual "key."

Cornett, C. F. "Reading for Fun...in Science Class?" *Science Teacher 42* (1975): 58-59.

Describes the incorporation of a free-reading period in a ninth-grade science classroom. The students were encouraged to read purely for enjoyment, not for grades. Provides a list of books and magazines at various levels of readability and interest.

Covey, R. and J. Carroll. "Effects of Adjunct Pictures on Comprehension of Grade-Six Science Texts under Three Levels of Text Organization," 1985. [ED 259 946]

Indicates, on the basis of a study involving 132 sixth-graders, that pictures may facilitate comprehension for some science texts.

Criscuolo, N. P. "Centering In on Books and Life Sciences," *Teacher 94* (1977): 82-85.

    Describes a year-long program in a sixth-grade classroom that used biology as a base for developing interest in reading. Details assorted science centers. Includes lists of reference materials.

Davis, S. J. "Applying Content Study Skills in Co-Listed Reading Classrooms," *Journal of Reading 33* (1990): 277-81.

    Reports that students involved in learning study skills using real content-area materials improved both their self-reported study habits and their grades in science and social studies classes.

Diller, C. and B. Glessner. "A Cross-Curriculum Substance Abuse Unit," *Journal of Reading 31* (1988) 553-61.

    Describes a unit on substance abuse that integrates many areas of the curriculum.

DiSibio, R. and J. Parla. "Expand Children's Limits in Reading, Integrate REAP: Reading Experiences Associated with Partners," 1985. [ED 268 479]

    Details a program in which teachers act as guides, facilitators, stimulators, and questioners. Students work together with partners to complete task cards.

Fehrenbach, C. R. *et al.* "LEA on the Moon," *Science and Children 23* (1986): 15-17.

    Suggests ways to use language experience activities to enhance the development of science concepts.

Fisher, R. J. and L. Fisher. "Reading, Writing, and Science," *Science and Children 23* (1985): 23-24.

    Asserts that reading and writing should be used along with science to develop important skills such as classifying, sequencing, drawing conclusions, and identifying main ideas.

Gionfriddo, J. "The Dumbing Down of Textbooks: An Analysis of Six Textbook Editions during a Twelve-Year Span," 1985. [ED 255 849]

    Shows that the reading levels of selected science texts dropped over a twelve-year period. Students performed significantly better with the newer texts at lower reading levels.

Grimaldi, C. "Can Improvement of Retention of the Science Content Area Be Had by the Addition of Study Skills?" 1987. [ED 281 169]

    Reports study of 32 seventh-grade students to determine the effect of study-skill instruction on retention of science material.

Guthrie, J. "Research: Scientific Literacy," *Journal of Reading 27* (1983): 286-88.

    Discusses the role of reading teachers in helping students gain scientific literacy. Outlines the components of scientific literacy.

Hewitt, A. M. and M. C. Roos. "Thematic-Based Literature throughout the Curriculum," 1990. [ED 314 718]

    Offers practical suggestions for using literature-based materials to teach content-area concepts. Presents a sample unit and a list of books appropriate for primary grades.

Kangas, P. C. "How To Do It: A Demonstration on the Role of Animals in Ecosystems," *American Biology Teacher 52* (1990): 50-52.

    Presents a demonstration in which students examine the role of animals through an analysis of books about ecosystems. Offers suggestions for devloping book analyses, and provides a list of appropriate books about related topics.

Kaplan, E. M. and A. Tuchman. "Vocabulary Strategies Belong in the Hands of Learners," *Journal of Reading* 24 (1980): 32-34.

    Describes five strategies that foster independent learning of content-area vocabulary: (1) Prior to reading the text, students read titles and headings to anticipate new words they may encounter. (2) The teacher presents key concept words to the class and elicits synonyms. (3) Key vocabulary concept words are listed on the board; the students then have two minutes to write as many synonyms that relate to the content area as they can. (4) The students predict the meanings of the words from the context. (5) Students construct a matrix of words with multiple meanings; before reading, they predict what the definitions will be, and they check their predictions afterward.

Karahalios, S. M. "Using Advance Organizers to Improve Comprehension of Content Textbooks," *Journal of Reading 22* (1979): 706-08.

Defines an advance organizer as a written aid to supplement in an explanatory manner the reading and studying of the text. Reports that seventh-graders who read a chapter in a science text using a written handout explaining major concepts, performed better on post-tests than did a group without the handout.

Keimig, R. T. "System for Integrating Reading into Content Areas (SIRCA): An Earth Science Application," paper presented at the annual convention of the International Reading Association, Anaheim, California, May 1976. [ED 122 214]

Examines a system for integrating reading into the earth-science curriculum. Concludes that student, parent, and teacher reactions to SIRCA have been positive.

Kurland, D. J. "The Nature of Scientific Discussion: Reading and the Introductory Science Course," *Journal of Reading 27* (1983): 197-201.

Urges developing scientific literacy by encouraging the students to become actively involved in critical-reading skills.

Lamb, W. G. "Ask a Higher-level Question, Get a Higher-level Answer," *Science Teacher 43* (1976): 22-23.

Discusses the need for stressing high-level types of questions to improve comprehension. Provides extensive references for further reading.

Lloyd, C. "How Ideas Are Elaborated in One Topic across Three Biology Textbooks," 1990. [ED 314 734]

Reports that textbooks designed for the least-able students presented the least amount of information. Other texts presented similar amounts of information and elaborated concepts to varying degrees.

Lloyd, C. V. and N. J. Contreras. "The Role of Experience in Learning Science Vocabulary," 1985. [ED 281 189]

Compares traditional and experiential approaches to science vocabulary instruction.

Manzo, A. V. "Three 'Universal' Strategies in Content Area Reading and Languaging," *Journal of Reading 24* (1980): 146-49.

Suggests three strategies to help students understand concepts in content-area reading: (1) using an oral reading strategy, (2) using the key concept, key terminology, and key question (C/T/Q) strategy, (3) using the question-only strategy.

Matz, K. A. "Look What Followed Me Home, Mom!" *Science and Children 27* (1990): 12-15.

Describes an interdisciplinary unit for elementary school students. Presents possible research strategies, semantic map, and ideas for integrating science and the language arts. Discusses the use of imagination to enhance learning.

Meyer, L. A. *et al. The Heuristic and Measurement Models during a Study of Reading Comprehension* (Technical Report 382), 1985. [ED 267 382]

Describes a longitudinal study in progress since 1983. Investigates how students comprehend science text.

Meyer, L. A. *et al. Elementary Science Textbooks: Their Contents, Text Characteristics, and Comprehensibility (Technical Report 386),* 1986. [ED 278 947]

Compares text structure, content, vocabulary, relative considerateness of the text, and use of diagrams of four science programs.

Miceli, C. "Developing a Useful Model for Teaching Vocabulary Concepts in Science," *Science Teacher 42* (1975): 21.

Reports that several junior high school teachers combined efforts and incorporated science vocabulary into their respective content areas. Games were devised and experimental booklets were prepared. Retention scores for those students who participated in the experimental program were higher than for other students.

Morrison, B. "The Identification of Reading Skills Essential for Learning in Seven Content Areas at Postelementary Levels," 1980. [ED 185 536]

Reports on a questionnaire designed to give content-area teachers an opportunity to review 35 reading/learning skills that are necessary for vocabulary development, comprehension of written materials, and the efficient use of study time.

Ohio Academy of Science. "Why? Student Research," 1988. [ED 289 717]

Offers suggestions for developing a research-based science program that integrates science, reading, language, writing, and critical-thinking skills. Stresses the importance of planning and management.

Perry, C. M. "Questions," *American Biology Teacher 41* (1979): 360-62.

Discusses good questioning techniques for classroom teachers: Encourages wait-time after asking questions, to allow for more comprehensive answers; urges that teachers monitor their own question-asking behavior; discusses the asking of higher-level questions *versus* recall-type questions.

Powell, G. H. and D. Isaacson. "Effects of Text Structure on Children's Recall of Science Text," 1984. [ED 251 826]

Encourages reading instructors to emphasize identification of supporting main ideas as well as major ideas, and to help students develop outlining and other organizational study skills.

Putnam, L. R. "Skills and Techniques Useful in Developing Reading Abilities in Science," 1979. [ED 184 089]

Incorporates methods primarily associated with teaching reading as an isolated subject. Recommends determining the student's reading instructional level, matching text material to that level, developing vocabulary through context clues and Latin and Greek roots, and developing main ideas through study outlines.

Rakow, S. J. and T. C. Gee. "Test Science, Not Reading," *Science Teacher 54* (1987): 28-31.

Illustrates some common problems in tests that might confuse students; offers suggestions and a systematic checklist to aid teachers in developing science tests.

Reid, D. J. *et al.* "The Effect of Pictures upon the Readability of a School Science Topic," *British Journal of Educational Psychology 53* (1983): 327-35.

Concludes that pictures in text may enhance comprehension performance on criterion-referenced tests. Suggests that science and reading teachers should use more than readability formulas when attempting to match students with textbooks.

Shuman, B. R. "Teaching Teachers to Teach Reading in Secondary School Content Classes," *Journal of Reading 22* (1978): 205-11.

Offers useful and practical ideas for all subjects. Recommends use of alphabetizing, cloze procedure to determine readability, a group approach to untangle sentence structure, glossing skills, and teaching techniques for special vocabulary.

Spector, B. and S. Kossack. "Use the News," *Journal of Reading 31* (1988): 566-68.

Provides sample activities that could be used to enhance the teaching of integrated subjects.

Spiegel, D. L. and J. D. Wright. "Biology Teachers' Preferences in Textbook Characteristics," *Journal of Reading 27* (1984): 624-28.

Delineates the characteristics of textbooks that biology teachers deem important, and suggests types of activities that would improve science text comprehension.

Strain, L. B. "Developing Interpretive Comprehension Skills in Mathematics and Science," 1984. [ED 253 854]

Discusses the roles of elementary teachers, reading specialists, and content-area teachers in helping students develop interpretive skills. Discusses questioning techniques and the uses of structured overviews.

Texas Education Agency. *Strategies for Improving Reading Skills in Science,* 1981. [ED 200 955]

Summarizes research, and suggests activities for improving student reading skills in the content area of science.

Thelen, J. D. *Improving Reading in Science.* Newark, Delaware: International Reading Association, 1984. [ED 250 675]

Addresses learning from science text, diagnosing in teaching science, pre-reading strategies, guides, vocabulary, and choosing appropriate materials for science and reading.

Williams, R. L. and L. D. Yore. "Content, Format, Gender, and Grade Level Differences in Elementary Students' Ability to Read Science Materials as Measured by the Cloze Procedure," *Journal of Research in Science Teaching 22* (1985): 81-88.

Insists that students need instruction in how to use visuals and how to extract important information from text. Recommends use of supportive instructional strategies to help students use science texts effectively.

Woolsey, D. P. and F. R. Burton. "Blending Literary and Informational Ways of Knowing," *Language Arts 63* (1986): 273-80.

Describes the differences between efferent and aesthetic reading; suggests that a variety of types of reading (narratives, journals, and transactional texts such as encyclopedias) be used in science instruction.

Wright, J. D. and D. L. Spiegel. "Teacher-to-Teacher: How Important Is Textbook Readability to Biology Teachers?" *American Biology Teacher 46* (1984): 221-25.

Stresses that when the text is appropriate for the students' reading abilities, attitudes will improve, and students will be much more able to meet the demands of the new task.

8

Reading in Social Studies

Darla K. Wilshire
The Pennsylvania State University
Altoona Area School District, Pennsylvania

Philip Berryhill
Fairmont State College
Fairmont, West Virginia

Global Considerations

Three groups of factors are important to reading in social studies:

- text factors (organization, technical vocabulary, and passage design)

- student factors (prior knowledge and motivation)

- teacher factors (the consideration of textual complexity, the teaching of technical vocabulary, techniques to expand unfamiliar context, and the writing-reading connection to interpretation)
  A distinct research base for each group may be useful to teachers practicing in the field.

Mapping the Terrain

The textbook remains a major tool of instruction in social studies classrooms, but studies show that teachers are spending little time helping students comprehend it.[1] In response to the demand for more student-friendly texts, textbook companies have included advanced organizers, subtitle headings, composition topics, and distinct passage structures such as comparison and chronological order. David Hayes suggested that social studies texts today are written "in clear expository language, but elementary school students are much more familiar with the narrative structure found in basal reading series."[2]

Citing research, Patrick Shannon concluded that the teaching of reading is strongly influenced by practices in basal reading series.[3] Students undergo a crucial transition from basal-reader prose to the prose in content-area textbooks. A large number of students have difficulty in reading and comprehending their texts.[4]

Most teachers fail to deal with the problems that their students encounter as a result of poor reading skills.[5] In addition, some texts provide little or no transition in essential reading skills.[6] Although publishers profess that their books teach reading-related skills, their programs rely primarily on having students practice or apply skills without the benefit of instruction in reading.[7]

Passage structure can be an aid to summarizing social-studies texts.[8] Focusing on the features of text can help students see structural characteristics: Is the text organized from the general to the specific, or by comparison and contrast? Are text aids available for the reader? Emphasizing comprehension as the construction of meaning by reading the text interactively can help the student bridge the gap between the known and the new.

An additional problem is the makeup of history texts. Current history books present a world of compartmentalized material rather than an integrated approach to learning.[9] Few texts paint sweeping panoramas of historical, social, political, and literary events; rather, each event has its own separate spot in the chapter.

Maps, charts, and pictures enhance newer texts. Traci Bliss pointed to the considerable increase in the volume of textbook visuals which now constitute nearly one-third of all content in U.S. history texts. She urged textbook publishers to make "explicit links between words and pictures and to limit the use of visuals to those occasions that can significantly enhance the students' understanding of information."[10]

David Armstrong suggested ways for teachers to help students grapple with textbook terminology. Even though modern texts do a reasonably good job of content-related vocabulary, aiding the reader with boldface print and definitions printed in margins, some students may have difficulty with words that carry the narrative discussion. Armstrong noted that it is more productive for a teacher to provide definitions for words carrying the discussion than to refer students to dictionaries. He recommended a "teacher glossary," a word list prepared by the teacher to supplement the text, in which familiar words are used to define the new terms. The teacher can scan the material, identify potential problem words, and develop and distribute a custom-made glossary to students. Armstrong also suggested that teachers help students establish a "purpose for reading."[11]

Textbook publishers continue to respond to the needs of teachers and of students. Patricia Cousin focused on taking advantage of textbook adaptations to help mainstreamed learning-disabled students and diverse groups of learners. She stressed three key teaching emphases that improve textbook use:

- prereading

- engaging students in the learning activity

- having students demonstrate competence and expand their knowledge[12]

Teachers usually need to help students interact with the text for better comprehension and retention of material. Teachers need to link students' existing knowledge to the concepts in the text, to organize the information that students read for retention, and to make the expository style of the text accessible to them.

Germinating Thought—Motivating Students

Not even a well-written textbook will solve all the comprehension problems in the classroom. Carla Mathison asked a common question: Why is it that students do not read their textbooks? If inability is the problem, then we need to teach strategies for reading. Mathison stated that "the focus of instruction needs to include an emphasis on the factors that motivate students to read their textbooks as well as factors that enhance reading ability." [13]

Interest can be stimulated by strategies that link the reader and the text:

- using analogies

- relating personal anecdotes

- disrupting readers' expectations

- challenging readers to resolve a paradox

- introducing novel and conflicting information or situations

The concept of students' prior knowledge and the application of that knowledge to new content, may be the link necessary for increasing students' motivation for reading and for comprehension.

Student Considerations in Research

Student-generated analogies show problem areas encountered in reading social-studies texts.[14] Examining student analogies about reading may offer clues to ways of overcoming difficulties. An example might be to make a comparison between the heart of the city and its transportation arteries and the heart in the physical body with its connecting arteries. Both the teacher and the students can generate these analogies.

Insufficient background knowledge contributes to students' inability to comprehend difficult text material.[15] A reader's schema provides a foundation for making predictions about incoming information. Personal context can help students appreciate the importance of text passages. Assessing what they already know about historical events or geographic localities adds meaning and familiarity to new content.

Students become bored when they are not challenged; by disrupting their learning expectations, teachers can surprise and confuse them and heighten their interest. Asking students to predict what would have happened to America if the South had won the Civil War, for example, makes students use their knowledge to predict consequences.

Challenging students to resolve a paradox by applying conflicting values or factual information that contradicts their present knowledge and beliefs, produces "dynamic disequilibrium," according to Bruce Joyce and Marsha Weil.[16] Etta Miller, Bill Vanderhoof, Henry Patterson, and Luther Clegg have amassed a dozen ways to turn social-studies students on to reading. One example is the "Phony Document" scenario, which presents students with the task of deciding the truth of material presented in a 'phony letter.'[17] Simulations may also provide students with the opportunity to use critical thinking and reading skills.

Introducing novel situations and conflicting information may attract student interest. Court cases in mock-trial style or the interpretation of the law from the individual's as well as the state's point of view, may encourage wider reading among students in the classroom. James Wells, Edward Reichbach, Sharon Kossack, and Joan Dungey recommended using newspapers to teach the difference between fact, opinion, and propaganda and to teach map and globe skills. Cause-and-effect patterns recur as history repeats itself; the newspaper is a good source of relevant issues.[18]

Unless the students are interested, they will learn little. With proper motivation and the imaginative use of available materials, students find history stimulating and relevant to their lives.

Climate Control—Teacher-Directed Strategy

The teacher plays an active role in interpreting text, in motivating the student, and in teaching the reading process. Strategies to promote student comprehension abound. The role of the teacher is to determine individual students' needs through cloze procedures or informal inventories, to assess the areas of weakness in their reading processes and to help them use strategies to improve their ability to read expository text. These learning-from-text strategies include mapping techniques or goal frames, summarizing techniques, graphic organizers, study guides, questioning strategies, the explication of texts, and the recognition of text structure. The writing process may be integrated into the classroom through the reading-writing connection. Computers can help.

Teachers' Considerations in Research

Many teachers feel that teaching historical content outweighs the importance of teaching critical-reading skills. These teachers may be unwilling to invest time in teaching reading. A change in attitude is occurring, however, because teachers have come to recognize the importance of reading comprehension, and they are beginning to assess student reading ability. If students do not develop cognitive abilities—reading, writing, thinking—they will not be able to grasp either the content of their social-studies lessons or its significance for their lives.

Because of the deep concern about the difficulty of the reading material, teachers need to be aware of their students' reading abilities. William Henk and John P. Helfeldt recommended a group reading inventory (GRI) for social-studies classrooms. The GRI is a reading evaluation tool that enables the teacher not only to survey an entire class of students but also to measure how well they have learned specific skills and concepts emphasized in the social-studies curriculum. With that information, the teacher can devise strategies to help students overcome deficiencies.[19] Cloze procedures for determining student reading abilities may also prove useful.[20] In a cloze test, every fifth word in a passage is omitted, and the reader must place a word in the blank that makes sense in that particular context. The test is then scored for the reader's ability to reconstruct the text's meaning.

Many reading deficiencies can be discovered through oral reading, according to William Welker. Do students decode new terms properly? Do they read with proper expression? Do they read in meaningful phrase units? Do they rely too heavily on context and fail to recognize terms, substituting words that distort the book's meaning?[21] Once reading assessment has taken place, teachers can address the skill areas of reading.

Experts in the reading field have identified skills that are necessary for student comprehension. By synthesizing current reading models, and through other investigative research, Barbara Lehman and David Hayes have found "a host of component skills" for critical reading:

- recognizing what is already known through prior learning and experience

- keeping an open mind

- becoming aware of attitudes and values

- developing an attitude of inquiry

- searching for relevant materials

- checking sources

- analyzing language and writing style

- comparing various sources

- developing and refining criteria for evaluating sources[22]

Critical-reading skills help the student read and understand social-studies texts and to make inferences from the material. Skilled readers anticipate what they will read, realize what they are reading, and contemplate the connections between what they know and what they are reading. Teachers must develop such reading strategies in students to help them make the transition from the literal comprehension of text to the formulation of critical thought.

Bonnie Armbuster and Beth Gudbrandsen delineated skills according to the following categories:

- comprehension—interpreting in light of personal experiences, and empathizing

- comprehension—recognizing main idea and details, summarizing and distinguishing fact from fancy, interpreting facts, skimming for information, and recognizing time order

- enriching vocabulary

- using textbook features such as the index, glossary, and appendix

- using reference tools

- organizing information by note-taking, constructing graphs and charts, and outlining.[23]

Teaching strategies appropriate for the social-studies classroom include explication of text passages, the use of computers, writing goal frames and study guides, the use of graphic organizers, the process of writing to learn, the use of literature, and oral reading.

In an effort to aid comprehension, Nancy Piore recommended explication—a way of learning from text.[24] In explication, a student selects a passage for close examination and gives a careful, elegant analysis of its style and content. Students read their passages several times and annotate them, asking questions, writing comments, and drawing arrows from one place to another to indicate connections in thought. Next, students are asked to determine the tone, the language, and the evidence that the authors use. They also examine the structure of the texts. After the work of explication, a student begins to understand the way one writer writes, and learns to read more carefully and to make decisions while reading.

Computers can help some students' reading ability in social studies. Kathlene Willing found that students are motivated by using computers to profit from instruction in reading texts. Find-ings from field tests on a series of computer simulations of history support the concept that well-designed computer pro-grams can provide historically correct content while actively engaging students as readers.[25]

Goal frames and study guides alike help students become better readers. Goal frames, also known as story grammars, provide a true narrative base for students; each frame includes a goal, a plan, an action, and an outcome. This kind of text analy-sis gives students a guide to reading history texts.[26]

Study guides prepare students for reading by focusing their attention on textually explicit material.[27] Social-studies teachers are well-advised to consider the potential that reading assign-ments have for fostering thinking beyond the literal level. Rich-ard Smith's study guide fosters further thinking by asking students to do more than read the text:

- Suggest a different title for the section you have just read.

- If the author of this selection were available to you, what questions would you ask, or what comments would you make to him or her?[28]

This interaction challenges students to work beyond the literal level of comprehension.

The use of graphic organizers, a visual hierarchy of related terms or events, tends to increase students' understanding of what they read. Students who use graphic organizers develop a schema for making predictions and are better able to predict events in history than those students who use only outlining and discussion.[29]

Judith Langer recommended writing as a means to under-standing and to processing content material. In a study of three common study tasks (completing short-answer study questions, taking notes, and writing essays), students were asked to read two social-studies passages covering material that they had not yet studied. When answering short-answer study questions, the students tended to focus on specific ideas that the teacher or textbook author had chosen. When taking notes, they focused on larger concepts, and they integrated ideas across sentence boundaries, but they still treated the subjects superficially. When writing essays, however, the students reconceptualized the content in ways that cut across ideas, focused on larger issues, and integrated the material.[30]

Students must anticipate, question, appreciate, confirm, and imagine as they write. To these purposes, units have been developed to help the reading and writing skills of low achievers in the field of social studies.[31] Mollee Sager recommended story writing as a way to engage students in text. The activity allowed students to write transcripts of narratives they read in class, and it provided a basis for assessing their comprehension of the reading assignment, including the degree to which the events, the geography, and the human drama were a part of the students' background knowledge. Within this approach, students could practice using language the way creative writers do as they develop plot and character.[32]

Sources other than textbooks play a role in developing students' knowledge skills: biographies, picture books, and literature can enhance student achievement and reading skills. Literary fiction can enhance students' understanding of a historical period.[33] Guidelines for selecting and using children's literature to teach social-studies concepts are available for teachers. Area study makes use of historical fiction, folklore, and biographies; the problems approach focuses on themes; and "worldmindedness" uses fiction describing history, geography, and life in other countries.[34] Dixie Spiegel recommended integrating social-studies and adolescent literature. Her strategies include sustained silent reading in the classroom, giving students "what I learned" cards to fill in, making displays on bulletin boards, and comparing a textbook description of a person with a description in literature.[35]

Having used literature as a framework from which to teach social studies, Patricia Crook concluded that the area of social studies offers a natural structure for working with literature. Trade books offer a wide variety of reading for the heterogeneous student population.[36] Trade books may be integrated into the social-studies area through a directed reading-thinking activity (DRTA).

By demonstrating the use of data charts, teachers can show students how to compare and synthesize information from several sources for both written and oral reports.[37]

The use of picture books may entice reluctant readers, non-readers, and poor readers to learn content material. Because they are short, picture books are easy to fit into hectic schedules. Peggy Sharp supplied book titles for consideration by teachers.[38] B. De Lin DuBois and Margaret McIntosh proposed oral reading by teachers in the classroom to promote student interest, imagination, motivation, and comprehension; they recommended that teachers rehearse their readings and keep the first encounter brief, because secondary students are unaccustomed to oral reading.[39]

Contemplations

Much of the research suggests that teachers need help in teaching reading within their own content areas. Bonnie Armbuster and Beth Gudbrandsen emphasized that really good instruction in content-area reading takes time to develop and time to practice.[40] Thomas Gee and Nora Forester noted that reading teachers are on one side of the building, and that content teachers are on the other; seldom do they share ideas, teaching strategies, or knowledge about how students function. Here are seven steps toward a solution of that division within the school:

1) establish schoolwide reading teams

2) offer services to content teachers

3) offer inservice education

4) pair reading teachers and content teachers

5) publish newsletters and other aids

6) subscribe to reading journals

7) furnish planning reminders to teachers.[41]

Reading instruction in reading class alone is not enough. If students are to be well-served, content and reading teachers must cooperate. A student's educational and practical life may depend on the social-studies teacher to be a teacher of reading, as well.

Notes

1. T. Kautsounis, "Interrelation between Social Studies and Other Curriculum Areas; a Review," *The Social Studies 81* (November/December 1990): 283-86.

2. D. Hayes, "Toward Students Learning through the Social-studies Text," *The Social Studies 79* (November/December 1988): 267.

3. P. Shannon, "The Use of Commercial Reading Materials in America's Schools," *Reading Research Quarterly 19* (1983): 68-75.

4. B. Taylor, "Improving Middle Students' Reading and Writing of Expository Text," *Journal of Education Research 79* (1985): 119-25; R. Anderson, "Role of the Reader's Schema in Comprehension, Learning and Memory," in R. Anderson, J. Osbourne and R. Tierney, editors, *Learning to Read in America's Schools* (Hillsdale, New Jersey: Erlbaum, 1984).

5. Y. Tixier y Vigil and James Dick, "Attitudes toward and Perceived Use of Textbook Reading Strategies among Junior and Senior High School Social Studies Teachers," *Theory and Research in Social Education 15* (1987): 51-59; B. Armbuster and B. Gudbrandsen, *Reading Comprehension Instruction in Social Studies Programs or, On Making Mobiles out of Soapsuds* (Report No. 309) (Washington: National Institute of Education, 1984).

6. W. Sesow and C. Sorensen, "A Strategy for Helping Pupils Understand Textbook Content," *The Social Studies 78* (May/June 1987): 140-42.

7. B. Armbuster and B. Gudbrandsen, "Reading Comprehension Instruction in Social Studies Programs," *Reading Research Quarterly 21* (1986): 36-48.

8. C. Roller, "Using Passage Structure As an Aid to Summarizing Social Studies Texts," *The Social Studies 74* (November/December 1984): 268-72.

9. T. Bean, H. Singer, H. Sorter, and C. Frazee, "Acquisition of Hierarchically Organized Knowledge and Prediction of Events in World History," *Reading Research and Instruction 26* (1987): 99-114.

10. T. Bliss, "Visuals in Perspective: An Analysis of U.S. History Textbooks," *The Social Studies 81* (January/February 1990): 10-14.

11. D. Armstrong, "Helping Youngsters Grapple with Textbook Terminology," *The Social Studies 75* (1984): 216-19.

12. P. Cousin, "Toward Better Use of Improved Textbooks," *Reading Research and Instruction 29* (1989): 61-64.

13. C. Mathison, "Activating Student Interest in Content Area Reading," *Journal of Reading 33* (December 1989): 170-176.

14. L. Kuse and H. Kuse, "Using Analogies to Study Social Studies Texts," *Social Education 50* (January 1986): 24-25.

15. D. Garrahy, *Development of Reading and Writing in the Social Studies, Teacher's Guide,* Vista Unified School District, California 1982. [ED 241 434]

16. B. Joyce and M. Weil, *Models of Teaching*, third edition, (Englewood Cliffs, New Jersey: Prentice-Hall, 1986).

17. E. Miller, B. Vanderhoof, H. Patterson, and L. Clegg, "One Dozen Ways to Turn Them On to Reading," *Social Education 51* (November/December 1987): 486-87.

18. J. Wells, E. Reichbach, S. Kossack, and J. Dungey, "Newspapers Facilitate Content Area Learning: Social-studies," *Journal of Reading 31* (December 1987): 270-72.

19. W. Henk and J. Helfeldt, "The Group Reading Inventory in the Social-studies Classroom," *Social Education 49* (March 1985): 224-27.

20. W. Taylor, "Cloze Procedure: A New Tool for Measuring Readability," *Journalism Quarterly 30* (Fall 1953): 415-33.

21. W. Welker, "The PACE Strategy: A Narrative Approach to Teaching," *Reading Today 7* (August/September 1990): 22.

22. B. Lehman and D. Hayes, "Advancing Critical Reading through Historical Fiction and Biography," *The Social Studies 76* (July/August 1985): 165-69.

23. Armbuster and Gudbrandsen, *op. cit.*: 41.

24. N. Piore, "Explication: Learning from Texts," *Social Education 51* (April/May 1987): 279-80.

25. K. Willing, "Computer Simulations: Activating Content Reading," *Journal of Reading 31* (February 1988): 400-09.

26. M. Gray, "One Route to Success in Reading History: The Goal Frame," *The Social Studies 78* (1987): 258-59.

27. D. Schneider and M. Brown, "Helping Students Study and Comprehend Their Social-studies Textbooks," *Social Education 44* (1984): 105-12.

28. R. Smith, "A Study Guide for Extending Students; Reading of Social-studies Material," *The Social Studies 78* (1987): 85-87.

29. Bean, Sorter, Singer and Frazee, *op. cit.*: 744.

30. J. Langer, "Learning through Writing: Study Skills in the Content Areas," *Journal of Reading 29* (February 1986): 400-06.

31. R. Mills, "Using *The Grapes Wrath* in the History Classroom," *Social Studies Review 26* (1987): 43-48.

32. M. Sager, "Exploiting the Reading-Writing Connection to Engage Students in Text," *Journal of Reading 33* (October 1989): 40-3.

33. Mills, *op. cit.*: 44.

34. A. Stoddard, "Teaching Social-studies in the Primary Grades with Children's Literature," paper presented at the annual meeting of the Florida Reading Association, Jacksonville, Florida, October 1984.

35. D. Spiegel, "Using Adolescent Literature in Social-Studies and Science," *Educational Horizons 65* (summer 1987): 162-64.

36. P. Crook, "Children Confront Civil-War Issues: Using Literature as an Integral Part of the Social-studies Curriculum," *The Social Studies 81* (March 1990): 489-503.

37. B. Lehman and P. Crook, "Content Reading, Tradebooks and Students: Learning about the Constitution through Nonfiction," *Reading Improvement 26* (spring 1989): 50-57.

38. P. Sharp, "Teaching with Picture Books throughout the Curriculum," *Reading Teacher 38* (1984): 132-37.

39. B. De Lin Dubois and M. McIntosh, "Reading Aloud to Students in Secondary History Classes," *The Social Studies 77* (September/October 1986): 210-13.

40. Armbuster and Gudbrandsen, *op. cit.* (1986): 47.

41. T. Gee and N. Forester, "Content Reading Programs: Meeting the Promises," *NASSP Bulletin 73* (May 1988): 95-101.

Annotated Bibliography

Anderson, Robert. "Role of the Reader's Schema in Comprehension, Learning, and Memory," in *Learning to Read in American Schools: Basal Readers and Content Texts*, edited by R. Anderson, J. Osborne, and R. Tierney. Hillsdale, New Jersey: Erlbaum, 1984.

   Suggests that a reader's schema based on prior knowledge plays an important role in predicting oncoming information from a text.

Armbuster, Bonnie and Beth Gudbrandsen. *Reading Comprehension Instructions in Social Studies Programs or, on Making Connections out of Soapsuds*. (Report No. 309). Washington: National Institute of Education, 1984.

   Reports on a study to determine whether publishers of texts purported to teach reading-related skills acknowledged the importance of reading in the social-studies curriculum. Found either too little direct-skill instruction or inadequate instruction. Reports that there is little consensus on what reading skills are, and that what is known about reading is not finding its way into content classrooms.

Armbuster, Bonnie and Beth Gudbrandsen. "Reading Comprehension Instruction in Social-studies Programs," *Reading Research Quarterly 21* (1986): 34-48.

   Examines how much, and what kind of, reading instruction is provided by texts in five social-studies books at the fourth- and sixth-grade levels. Concludes that direct instruction is rare in texts examined.

Armstrong, David. "Helping Youngsters Grapple with Textbook Terminology," *The Social Studies 75* (1984): 216-19.

   Suggests methods of enhanced vocabulary instruction. Methods include pointing out specialized use of terms and potential areas of confusion, giving instructions, and glossary preparation.

Bean, Thomas, Harry Singer, Harry Sorter, and Charles Frazee. "Acquisition of Hierarchically Organized Knowledge and Prediction of Events in World History," *Reading Research and Instruction 26* (1987): 99-114.

Indicates that students must be taught how to construct text-based information into a hierarchy, and use it for making predictions in social studies.

Bliss, Traci. "Visuals in Perspective: An Analysis of U.S. History Textbooks," *The Social Studies 81* (January/February 1990): 10-14.

Examines changes in visuals used in U.S. history textbooks through three time periods (1890 to 1920, 1920 to 1940, 1940 to 1960). Examines history texts from 1960 to the present for their use of visuals (illustrations, diagrams, original works of art, and portraits).

Cousin, Patricia. "Toward Better Use of Improved Textbooks," *Reading Research and Instruction 29* (1989): 61-64.

Suggests that textbooks will begin to address the needs of mainstreamed learning-disabled students. Gives suggestions to teachers to help students in content areas.

Crook, Patricia. "Children Confront Civil-War Issues: Using Literature As an Integral Part of the Social-studies Curriculum," *The Social Studies 81* (March 1990): 489-503.

Recommends the use of trade books to supplement textbook presentations. Provides unit instruction for teachers. Includes a bibliography of children's books on the Civil War.

Dubois, B. De Lin and Margaret McIntosh. "Reading Aloud to Students in Secondary History Classes," *The Social Studies 77* (September/October 1986): 210-13.

Recommends that teachers read aloud to students to increase motivation. Suggests some tips for reading orally.

Garahy, Dennis. *Development of Reading and Writing in the Social Studies. Teacher's Guide.* Vista, California, Unified School District, 1982. [ED 241 434]

Outlines a series of social-studies units designed to develop the reading and writing skills of below-average students.

Gee, Thomas and Nora Forester. "Content Reading Programs: Meeting the Promises," *NASSP Bulletin 72* (May 1988): 95-101.

Suggests ways of connecting reading teachers with content-area teachers to improve student reading skills. Recommends a district-wide team program.

Gray, Mary. "One Route to Success in Reading History: The Goal Frame," *The Social Studies 78* (1987): 258-59.

Identifies the "goal frame" as a method of analyzing text by providing a schema of goal, plan, action, and result. Recommends reading for a purpose, and the use of frames for better comprehension and organizational skills.

Hayes, David. "Toward Students Learning through the Social-Studies Text," *The Social Studies 79* (November/December 1988): 226-70.

Recommends that teachers link students' existing knowledge to concepts in text, organize the information, and make the expository style of text accessible to students.

Henk, William and John Helfeldt. "The Group Reading Inventory in the Social-studies Classroom," *Social Education 49* (March 1985): 224-27.

Suggests using the group-reading inventory to evaluate functional reading levels of groups of students. Uses three short questions.

Joyce, Bruce, and Marsha Weil. *Models of Teaching,* third edition. Englewood Cliffs, New Jersey: Prentice-Hall, 1986.

Discusses models of teaching practice for the classroom. Includes strategies for classroom use.

Kautsounis, Theodore. "Interrelation between Social-studies and Other Curriculum Areas: A Review," *The Social Studies 81* (November/December 1990): 283-86.

Evaluates the section of the Handbook of Research on Social-studies Teaching and Learning that deals with the interrelations between social-studies and other curriculum areas (art, music, and literature; science technology; society). Looks at reading research, and writing for social studies. Recommends the integration of social studies into other subject areas.

Kuse, Loretta and Hildegard Kuse. "Using Analogies to Study Social-studies Texts," *Social Education 50* (January 1986): 24-25.

Suggests a strategy to help students overcome reading problems in social studies by formulating analogies and using them to find ways to study the text.

Langer, Judy. "Learning through Writing: Study Skills in the Content Areas," *Journal of Reading 29* (February 1986): 400-06.

Examines how six high-school juniors approached three common study tasks: completing short-answer study questions, taking notes, and writing essays. Reports that different study habits motivate students to use different writing skills and thinking patterns.

Lehman, Barbara and David Hayes. "Advancing Critical Reading through Historical Fiction and Biography," *The Social Studies 76* (July/August 1985): 165-69.

Suggests ways to help social-studies teachers use historical fiction to teach critical-reading skills to intermediate grade students.

Lehman, Barbara and Patricia Crook. "Content Reading, Trade-books and Students: Learning about the Constitution through Nonfiction," *Reading Improvement 26* (Spring 1989): 50-57.

Recommends the use of trade books to help motivate students. Suggests ways to integrate reading into a social-studies unit on the

Constitution. Provides strategies for the use of nonfiction works in the social-studies classroom.

Mathison, Carla. "Activating Student Interest in Content Area Reading," *Journal of Reading 33* (December 1989): 170-76.

Gives five strategies to stimulate student interest in content reading. Includes examples such as the use of analogies for students and the use of prediction.

Miller, Etta, Bill Vanderhoof, Henry Patterson, and Luther Clegg. "One Dozen Ways to Turn Them On to Reading," *Social Education 51* (November/December 1987): 486-87.

Gives twelve strategies for helping students read social-studies material with greater comprehension. Strategies include simulations, debates, and using documents and differing accounts of history.

Mills, Randall. "Using *The Grapes of Wrath* in the History Classroom," *The Social Studies 78* (1987): 43-48.

Shows how to use literary fiction to enhance students' understanding of a historical period. Shows the human side of problems in a historical context.

Piore, Nancy. "Explication: Learning from Text," *Social Education 51* (April/May 1987): 279-80.

Describes a reading/writing technique to have students read a page of text carefully and respond to it. Suggests how to eliminate superficial reading of material while helping students read critically.

Roller, Cathy. "Using Passage Structure as an Aid to Summarizing Social-studies Texts," *The Social Studies 75* (November/December 1984): 268-72.

Discusses problems encountered by students unfamiliar with the structure of the passage. Suggests how to help students overcome difficulties with a specific strategy.

Sager, Mollee. "Exploiting the Reading-Writing Connection to Engage Students in Text," *Journal of Reading 33* (October 1989): 40-43.

> Recommends that students write transcripts of narratives that they read in class, using the teacher as a mentor, and practicing writing as they learn.

Scheider, Donald and May Brown. "Helping Students Study and Comprehend Their Social-Studies Textbooks," *Social Education 44* (1984): 105-12.

> Suggests strategies and activities for developing structured overviews and study guides as a means of organizing content. Presents three phases: prereading, reading, and postreading.

Sesow, William and Carrie Sorensen. "A Strategy for Helping Pupils Understand Textbook Content," *The Social Studies 78* (May/June 1987): 140-42.

> Suggests a need for teachers to help students relate their concrete, nonschool experiences to the abstract content of textbooks. Provides a strategy to relate the content of the text to student experiences.

Shannon, Patrick. "The Use of Commercial Reading Materials in America's Schools," *Reading Research Quarterly 19* (1983): 68-85.

> States that the teaching of reading is strongly influenced by the reading practices suggested in basal readers.

Sharp, Peggy. "Teaching with Picture Books throughout the Curriculum," *Reading Teacher 38* (1984): 132-37.

> States that picture books can be used effectively in teaching all areas of the elementary curriculum. Describes lessons for use in social studies and in other areas.

Smith, Richard. "A Study Guide for Extending Students' Reading of Social-studies Material," *The Social Studies 78* (1987): 85-87.

> Proposes that study guides contain questions that require the type of critical reading that promotes interactive, constructive, and

dynamic cognitive behaviors. Advocates interaction between student and text.

Spiegel, Dixie. "Using Adolescent Literature in Social Studies and Science," *Educational Horizons 65* (Summer 1987): 162-64.

Suggests that literature be used to supplement content-area study. Emphasizes the use of adolescent literature units to motivate and enhance the understanding of students in grades 5 to 8.

Stoddard, Ann. "Teaching Social Studies in the Primary Grades with Children's Literature," paper presented at the annual meeting of the Florida Reading Association, Jacksonville, Florida, October 1984.

Offers guidelines for selecting and using children's literature to teach social-studies concepts. Focuses on area study (using folklore, historical fiction, etc.); problems approach; and "world-mindedness," using fiction to describe history, geography, and other cultures.

Taylor, Barbara. "Improving Middle-Grade Students' Reading and Writing of Expository Text," *Journal of Educational Research 79* (1985): 119-25.

Reports on a study of the effectiveness of reading and/or writing instruction in sixth-grade social studies that focused on text organization, main ideas, and supporting details. Students who received reading instruction did better on recall of textbook material than did others.

Taylor, W. "Cloze Procedure: A New Tool for Measuring Readability," *Journalism Quarterly 30* (Fall 1953): 415-33.

Introduces cloze as a new tool to measure the readability of social-studies textbooks.

Tixier y Vigil, Yvonne, and James Dick. "Attitudes toward and Perceived Use of Textbook Reading Strategies among Junior and Senior High School Social-studies Teachers," *Theory and Research in Social Education 15* (1987): 51-59.

Reports the results of a study surveying 237 junior and senior high school teachers' endorsement and use of selected content-area reading strategies. Shows a gap between perceived attitude toward reading practices and use in the classroom.

Welker, William. "The PACE Strategy: A Narrative Approach to Teaching," *Reading Today 7* (August/September 1990): 22.

Discusses a prereading activity for concept enhancement, an offspring of the advanced organizer technique.

Wells, James, Edward Reichbach, Sharon Kossack, and Joan Dugey. "Newspapers Facilitate Content Area Learning: Social-studies," *Journal of Reading 31* (December 1987): 270-72.

Recommends that newspapers be read in social-studies classrooms to compare and contrast issues, find cause-and-effect patterns, determine fact *versus* opinion, identify propaganda, and learn map skills.

Willing, Kathlene. "Computer Simulations: Activating Content Reading," *Journal of Reading 31* (February 1988): 400-09.

Presents four field tests of Canadian software, which show that computerized interactive fiction teaches both history and study skills in social studies and enhances student motivation.

9

Reading in Business Education

Linda H. Merchant
The Pennsylvania State University

Overview

Workplace literacy is one of the most pressing demands in education today. If we fail to educate our students so that they can maintain a competitive edge when they enter the professional world, we have failed them educationally, economically, and personally. The demands of the marketplace change quickly with the rapid advances in current technology. Business educators who prepare their students to enter a highly technological, fast-paced workplace, must model the real-world environment in their classrooms.

People who work in business must cope with texts from application forms to tax forms, from explanations of benefits packages to computer documentation, from in-house memos to glossy image-piece corporate reports. Equipping students with the reading and writing skills they need to work efficiently with this variety of texts is the literacy business of a business-education curriculum. Students need more than skills in typing and word processing, shorthand, and transcription, filing and operating business machines. Students need critical-thinking and problem-solving skills to comprehend text in courses such as consumer education, general business education, business law, marketing, and accounting. These academically oriented subjects require high-level critical-reading skills. Literacy skills (listening, speaking, writing, problem-solving, and reasoning) are extremely important for today's *beginning* office worker.

Business educators have been aware for decades of the need for manual skills; they are newly aware of the need for literacy skills and thinking strategies that must become an important component of the business education curriculum.

Research Review

Empirical research on reading-skill development in business education has focused primarily on the readability of textbooks used in business education courses. According to *A Dictionary of Reading*, "readability" is the ease of understanding or comprehension because of writing style, and it is an objective estimate or prediction of reading comprehension, usually in terms of reading-grade level, based on selected and quantified variables in a text, namely vocabulary difficulty and sentence difficulty.[1] Many factors in a text influence readability:

- sentence length and complexity

- vocabulary

- abstractness of concepts

- format

- print size

What the reader brings to the text also plays an important role: ability, motivation, interest, and background knowledge.

Nevertheless, of the more than 30 quick, easy-to-use formulas available to assist teachers in calculating readability, most predict the difficulty of a text from its vocabulary and sentence length.

Gary L. Clark and Peter F. Kaminski investigated the readability of 21 textbooks on marketing. They began with the premise that students form a negative or positive attitude toward the study of marketing as a result of their early exposure to marketing textbooks. They used Gunning's "Fog Index," a commonly used readability formula, as an objective method for estimating and predicting the difficulty level of the reading materials. (The higher the *fog* score, the more difficult the text.) Results of the study revealed that seven of the 21 textbooks were appropriate for college graduates, nine for college seniors, two for college juniors, three for college sophomores, and none for secondary-school students. Writing styles that were difficult for students to read caused frustration and indifference. Because marketing concepts can, however, be communicated easily, writing styles that result in high *fog* scores were viewed as unnecessary. Clark and Kaminski found stylistic variation within and among chapters, and they faulted some authors for failing to maintain a range appropriate for the intended audiences.[2]

Low *fog* scores alone, however, are not enough. As Clark and Kaminski cautioned, teachers need to consider additional factors when selecting a text for classroom use:

- organization of the content

- number and difficulty of abstract concepts

- physical features of the text such as typeface

- aids to learning such as graphs, charts, and tables

Gerald Smith, Claire Smith, and Gladys Dronberger applied the Flesch Readability Formula to accounting textbooks.[3] Results varied from a mean reading-grade level of 9.4 to one as high as 12.1. The purpose of this study was threefold:

- to acquaint teachers with the application of the Flesch formula

- to encourage teachers to consider readability results when selecting a text

- to provide quantifiable data on the readability of the 15 textbooks.

Gerald Salzman investigated readability of job-related materials used in insurance and financial institutions.[4] By the FORCAST readability formula, these documents had reading-grade levels from 10.2 (form letters) to 12.0 (reference materials). Salzman's study has strong implications for business educators. Developing reading skills must be an integral part of the business curriculum if graduates are to comprehend the reading materials they encounter in the workplace.

In 1977, Novella Ross compared reading materials handled by beginning office workers to those used in business education classes. Applying the FORCAST formula, she found no significant differences in their readability. Even so, an examination of the instructional materials led Ross to conclude that students should be exposed to more job-related materials, including handwritten and rough-draft materials, notes, memos, and invoices.[5]

In the late 1970s, materials were not so technical as those found in offices today. Replicating Ross's study in the 1990s might reveal a significant discrepancy between the readability of workplace materials and of those used for instruction in business education classes.

Most objective and quantifiable studies have focused on the readability of written materials in the content area of business education. What of developing the skills needed to read the documents? Journals are replete with "I tried this; it worked for me" articles, but there is little research to validate any particular strategy or technique. What is needed is systematic action research by teachers in their own classrooms. Teachers then will be able to say, "I developed this strategy; it worked for me. Here are the data to prove its effectiveness."

Literacy Skills for Business Education

Teachers want their students to become independent, to become critical thinkers and problem solvers, to apply the basic skills they learned in school to the workplace.[6] To accomplish these goals in the business education curriculum, teachers must consider four general categories of literacy skills: vocabulary, comprehension and problem-solving skills, selected learning skills, and writing-to-learn strategies. By helping their students develop strong literacy skills in school, business educators can prepare them to be competent members of the working community.

Vocabulary Skills

To comprehend business education texts, students need the ability to understand specialized technical vocabulary. The style of these texts is often terse, and they are laden with highly specialized terms that represent new or unfamiliar concepts. Many of these terms have multiple meanings, but the student must focus on the precise meaning that applies to the business content.

Betty Roe, Barbara Stoodt, and Paul Burns reasoned that direct instruction of this technical vocabulary is essential.[7] But students need something more—they need to be able to learn new vocabulary on their own when they leave school. William Nagy suggested the following ways of helping students derive meaning from new terms:

- Use the term in context before reading the text.

- Ask students to decipher the meaning from context clues.

- Encourage students to use structural clues (base words and affixes).

The motivation for asking students to figure out word meanings from context is to help them develop word-learning strategies that they can transfer to the workplace.[8]

Instruction that most effectively improves comprehension goes far beyond these contextual and definition approaches. Nagy suggested that integration is a property of vocabulary instruction that is effective in increasing reading comprehension.[9]

A prime example of an integration technique is semantic mapping, also commonly known as networking, webbing, concept mapping, or clustering. In semantic mapping, students integrate any existing knowledge with the new term. They first list other words that are in any way related to the new term. Then they group the words by categories, and they map the relationships among them. With a semantic map, students are able to see the relationships among the words. With a semantic map, students are able to see the relationships between what they already know and the new information they are learning.

SEMANTIC MAP

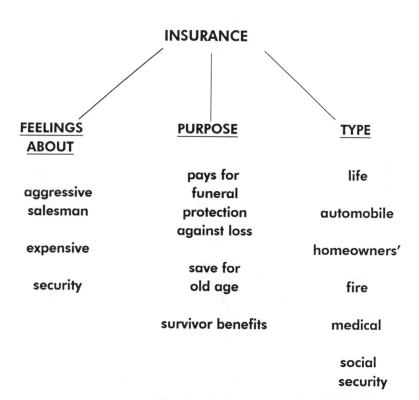

Another highly effective strategy for integrating and rein-forcing the vocabulary essential to understanding new concepts is semantic feature analysis.[10] When using this strategy, stu-dents and teachers together work to construct a grid with essen-tial vocabulary words along one dimension, and major features or characteristics along the other dimension. Students complete the grid by indicating how the vocabulary terms relate to the features or characteristics. They are then able to examine the grid to discover the special characteristics of each new term. Again, students are able to learn the relationships among the concept-laden vocabulary terms.

SEMANTIC FEATURE ANALYSIS

TYPES OF TAXES	PAID TO		
	FEDERAL	STATE	LOCAL
INCOME	X	X	X
SALES		X	X
PROPERTY			X
POLL			X
OCCUPATION			X
EXCISE	X	X	

Joyce Johnston advocated using structural analysis skills to teach new technical vocabulary. The new words for this instruc-tion should be obtained from workplace materials: insurance policies, product warranties, business machine instruction manuals.[11]

Carol Lundgren encouraged business educators to reinforce new vocabulary with games: enjoyable, non-threatening experi-ences that increase skills while teaching content.[12]

A great deal of vocabulary instruction focuses on definitions:

- "Look for the word in the dictionary or glossary."
- "Copy the definition in your notebook."
- "Memorize it for a test on Friday."

Teachers and students alike testify that the meaning of words learned this way usually disappears from memory by the following Friday. With this method, vocabulary knowledge does not increase; reading comprehension does not improve. Students do not acquire basic skills to transfer to the workplace.

What does work, however, is a combination of the context and the definition approaches. Working together on semantic maps and semantic feature analyses, emphasizing concepts, providing repeated exposure to new terms, and employing motivational activities are techniques that, taken together, aid students in the long-term acquisition of new vocabulary.

Comprehension and Problem-Solving Skills

Business education attracts a wide cross section of students, from the potential dropout to the college-bound.[13] This population includes both unmotivated, disabled readers and readers who are highly motivated and competent. This diversity, coupled with the complexity of the business curriculum, poses problems for business educators, particularly in the area of reading comprehension. Individualization of instruction appears to be the key to helping all students gain meaning form print.[14]

Most researchers in content-area reading advocate the directed reading lesson (DRL), sometimes called the directed reading thinking activity (DRTA), as a means to improve reading comprehension of content material. The three steps of this comprehension strategy can easily be employed with business education texts.

1) prereading: providing motivation, activating prior knowledge, introducing key concepts and vocabulary, developing awareness of the task demands of the assignment, and learning the strategies necessary for efficient learning

2) guided reading: leading the search for, and retrieval of, new information through questioning, using study guides if necessary, predicting outcomes, emphasizing silent reading

3) postreading: extending thinking about the new ideas, reinforcing new concepts by using writing as a means of elaboration.[15]

The language experience approach (LEA) is an excellent strategy for students with underdeveloped or depressed reading skills.[16] This approach, originally used with early readers, can easily be adapted to secondary students who are experiencing difficulty with content material.[17] When, for example, students are having trouble understanding the instructions for operating a sophisticated piece of duplication machinery, the instructor demonstrates the operation in a step-by-step manner. As the students watch, they write the instructions in their own words. In doing so, they formulate their own text. They might then keystroke their instructions, thus producing a simplified version of the manual, a version they will understand.

Researchers on comprehension of business-education materials have emphasized using job-related materials rather than, or in addition to, published textbooks.[18] Classroom units about real-world concerns (buying a home, estimating the cost of home insurance, investing money wisely, buying a car, and procuring insurance) have stimulated interest in, and enthusiasm for, business education content. These units provided successful reading experiences, especially for those with underdeveloped reading skills. Newspapers, magazines, brochures, and information gleaned from personal interviews formed the bases of the reading material. Carol Lundgren suggested using magazines and periodicals that deal with timely business issues to teach main-idea comprehension.[19] Claudia McIsaac used similar material to teach summarizing to her students.[20]

If teachers are to facilitate the comprehension of expository text, such as that encountered in the business education curriculum, they need to provide students with a wide variety of reading materials: job-related materials, magazines, journals, newspapers, textbooks, literature. Incoming business students are often enthusiastic about their coursework; however, this enthusiasm may quickly wane.[21] Using literature to teach business content can help maintain enthusiasm. Books such as *Iaccoca: An Autobiography,* by Lee Iaccoca, would be excellent for an introductory course in economics or business practices. Carolyn Hagler and Bobbye Davies suggest the following short list:

Swim with the Sharks without Being Eaten Alive
by Harvey Mackay

Trump: The Art of the Deal,
by Donald Trump

Thriving on Chaos
by Tom Peters

One Small Cookie
by Debbi Fields and Alan Furst

McDonald's: Behind the Golden Arches
by John F. Loru[22]

We praise literature-based programs in elementary school and secondary developmental reading classes these days. Why not in business education, as well?

Another way to maintain interest is to use a wide variety of questioning strategies:

- literal questions (answered in print)

- inferential questions (answered by reading between the lines)

- evaluative questions (answered by making judgments, going beyond the print)

- appreciative questions (answered by assuming the role of a literary critic)[23]

Sound comprehension instruction requires use of these questioning strategies *before* reading when we ask students to set purposes *for* reading and relate the new materials to prior knowledge; *during* reading, when we ask them to monitor their own comprehension; and *after* reading, when we expect them to recall, analyze, and synthesize what they have learned.

Saying, "Read chapter 17 and answer the questions at the end of the chapter," short-changes students' reading comprehension. We need to teach specific strategies, such as semantic mapping, the DRTA or the LEA technique, so that students will internalize these methods and use them, at least in part, for lifelong learning.

Note-taking

Office personnel, especially secretaries and receptionists, must master note-taking skills. Annette Nuñez and Fran Norwood emphasized that note-taking is a complex process involving many factors: mental processes, manual dexterity, organizational skill, and listening ability.[24]

Students do not instinctively know how to take good notes. The skill must be taught, practiced, and reinforced; therefore, most content-area texts contain discussion of note-taking in detail. Thomas Devine offered numerous suggestions for instruction in note-taking.[25] He emphasized that practice with this skill should include materials and activities relevant to the job.

Listening

Although taking notes from printed texts is essential for efficient office practice, taking notes from verbal instruction is of primary importance to the secretarial student or secretary who must possess highly developed listening skills. To help students become efficient listeners for discrete information, Thomas Devine suggested classroom activities in listening for, and identifying, the main ideas of a selection, listening to follow directions, and listening to follow a sequence of events. He encouraged teachers to incorporate carefully structured listening-skill activities into each classroom presentation, progressing from the simple to the complex.[26] Teachers should consider the listening-skill demands of the workplace and use these real-world examples as the basis for their students' exercises.

Vicky L. Crittendon and William F. Crittendon outlined a three-step process for improving listening skills. First, the student must acknowledge that listening skills need to be sharpened. Second, personal strengths and weaknesses are assessed. Finally, strengths must be further developed and weaknesses must be overcome.[27] The Crittendons proposed using exercises similar to those suggested by Thomas Devine.[28]

Following Written Directions

Following written directions is another skill that business-education students must acquire.[31] Skills classes such as typing, word processing, filing, and operation of office machines rely heavily on the ability to follow directions accurately. In spite of good intentions, teachers often foster dependence rather than developing students' independence in deciphering written directions. When a teacher assigns a learning activity to the class, accompanied by detailed written instructions for completion, but then reads the directions aloud, explaining them step by step, the teacher has undermined the purpose of the lesson. The students learn to rely on the teacher's oral explanation rather than on the print.

Because many aspects of office workers' jobs require them to read and follow directions, business educators need to instruct students in techniques for reading and following directions with understanding.

Following directions involves two comprehension skills: locating details and detecting sequence. Just as in proofreading, slow and deliberate reading is required; rereading is often necessary.

It is advisable to present easy activities first, and then proceed to more difficult ones. Using job-related materials (manuals, tax forms, instruction books) enables the students to connect their school activities with the work they will be doing at a "real" job.

"The office worker who cannot comprehend and follow written directions will be at a disadvantage that is immediately evident. When a set of instructions (oral or written) becomes a hurdle instead of a help, the project he or she is working on will not materialize."[32]

Proofreading

"Proofreading has a place in every business course or program. It is imperative that it be a major objective. The quality of materials produced in offices will be only as good as the proofreader."[33] This quality-control skill must be taught carefully and skillfully, for it involves more than simply searching for typographical errors. The proofreader makes sure that a document is correct in format, spelling, grammar, punctuation, syllabication, and number usage. The typist or secretary must have a strong background in mechanics and grammar.

Proofreading also requires special reading skills. Speed reading does not help. A slow, deliberate rate is required to find errors; reading the material twice (once for content and once to detect errors) is necessary; reading from right to left can detect otherwise invisible errors.[34]

Writing to Learn in Business Education: A Tool for Thinking

For business students to process information and think their way through academic business education courses (marketing, business law, accounting, consumer education), they need to see the connections between what they already know, what they want to know, and what they are about to study. A powerful tool for making these connections is writing in the classroom, especially if teachers provide them with concrete classroom activities such as the guided-writing activity and the learning lab or journal.

The guided-writing activity is an instructional strategy that employs all four of the communication processes. The steps are as follows:

Day 1

- Propose a topic, such as taxes or marketing or insurance. Activate prior knowledge by brainstorming and listing students' responses on the chalkboard.

- Ask the class to organize, categorize, and label the responses. Make a semantic map, cluster, or web.

- Ask the students to write about the new topic, using the information from the map.

Day 2

- Have students read a textbook selection about the topic and revise their original writing. Cooperative learning groups often work well in the revision stage.

Day 3

- Ask students to share and discuss their writing with one another or with the entire class.[35]

In addition to making connections, the writing process helps students learn content. Passive learners can become active learners as they struggle with putting the content into their own words.[36] The guided-writing activity helps them prepare for reading new material, summarize and react to new concepts, and share and discuss their new learning with their classmates and teachers.

Another writing-to-learn technique is the learning log. Steven Zemelman and Harvey Daniels listed eight learning-log assignments that teachers might consider—everything from reflections on homework, including questions and puzzles about the reading, to explaining the student's thinking processes and any difficulties the student has encountered.[37] Learning logs can be used to stimulate class discussions, to clarify hazy concepts, and to provide the rationale for grouping students together to investigate an interesting or perplexing problem. This kind of journal writing encourages students to become active learners, critical thinkers, and problem solvers. English teachers have known the value of learning logs for some time. Why not transfer this instructional strategy to the business-education classroom?

Employers often complain that new graduates have deficient written-communication skills.[38] Doug Laufer and Rick Crosser advocated writing-intensive courses in which students work through the steps of writing:

- prewriting

- preparing a rough draft

- peer feedback

- revision

- publication

Integrating these writing steps with the course work not only helps students learn to write but also helps them write to learn the content of their business courses.

Final Thoughts

It is the responsibility of the business educator to make students aware that literacy skills (reading, writing, speaking, listening, problem solving, and critical thinking) are vital for survival in our fast-paced high-tech society. A few years ago, many high-school graduates were hired for clerical positions that required only minimal basic skills.[39] Advances in technology have eliminated most of these positions. Today, even the beginning office worker must possess highly developed literacy skills. Business educators must accept the challenge to provide instruction in these skills so that their students will enter the workplace well-equipped to face today's demands and sufficiently literate to read about, and cope with, tomorrow's new demands.

Many of the strategies and techniques presented in this chapter are not unique to business education. These research-based, content-area reading strategies are also employed in areas such as science, social studies, English, and mathematics. It is logical to apply them to the diverse courses in the business education curriculum. The need is clear for experimentally designed research to assess the effectiveness of incorporating literacy skills into business education.

Notes

1. T. Y. Harris, and R. E. Hodges, editor, *A Dictionary of Reading and Related Terms* (Newark, Delaware: International Reading Association, 1983): 262-63.

2. G. L. Clark and P. F. Kaminski, "Readability of Marketing Principles Textbooks: Another Look at the Data," *The Delta Pi Epsilon Journal 4* (fall 1986): 192.

3. G. Smith, C. Smith, and G. Dronberger, "An Analysis of the Readability of Financial Accounting Textbooks," *The Delta Pi Epsilon Journal 23* (fall 1986): 12-22.

4. G. R. Salzman, "A Descriptive Study of the Reading, Writing, and Math Tasks of Beginning and Experienced Secretarial Workers," doctoral dissertation, Ohio State University, 1979.

5. N. M. Ross, "An Analysis of the Nature and Difficulty of Reading Tasks Associated with Beginning Office Workers' Jobs in the Columbus, Ohio, Metropolitan Area," doctoral dissertation, Ohio State University, 1977.

6. L. Mikulecky, "Real-world Literacy Demands," in *Content Area Reading and Learning,* D. Lapp, J. Flood, N. Farnan, editors. (New Jersey: Prentice Hall, 1989): 123-36.

7. B. Roe *et al., Secondary School Reading Instruction,* fourth edition (Boston: Houghton Mifflin, 1991): 362.

8. W. E. Nagy, *Teaching Vocabulary to Improve Reading Comprehension.* (Urbana, Illinois: ERIC, NCTE, IRA, 1988):8.

9. *Ibid.*: 8-10.

10. W. G. Bronzo and M. L. Simpson, *Readers, Teachers, Learners: Expanding Literacy in Secondary Schools* (New York: Macmillan, 1991): 126-30.

11. J. D. Johnston, "The Reading Teacher in the Vocational Classroom," *Journal of Reading 25* (October 1974): 27-29.

12. C. S. Lundgren, "Practical Approaches for Improving Reading Skills," *The Balance Sheet 68* (November/December 1986): 35-39.

13. D. L. Shepherd, *Comprehensive High School Reading Methods*, third edition (Columbus, Ohio: Charles E. Merrill, 1982): 330.

14. W. H. Miller, *Teaching Reading in the Secondary School* (Springfield, Illinois: Charles E. Thomas, 1974): 401-28.

15. R. T. Vacca and J. A. L. Vacca. *Content Area Reading*, second edition (Boston: Little, Brown, & Company, 1986): 349-50.

16. R.G. Stauffer. *The Language Experience Approach to the Tracking of Reading* (New York: Harper & Row, 1980).

17. E. N. Askov and J. W. Lee, "The Language Experience Approach in the Content-Area Classroom," *Journal of Language Education 2* (January 1980): 13-20.

18. J. C. Schaefer and E. Paradis, "Help the Student with Low Reading Ability," *Journal of Business Education 52* (January 1977): 160-62.

19. Lundgren, *op. cit.*: 35-38.

20. C. McIsaac, "Improving Student Summaries through Sequencing," *The Bulletin 50* (September 1987): 17-20.

21. D. Labonty, "Getting Your Students Interested in Reading," *Business Education Forum 43* (March 1989): 13-14.

22. C. M. Hagler and B. J. Davis, "The Why and How of Promoting Reading in Secondary Business Education," *Journal of Education for Business* (September/October 1990): 15.

23. T. C. Barrett, "Taxonomy of Reading Comprehension," *Reading 360 Monograph* (Lexington, Massachusetts: Ginn, 1972).

24. A. V. Nuñez and F. Norwood, "Succinct Tips for Those Who Take and Give Notes," *Journal of Education for Business 61* (December 1984): 132-35.

25. T. G. Devine, *Teaching Study Skills* (Boston: Allyn & Bacon, 1981).

26. T. G. Devine, "Listening, What Do We Know after 50 Years of Research and Theorizing?" *Journal of Reading 28* (January 1978): 296-304.

27. V. L. Crittendon and W. F. Crittendon, "Improving Listening Skills—A Three-Step Process," *Journal of Business Education 58* (March 1983): 226-28.

28. T. G. Devine, *op. cit.*

29. M. S. Seitz, "Teaching Proofreading for Quality Control," *Business Education Forum 40* (March 1986): 18-20.

30. B. D. Roe, *op. cit.:* 377.

31. M. G. Conroy and C. Hedley, "Communication Skills: The Technology—Education Student and Whole Language Strategies," *The Clearing House 63* (January 1990): 231.

32. J. C. Simon. "Proofreading Skill Can Be Improved," *Journal of Business Education 55* (November 1979): 64-65.

33. Bronzo and Simpson, *op. cit.:* 155.

34. *Ibid.:* 173.

35. S. Zemelman and H. Daniels, *A Community of Writers* (Portsmouth, New Hampshire: Heinemann, 1988): 109-11.

36. D. Laufer and R. Crosser, "The Writing across the Curriculum Concept in Accounting and Tax Courses," *Journal of Education for Business* (November/December 1990): 83-85.

37. J. C. Scott, "Basic Skills and Business Communication," *The Balance Sheet 66* (May/June 1985): 10.

Annotated Bibliography

Askov, E. N. and J. W. Lee. "The Language-Experience Approach in the Content-Area Classroom," *Journal of Language Experience 2* (1980): 13-20.

    Briefly outlines the steps in a language-experience lesson. Advocates this reading approach in secondary content-area classes: English, social studies, science, home economics, music and art, industrial arts. Suggests methods for applying the approach to secondary content.

Barrett, T. C. "Taxonomy of Reading Comprehension," *Reading 360 Monograph*. Lexington, Massachusetts: Ginn, 1972.

    Uses Barrett's four levels of questions. Gives explanations, details, and examples for each level.

Bronzo, W. G. and M. S. Simpson. *Reading, Teaching, Learning: Expanding Literacy in Secondary Schools*. New York: Macmillan, 1991.

    Content-area reading textbook that communicates to teachers and students through the experiences of classroom teachers and teachers as researchers. Has well-developed sections concerning comprehension, vocabulary, writing, and literature.

Clark, G. L. and P. F. Kaminski. "Readability of Marketing Principles Textbooks: Another Look at the Data," *The Delta Pi Epsilon Journal 4* (1986): 181-96.

    Reports the results of an investigation of 21 marketing textbooks to determine their predicted readability using a *fog* index.

Conroy, M. G. and C. Hedley. "Communication Skills: The Technology-Education Student and Whole-Language Strategies," *The Clearing House 63* (January 1990): 231-34.

    Discusses the literacy skills (reading, writing, speaking, listening) within the context of technology education. Advocates the whole-language approach for this specialized curriculum.

Crittendon, V. L. and W.F . Crittendon. "Improving Listening Skills—A Three-Step Process," *Journal of Business Education* 58 (1983): 226-28.

> Discusses the role of listening in the communication process. Outlines a three-step process for teaching listening skills. Encourages business educators to include listening-skill development in all business classes.

Devine, T. G. "Listening: What Do We Know after Fifty Years of Research and Theorizing?" *Journal of Reading 28* (1978): 296-304.

> Summarizes 50 years of research in the area of listening in one comprehensive article. Defines listening. Discusses listening tests and the influence of intelligence on listening. Recommends listening activities for reading and thinking.

Devine, T. G. *Teaching Study Skills*. Boston: Allyn and Bacon, 1981.

> A comprehensive how-to book focused on teaching study skills in all content areas. Offers step-by-step procedures along with the research base for each prescribed skill.

Hagler, C. M. and G. B. Davis. "The Why and How of Promoting Reading in Secondary Business Education," *Journal of Education for Business* (September/October 1990): 13-16.

> Promotes reading-skill development in the business curriculum. Suggests activities that center on real-world materials, particularly literature selections.

Harris, T. L. and R. E. Hodges, editors. *A Dictionary of Reading and Related Terms*. Newark, Delaware: International Reading Association, 1983.

> A convenient desk reference.

Johnston, J. D. "The Reading Teacher in the Vocational Classroom," *Journal of Reading 25* (1974): 27-29.

> Deals primarily with vocational education classes, but includes an interesting strategy for teaching technical vocabulary through structural analysis. Provides sample exercises.

Labonty, D. "Getting Your Students Interested in Reading." *Business Education Forum 43* (1989): 13-14.

> Advocates introducing reading into the business curriculum by using current literature selections. Details the use of Lee Iaccoca's autobiography as the text for "Introduction to Business." Provides a study guide to accompany the strategy.

Lapp, D., J. Flood and N. Farnan. *Content Area Reading and Learning: Instructional Strategies.* Englewood Cliffs, New Jersey: Prentice-Hall, 1989.

> Suggests activities for integrating real-world activities into the business curriculum.

Laufer, D. and R. Crosser. "The Writing across the Curriculum Concept in Accounting and Tax Courses," *Journal of Education for Business* (November/December 1990): 83-87.

> Emphasizes written communication skills for business majors. Promotes the "writing process" as a viable way to teach these skills. Provides sample lessons and procedures.

Lundgren, C. A. "Practical Approaches for Improving Reading Skills," *The Balance Sheet 68* (1986): 35-39.

> Outlines practical and easily implemented suggestions for reading-skill development. Suggests student-selected materials (articles from journals, magazines, and newspapers) as sources for learning content. Advocates integrating humor and games as a motivating strategy to promote literacy.

McIsaac, C. "Improving Student Summaries through Sequencing," *The Bulletin of the Association for Business Communication 50* (1987): 17-20.

> Details a strategy to help students write summaries and abstracts. Emphasizes using job-related materials to teach the skill.

Mikulecky, L. "Real-World Literacy Demands," in *Content Area Reading and Learning*, D. Lapp, J. Flood, and N. Farnan, editors. New Jersey: Prentice-Hall, 1989.

Discusses real-world literacy demands, the changing nature of work, and the problems facing those entering the workforce. Outlines specific activities for business-education students.

Miller, W. H. *Teaching Reading in the Secondary School.* Springfield, Illinois: Charles C. Thomas, 1974.

Details specific reading skills that are necessary in business eduction. Discusses efficient use of textbooks, individualizing instruction, use of the language-experience approach, and directed reading activities.

Nagy, W. E. *Teaching Vocabulary to Improve Reading Comprehension.* Urbana, Illinois: ERIC, NCTE, IRA, 1988.

Provides teachers with knowledge of how to adapt vocabulary instruction to the content areas.

Nuñez, A. V. and F. Norwood. "Survival Tips for Those Who Take and Give Notes," *Journal of Education for Business 61* (1985): 132-35.

Discusses research in note-taking and offers guidelines for taking notes. Offers suggestions to teachers for preparing the lecture so that information can be efficiently transmitted.

Roe, B. D., D. B. Stoodt, and P. C. Burns. *Secondary School Reading Instruction,* fourth edition. Boston: Houghton Mifflin, 1991.

Suggests strategies and techniques for developing skills in following directions, solving problems, vocabulary, and comprehension. Provides examples of reading guides.

Ross, N. M. "An Analysis of the Nature and Difficulty of Reading Tasks Associated with Beginning Office Workers' Jobs in the Columbus, Ohio, Metropolitan Area," doctoral dissertation, Ohio State University, 1977.

Compared reading materials of beginning office workers with the reading activities in business-education classes.

Schaefer, J. C. and E. Paradis. "Help the Student with Low Reading Ability," *Journal of Business Education 52* (1977): 160-62.

Explains four proven techniques to help disabled readers succeed in business education classes: establishing purposes for reading, using SQ3R, using real-world materials, and using materials written at a lower level of difficulty.

Schmidt, J. "Preparing Business Students to Use Office Documents," *Delta Pi Epsilon Journal 4* (1987): 111-24.

Attempts to identify office documents that could be used successfully in the business-education classroom.

Scott, J. C. "Basic Skills and Business Communication: Are We Doing Enough?" *The Balance Sheet 66* (1985): 10-14.

States that the nature of work is quickly becoming more technically oriented, yet the basic skills of those entering the workforce are declining. Suggests ways to improve basic skills within the business curriculum. Stresses basic literacy skills.

Seitz, M. A. "Teach Proofreading for Quality Control," *Business Education Forum 40* (1986): 18-20.

Discusses the elements of efficient proofreading, the skills needed, and the strategies for teaching this ability.

Shepherd, D. L. *Comprehensive High School Reading Methods,* third edition. Columbus, Ohio: Charles E. Merrill, 1982.

Presents a chapter concerning applications of reading skills to business, industrial arts, and home economics. Emphasizes reading materials, vocabulary development, and the unit approach.

Simon, J. C. "Proofreading Skill Can Be Improved," *Journal of Business Education 55* (1979): 64-65.

States that the proofreading skill of typists can be improved through directed proofreading practice. Gives specific suggestions for implementing this practice, with emphasis on the type of materials to use.

Smith, G., C. Smith, and G. Dronberger. "An Analysis of the Readability of Financial Accounting Textbooks," *The Delta Pi Epsilon Journal 23* (1980): 12-22.

>Analyzes 15 accounting textbooks using the Flesch Readability Formula. Urges teachers to use the results when selecting books for classroom use.

Stauffer, R. G. *The Language Experience Approach to the Teaching of Reading*, second edition. New York: Harper and Row, 1980.

>Discusses language experience, directed reading-thinking activities, and the foundation and universality of the approach.

Vacca, R. D. and J. A. L. Vacca. *Content Area Reading*, second edition. Boston: Little, Brown, & Company, 1986.

>Discusses the use of the directed reading lesson as an aid to comprehension of business-education texts.

Zemelman, S. and H. Daniels. *A Community of Writers*: *Teaching Writing in The Junior and Senior High School*. Portsmouth, New Hampshire: Heinemann, 1988.

>Applies the process paradigm for all aspects of teaching writing. Defines terms, presents the challenge, provides various learning activities at all stages of the writing process, including evaluation and "writing to learn."

10

Reading in
Home
Economics

Michele L. Irvin
State University of New York
Cortland, New York

Overview

It has been said that the home economics class is the "last dumping ground" for poor readers. Many administrators and guidance counselors assume that it is safe to put these students in a class in which most of the attention deals with manual skill development.[1]

But a very different picture of the home economics classroom appears in the current literature on home economics education.

Kister noted that home economics programs continually respond to the changing needs of society. American society has changed drastically—from an industrial society to an information-based, technological society that demands the knowledge of critical thinkers.[2]

According to James Pellegrino, home economics programs require "advanced skills in technical reading, decoding, comprehension, analysis, synthesis, and troubleshooting which are part of the daily working environment."[3]

If Kister and Pellegrino are correct, then we must stop dumping poor readers into home economics classrooms. The earlier, inadequate perceptions of these classes have caused a multitude of problems for home economics teachers.

Many students who have difficulty with reading are frustrated, lack positive self-esteem, and have a poor attitude toward education. These students usually find their successes in other ways—ways that lead to disruption of class, detention, or suspension.[4] The home economics teacher is faced with the task of dealing with these problems while simultaneously making the content relevant and motivating, and likewise teaching the reading skills that students need to succeed in school and society.

Gary Cranney suggested that home economics presents eight problems when it comes to teaching reading:

1) Home economics classrooms are filled with students who have difficulty reading.

2) The subject matter can be very difficult for students.

3) The reading materials used in home economics classrooms are limited.

4) Few home economics teachers have the training to teach reading effectively in their classrooms.

5) Information regarding reading and home economics is skimpy.

6) The field of home economics requires a wide range of reading skills.

7) Because of technical advancements, home economics materials have become more difficult to read—both in the classroom and on the job.

8) The perception of home economics as an easy, non-academic subject is misleading.[5]

Research

Research on reading and home economics is scant but valuable to the home economics teacher.

Linnie Sue Comerford reported that students who are poor in reading and lack self-esteem can improve in these areas with an individualized home economics reading lab.[6]

The participants in her study were eighth-grade pre-vocational home economics students with a wide range of reading abilities. Their reading ability was evaluated, and instruction was planned in light of those evaluations. According to Comerford, students became involved and motivated when working at a level at which they could succeed.

Mastering the practical skills offered in home economics increases students' level of motivation and self-esteem, which in turn improves their listening, writing, and reading skills.

In a study focusing on instruction, Beverly Morrison used a questionnaire to assess which reading/learning skills teachers deemed important to developing vocabulary, comprehension, and study skills in home economic classrooms. The results showed that basic reading skills, such as prereading, guided reading, postreading, and effective questioning, are essential to effective reading in the home economics classroom.[7]

Home economics educators know that reading is a valuable life skill that might make the difference in their students' future success.[8]

Skills and Strategies

Succeeding in home economics requires students to use a variety of reading skills:

- advanced skills in technical reading, decoding, comprehension, analysis, synthesis, and troubleshooting

- the ability to read detailed, precise directions, as in reading recipes and preparing food; reading directions for the care and use of machinery; and reading and following training plans

- the ability to detect subtle inferences and interpretations of family dynamics such as appear in adolescent novels

- the ability to read for new information

- the ability to use reference materials such as FFA, VICA, and FHA guidebooks

- the ability to interpret graphs, charts, diagrams, and patterns as in nutrient source charts, process charts, and house plans[9]

Reading the technical vocabulary and concepts of home economics requires sophisticated skills such as the ability to compare and contrast different methods of food preparation or clothing and design techniques. Students must be able to distinguish between cause and effect, whether in family relations and child development or in the economics of supply and demand. They need the ability to expand authors' thoughts beyond statements on a printed page.[10]

To aid comprehension of these varied materials, both Julie Johnson and Karen Lundstrom recommended the use of a three-step process that involves prereading, silent reading, and postreading strategies. During prereading, teachers need to stimulate students' curiosity, develop their interest, and guide them in setting purposes for their reading and making connections between previous learning and new information. During silent reading, teachers can help in several ways as students become actively involved in their reading. In postreading, the teacher and students elaborate on the material with discussions, activities, and projects.[11]

The following skills and strategies expand on the three steps suggested by Johnson and by Lundstrom. Each step includes activities that will help the home economics teacher integrate reading instruction effectively with home economics content.

Prereading Strategies

Teachers can stimulate students' interest in reading by developing their curiosity about concepts contained in the reading material. Concept development starts out best at a concrete level, and gradually progresses to a more abstract level. Whenever possible, hands-on activities, field trips, labs, experiments, films, cooking demonstrations, etc., will involve students with the concept. Simply talking about a particular concept will not be enough for many students to comprehend thoroughly.

Another important prereading strategy is to help students set purposes for reading and make connections between what they have already learned and what they are about to read. Teachers need to survey the material with the students, drawing their attention to the title, illustrations, diagrams, subtitles, summaries, and anything else that suggests content. Posing questions causes students to think about the material and its relevance to information they have already learned, and new information they will learn through reading. This procedure requires students to draw on their prior knowledge to help them make connections and predictions about the new information. Using predictions, the thoughtful reader then sets purposes for reading the material.

The teacher might ask some of the following questions:

- "After looking at the title and subtitles of this chapter, what do you think it will tell us?"

- "How does the diagram on p. 59 relate to the title?"

- "Read the introduction on p. 8 and the summary on p. 20. What new information will we learn from this chapter?"

- "What do we already know? "

To facilitate comprehension, new vocabulary terms need to be presented to students during a prereading discussion. Vocabulary development can take a variety of forms. Johnson uses the following example to have students classify words under general topics:

parts of each grain kernel
   bran
   endosperm
   germ
types of flour
   patent flour
   clear flour[12]

This type of classification helps students relate a new term to a general category already familiar to them.

Another strategy for vocabulary development is a concept of definition developed by Robert Schwartz and Taffy Raphael. Teaching students words through this strategy helps them realize what information makes up a good definition. Asking students "What is it?" "What are its characteristics?" and "What are some examples?" will make them think through important aspects of new words. These three questions help students develop 1) the general class to which the concept belongs, 2) the primary properties of the concept and those distinguishing it from other members of the class, and 3) examples of the concept.[13]

A third strategy for vocabulary development—word-attack skills—includes four components, elaborated by Mary Dupuis and her associates. These four attack skills will help students read technical materials independently and unlock the meanings of unfamiliar words:

- context clues

- structural analysis

- sound patterns

- outside references

Teachers will need to instruct students in the use of context clues to clarify what they read.

Context clues, the information surrounding an unknown word, can be organized according to seven categories:

1. Definition—the descriptive context defines the unknown word.

2. Experience—students use their past experiences to complete the thought.

3. Comparison with known ideas—students compare the unknown word to something they know.

4. Synonym—the preceding context offers a synonym of the unknown word.

5. Familiar expression—our language is filled with expressions that are meaningful to native speakers but confusing to those learning the language.

6. Summary—an unknown word summarizes previous concepts.

7. Reflection of a mood or situation—the author creates a mood with language.[14]

Structural analysis is the process of dividing words into their roots and affixes. A term such as "nonjudgmental," for example, can be more easily understood when it is analyzed into its root, prefix/suffix, and ending: non-judg[e]-ment-al.

Sound patterns help students pronounce new words. They are usually taught in the early elementary grades. The task of the home economics teacher is not to reteach these patterns, but to transfer students' skill in using them to longer, more technical terms—such as the important nutritional terms "carbohydrate" and "riboflavin."

The last word-attack skill, using outside references such as dictionaries, glossaries, encyclopedias, is last for good reason. Teachers often tell students to consult a dictionary when figuring out an unknown word. When the word has only one meaning, and the dictionary entry happens to be understandable, this may be good advice; however, if the word has multiple meanings, and the student is unsure of its usage, problems will occur.

All of the above strategies should be taught within the context of the materials being read. Understanding the information is the ultimate goal.

Silent Reading Strategies

To help students become actively involved in reading the material, teachers can guide them in answering the purpose-setting questions previously mentioned by encouraging them to answer these questions as they read. Other strategies that encourage active participation while reading silently are the use of study guides,[15] [16] and thought maps.[17]

Statements in study guides lead students through a reading selection. Study guides appear in various formats:

- category guides that help students organize information in a chart format

- open-ended guides that force students to think and respond to the material

- guides for difficult material that are explicit and tell the students what to read and what not to read.[18]

Teachers need to model the use of these strategies and provide guided practice before encouraging students to use them independently. It is important that not all study-guide questions be at the level of literal thinking. Higher-level questions encourage students to apply critical thinking skills. The following questions facilitate critical thinking, and they guide students in connecting new information with old.

"Is the cooking time for muffins the same as for the biscuits we made last week? Why is it different?" "Are the ingredients we used in muffins the same as those in biscuits? If not, what is different, and what difference would this make in the product?" "What nutritive values do muffins contribute to the diet? Is this different from that of other breads? Why or why not?"[19]

Semantic maps and thought maps help students organize the information in a visual format. The following is an example of a thought map.[20]

THOUGHT MAP

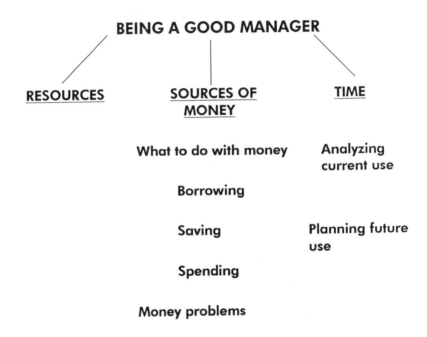

BEING A GOOD MANAGER

RESOURCES   SOURCES OF   TIME
                     MONEY

What to do with money   Analyzing
                               current use

Borrowing

Saving   Planning future
                               use

Spending

Money problems

Post-reading Strategies

Postreading strategies expand on the reading material. The teacher and the students might analyze the material by answering the purpose-setting questions they developed before reading, and discuss how the new information is related to subject matter studied previously.[21] They may review study guides, semantic maps, and thought maps.

At this point, the teacher may want to have students apply the new information through such activities as demonstrations, projects, reports, role playing, arts and crafts, labs, and experiments. In these activities students will use the information learned through reading, and the teacher can check comprehension.

The teacher needs to provide students with strategies that will permit them to read and comprehend material independently. The SQ3R (Survey, Question, Read, Recite, and Review) study strategy incorporates prereading, silent reading, and postreading steps in a student-directed format, as follows:[22]

Survey—students quickly skim through the reading material, reading headings, introductory and summary paragraphs, charts, graphs, and any other information that will give them an overview of the material.

Question—students formulate questions that they expect will be answered during reading. These questions, based on the survey, give the students a purpose for reading the material.

Read—students read the material to answer their own questions.

Recite—students answer the questions. Written answers can become study notes for the material.

Review—Students review their own questions and answers.

This prereading, reading, postreading strategy is very effective as an aid to comprehension; it also helps develop metacognitive skills—skills used to assess one's own processes of comprehension and learning.

Conclusion

Home economics educators prepare students to feed, clothe, and house themselves and their families and to contribute actively to society; therefore, home economics educators know that reading is an important life skill that will make the difference in their students' success in the grown-up world of words, both at home and outside the home.[23] Few jobs in today's society—and no high-paying ones—require no reading as a part of the job description. Clearly, reading is both a life skill and also a vocational skill.

Although the literature on teaching reading skills in home economics classrooms is plentiful, more research is needed on *specific needs*. Further research may identify exact relationships between home economics and reading instruction, and facilitate the successful teaching of both subjects.

Notes

1. C. J. Ley, "Reading: Its Place in the Home Economics Classroom," *Illinois Teacher of Home Economics 22* (1978): 48-50.

2. J. Kister, "Home Economics Education: We Need It!" *Vocational Education Journal 64* (1989): 35-36.

3. J. P. Pellegrino, "Literacy Is Vital to Survival in the Technical Classroom and Workplace," *NASSP Bulletin 72* (1988): 90.

4. L. S. Comerford, "Teaching Home Economics Content Material in an Individualized Reading Skills Laboratory," 1980.

5. A. G. Cranney, "The Reading Skills of Home Economics: Problems and Selected References," 1984.

6. L. S. Comerford, *op. cit.*

7. B. Morrison, "The Identification of Reading Skills Essential for Learning in Seven Content Areas at Postelementary Levels," 1980.

8. P. Incardone, "Teaching Students to Read Better," *Professional Development Series 8* (Arlington, Virginia: American Vocational Association, Inc., 1982).

9. P. Pellegrino, *op. cit.*; C. Thompson, P. Davis, and B. Wade, *Home Economics Reading Strategies. Vocational Reading Series*. College Park: The Pennsylvania State University, 1982; P. J. Hallman, *Teaching Basic Skills in Secondary Vocational Classes,* 1986; A. G. Cranney, 1986; A. G. Cranney, *op. cit.*

10. B. Parrish, editor, *A Home Economics Teacher's Primer to Reading* (Tempe: Arizona State University, College of Education, 1987).

11. J. M. Johnson, "Reading: A Basic Skill for Home Economics," Illinois Teacher of Home Economics 32 (1988): 63-65; K. Lundstrom, "Teaching Reading in Home Economics," *Illinois Teacher of Home Economics 30* (1986): 50-53.

12. J. M. Johnson, *op. cit.*

13. R. M. Schwartz and T. E. Raphael, "Concept of Definition: A Key to Improving Students Vocabulary," *The Reading Teacher 39* (1985): 200.

14. M. M. Dupuis, *et al.*, *Teaching Reading and Writing in the Content Areas* (Glenview, Illinois: Scott, Foresman and Co., 1989).

15. Dupuis, *op. cit.;* Thompson, Davis, and Wade, *op. cit.*, semantic maps.

16. D. D. Johnson and P. D. Pearson, *Teaching Reading Vocabulary*, second edition (Fort Worth, Texas: Holt, Rinehart and Winston, Inc., 1984).

17. Johnson, *op. cit.*

18. Dupuis, *op. cit.*

19. H.T. Spitze, "Helping Students Learn to Think, or the Purpose of the Muffin Lesson," *Illinois Teacher of Home Economics 29* (1986): 123.

20. Johnson, *op. cit.*

21. Johnson, *op. cit.*

22. Dupuis, *op. cit.*; B. D. Roe, B. D. Stoodt, and P. C. Burns, *Secondary School Reading Instruction: The Content Areas* (Boston: Houghton Mifflin Co., 1983); R. T. Vacca and J. A. Vacca, *Content Area Reading*, third edition (Glenview, Illinois: Scott, Foresman and Company, 1989); P. J. Hallman, "Teaching Basic Skills in Secondary Vocational Classes," paper presented at the National Home Economics Education Conference, Columbus, Ohio, 1986.

23. Incardone, *op. cit.*

Annotated Bibliography

Colwell, C. G. *et al*. *A Reading Guide: Assisting Content-Area Teachers*. Manhattan: Kansas State University, Manhattan Unified School District, 1983. [ED 228 633]

> Deals with ideas to help content-area teachers design lessons that include reading and study strategies. Includes two sample lessons that incorporate two reading strategies—Guided Reading Procedure (GRP) and Modified ReQuest.

Comerford, L. S. "Teaching Home Economics Content Material in an Individualized Reading Skills Laboratory," 1980. [ED 209 632]

> Reports on eighth-grade students who fell below level in reading, had poor self-concepts, and received disciplinary action consisting of a six-week individualized home-economics reading lab, which included work in improving self-concept and improving and individualizing reading skills. Students showed success in both areas.

Crabtree, M. P. and C. C. T Maltby. *Teacher's Guide for Home Economics Curriculum Competency Based Modules for Integrating Basic Skills in Reading, Writing, and Mathematics*. Miami: Florida International University, 1982. [ED 223 819]

> Encourages home economics educators to incorporate basic skills in their instruction of home economics.

Cranney, A. G. *et al*. "The Reading Skills of Home Economics: Problems and Selected References," 1984. [ED 249 476]

> Discusses eight problems that occur in home economics classes regarding reading, including large numbers of poor readers enrolled in home-economics classrooms, too few home-economics teachers trained in the area of reading, and the diversity of reading skills needed to be successful in the home economics classroom. Concludes with selected references in the area of reading and home economics.

Davis, A. B. and S. J. Gill. "Teaching Critical Thinking through Questioning and Concept Attainment," *Illinois Teacher of Economics 32* (1989): 186-87.

Provides examples of questions to ask when developing critical thinking, and an example of a "concept attainment model" to improve thinking and reading skills.

Dupuis, M. M., J. W. Lee, B. J. Badiali, and E. N. Askov. *Teaching Reading and Writing in the Content Areas.* Glenview, Illinois: Scott, Foresman and Company, 1989.

Deals with background information and strategies for teaching reading and writing in content-area classrooms. Suggests ways to incorporate the use of the "language-experience approach" in the home-economics classroom.

Hallman, P. J. "Teaching Basic Skills in Secondary Vocational Classes," paper presented at the National Vocational Home Economics Education Conference, Columbus, Ohio, 1986. [ED 267 233]

Identifies the resources available through the National Archives, including learning packages that contain primary-source documents for use by students; columns from *Social Education* that reproduce a document, offers historical background, and suggests learning activities; and summer workshops on instructional uses of primary sources. Presents a sample lesson on Constitutional amendments.

Harbour, M. J. "Back to Basics: Teaching Reading in Home Economics," *Illinois Teacher of Home Economics 28* (1984): 56-57.

Briefly discusses a cooperative content-area reading program that proved effective (based on twelfth-grade reading comprehension test scores). The participants in the program spent a semester learning about reading theory and strategies that could be used in their classrooms. Discusses many reading strategies that can be adapted for use in the home-economics classroom; provides two sample lesson plans using a Modified Guided Lecture Procedure and a Modified ReQuest Technique.

Incardone, P. *Teaching Students to Read Better*. Professional Development Series, No. 6. Arlington, Virginia: American Vocational Association, Inc., 1982. [ED 252 665]

Covers causes of reading difficulties; techniques to teach reading skills in vocabulary, comprehension, and textbook usage; methods used for bilingual students; resource personnel within the school setting; and a model reading unit for an entire school year.

Johnson, D. D. and P. D. Pearson. *Teaching Reading Vocabulary*, second edition. Fort Worth, Texas: Holt, Rinehart and Winston, Inc., 1984.

Provides teachers of any content area with sound strategies for teaching reading vocabulary. Provides a rationale for the use of each topic.

Johnson, J. M. "Reading: A Basic Skill for Home Economics," *Illinois Teacher of Home Economics 32* (1988): 63-65.

Discusses reading as a process that should be integrated into every class. Suggests prereading activities, reading activities, and postreading activities.

Kister, J. "Home Economics Education: We Need It!" *Vocational Education Journal 64* (1989): 35-36.

Discusses work, family, and economic trends, and the response of home-economics education programs to the needs of family and society.

Ley, C. J. "Reading: Its Place in the Home Economics Classroom," *Illinois Teacher of Home Economics 22* (1978): 48-50.

Discusses reading in the home economics classroom. Makes the point that effective content-area teachers need to help students read better and assist those students who need help overcoming reading obstacles. Discusses two steps in helping students improve their reading skills: evaluate the reading materials that actually exist in the classroom, and help students develop comprehension skills that will enable them to read the materials critically.

Lundstrom, K. "Teaching Reading in Home Economics," *Illinois Teacher of Home Economics 30* (1986): 50-53.

Focuses on prereading activities consisting of motivational activities that pique students' interest, preview activities that provide students with information relevant to the reading selection, vocabulary development that employs the strategy of learning word meanings through context, and prequestioning that helps focus on the essential information to be gained from the selection.

Moore, D. W., J. E. Readence, and R. J. Rickelman. *Prereading Activities for Content-Area Reading and Learning*. Newark, Delaware: International Reading Association, Inc., 1983.

Supplements any content-area textbook and teacher's manual. Provides the content-area teacher with information on reading readiness, questioning, predicting, and vocabulary development.

Morrison, B. *The Identification of Reading Skills Essential for Learning in Seven Content Areas at Postelementary Levels*. Madison: University of Individualized Schooling, 1980. [ED 185 536]

Presents data analyzed from a questionnaire sent to content-areas classrooms. Reports that home-economics educators view the following reading and learning skills to be important in their classrooms: the use of context clues to determine word meaning, determining main ideas, ability to apply information from reading, setting purposes for reading, and formulating purpose-setting questions.

Parrish, B., editor. *A Home Economics Teachers' Primer to Reading*. Tempe: Arizona State University, College of Education, 1978. [ED 225 986]

Written by home-economics teachers to aid and promote reading in secondary curriculum programs. Covers reading skills and habits needed in home-economics classrooms, evaluation of students' reading abilities, selection of appropriate instructional materials; techniques to improve vocabulary, comprehension, and study skills; and techniques to stimulate reading in the home-economics classroom.

Pearson, P. D and D. D. Johnson. *Teaching Reading Comprehension.* New York: Holt, Rinehart, and Wilson, 1978.

Provides teachers of any content area with examples of instructional activities that cut across the primary-intermediate-secondary continuum.

Pellegrino, J. P. "Literacy Is Vital to Survival in the Technical Classroom and Workplace," *NASSP Bulletin 72* (1988): 88-94.

Discusses upsurge of interest in literacy and its relevance for vocational education.

Peterate, L. "Cartoons and Comics in the Classroom," *Illinois Teacher of Home Economics 32* (1988): 59-62.

Discusses the uses of cartoons and comics in the home economics classroom to introduce a lesson, promote thinking and writing, and make bulletin boards interesting.

Piercy, D. *Reading Activities in Content Areas: An Ideabook for Middle and Secondary Schools,* second edition. Boston: Allyn and Bacon, 1982.

Contains strategies for developing vocabulary and reading/thinking skills in many content classrooms. Provides information on developing home-economics vocabulary and concepts using visuals, games, and activities.

Roe, B. D., B. D. Stoodt, and P. C. Burns. *Secondary School Reading Instruction: The Content Areas.* Boston: Houghton Mifflin Co., 1983.

Provides information on reading in the secondary school, specifically the reading process, vocabulary development, comprehension, and study skills. Provides sample study guides used in home economics instruction.

Schwartz, R. M. and T. E. Raphael. "Concept of Definition: A Key to Improving Students' Vocabulary," *The Reading Teacher 39* (1985): 198-205.

Describes a way to help students develop a concept of definition through the use of semantic maps.

Spitze, H. T. "Helping Students Learn to Think, or the Purpose of the Muffin Lesson," *Illinois Teacher of Home Economics* 29 (1986): 123-24.

Compares two approaches used in teaching students to make muffins: a training session to "follow the recipe," and an exercise in helping students learn to think, ask questions, analyze, and solve problems, and thereby become independent learners.

Thompson, C., P. Davis, and B. Wade. *Home Economics Reading Strategies*. Vocational Reading Series. College Park: The Pennsylvania State University, 1982.

Helps home-economics instructors integrate reading instruction with home-economics content. Sample lessons are clear and easy to follow.

Vacca, R. T. and J. A. Vacca. *Content Area Reading*, third edition. Glenview, Illinois: Scott, Foresman and Company, 1989.

Contains background information and strategies that deal with content-area reading. Includes extending and reinforcing home-economics concepts and vocabulary, and use of context clues.

Wagner, E.H. "Recipe for Reading Comprehension," *Journal of Reading* 20 (1977): 498-502.

Discusses the possibilities of using recipes from the early pioneer days to teach reading in the classroom. Suggests using recipes to teach sequencing, following directions, building vocabulary, drawing inferences and conclusions, and making comparisons.

11

Reading in Vocational Education

Sonja Brobeck
The Pennsylvania State University

Overview

"Stop!"

"Insert screw B into slot C."

"Use the control codes and escape sequences discussed in Section 6."

"This lever moves in a 1:1 ratio with the rotation of the lens aperture ring to transmit the preset aperture to the camera meter when performing full-aperture metering."

"If you have an open beam ceiling with a 6" wide Hip and 5" rise, then to figure the amount to drop Hip, or amount of chamfer (or bevel) off each edge of Hip, use this formula..."

As can be seen from these examples taken from a variety of occupations, reading is absolutely vital for vocational education and for success in job performance. No matter what career one may choose, the inability to read places severe constraints on one's success. If special-needs students cannot read, they will suffer both reduced employment opportunities and lowered work performance.[1]

· Because reading is considered a prerequisite for vocational education programs, no effort is usually made to identify reading as a vocational skill.[2] On the false assumption that most students already know how to read when they enter their vocational programs, many teachers believe that their students do not have to be taught reading. On the contrary, many vocational students are disadvantaged because of cultural and language difficulties[3] or physical, mental, or emotional handicaps. It is necessary, therefore, that vocational teachers teach reading.

About one-third of students leave school without being able to read well enough to meet the demands of employment.[4] Because many students enter their vocational programs with skill deficiencies and, in many cases, poor attitudes resulting from years of failing to read and write adequately, a caring, supportive teacher is especially important for them. This is a teacher who will teach them not only the vocational skills they need but also the other essential skills, especially reading.

While the experts in both vocational and reading education agree that it is vital for vocational students to be able to read, nobody wants to accept the primary responsibility for teaching them. Vocational teachers—in many states hired as expert, experienced, practicing trade persons but with minimal training in professional education—often protest that they have not been trained as reading teachers,[5] and they do indeed usually have limited opportunities for staff development. Most reading teachers, on the other hand, neither know nor want to know anything about vocational schools.[6] They may, in fact, dislike having vo-tech students in their classes.

A mutual lack of understanding for each other's experiences and expertise prevails, in part because the reading teachers and vocational teachers alike tend to oversimplify each other's fields.[7] In addition, acceptable reading models are lacking because reading models for the content areas have usually been developed by reading teachers without any input from technical vocational content area specialists.[8]

If the vocational teachers choose not to teach reading, the problem persists: Who *does* teach reading? Is it always the job of the English teacher? The reading teacher? Are reading specialists or coordinators available? Where reading teachers and vocational teachers are in different schools under different administrative units, the teachers, the administrators, and the school boards must coordinate their programs.

Assessing the readability levels of the materials used and the reading levels of the vocational students poses another problem. Scales such as the Dale-Chall and Fry readability scales are calibrated to sentence complexity and vocabulary diversity; they, therefore, probably overestimate the difficulty of technical materials.[9] Vocational words like "carburetor" and "thermometer" tend to inflate the reading levels,[10] although students seem to have little difficulty with these kinds of words.[11]

Jay assessed average readability levels for written matter about carpentry, and he found the average to be from the ninth to sixteenth level, with other vocations nearly as high. One reason the reading levels for carpentry are so high is because carpenters must read what lawyers (retained by some of the major construction suppliers to write the instructions for installing their products in such a way as to avoid litigation) have written. Because vocational students characteristically read at a junior-high level, real problems exist.[12]

Vocational students typically cope with materials written at a level that is too difficult for them.[13] They are able to do this for one or more of the following reasons:

- Some occupations do involve little reading.

- Reading content is of high interest to students who have experience and specialized knowledge.[14]

- Vocational reading tends to be repetitive.

- The reading can be done slowly.

- Students read while interacting with the hands-on aspects of their jobs, computers, or interactive videos.

Reading demands in vocational technical schools, by contrast, typically do not match the reading demands of the job.[15] "Compared to workers, students read less frequently and less competently. The reading strategies of students are less effective, and their reading materials less difficult than those of workers."[16] Of the two and one-half hours per day that workers spend reading, twice as much of their time is spent in following directions as in fact-finding; students' time is allocated in the opposite direction. Much on-the-job reading is no more difficult than short imperatives: "Find the manual," "Look it up," and "Use the information"—but in schools, the emphasis falls on the textbook. On-the-job writing tasks also do not match writing tasks in the school, for on-the-job writing is informal and done in an abbreviated, telegraph style.[17]

The world in which the vocational-education graduate will work is changing rapidly, becoming increasingly more technical.[18] Greater change takes place in industry in a year than happens in education in a generation. This rapid change means that textbooks cannot possibly keep up, so teachers must rely on technical manuals and instructional materials written for the actual workplace.

Research

Textbooks, and the ways they are chosen and used in vocational schools, have been examined in a number of studies. Teaching technical material is often difficult because of the vocabulary involved, the interaction with materials necessary for the learning process, and the importance of the students' past experiences. J.D. Scarborough studied effects of text organization, visuals, and actually doing an activity on the comprehension of technical discourse. He found that each of these presentation techniques, when used individually, helped students more than did combinations of the presentation techniques.[19]

G. A. Negin examined logical connectives and found that those in industrial arts texts were different from those in academic texts. This finding led him to suggest a framework of connectives to help industrial arts teachers plan lessons.[20]

Stephen Matt reported a study in which he surveyed teachers to find out how best to select vocational education textbooks. The teachers responded that a good textbook explains technical vocabulary, has accurate illustrations and representation of symbols, has good visual qualities, indicates reading levels, and has a usable index.[21]

Research on developing materials to help vocational teachers teach reading has resulted in the publication of a variety of learning "modules" for teachers. These modules often discuss difficulties that vocational students experience in reading, and they suggest reading skills, strategies, and methods to improve teaching. The modules of Glen Fardig and Gail West were designed to help teachers help students develop technical reading skills.[22] The modules of Michael Wonacott and Elizabeth Kendall can help teachers help students develop basic skills.[23] A primer developed by Berta Parrish and others will help industrial arts teachers teach reading.[24] Peter Incardone pointed out that teachers need to teach technical vocabulary; he discussed how to use a textbook and shop skills such as tool identification to build this technical vocabulary.[25]

Incardone also wrote a guide to textbook usage, vocabulary, study skills, and reading skills for students who might have difficulties in reading.[26]

Materials have been developed to help disadvantaged learners in vocational education. Liveleen Gujral and others used a Vocational English as a Second Language (VESL) program to teach welding to refugees. Not only did the refugees learn the welding skills but also they learned to carry on conversations, identify tools, and ask for help in English.[27]

Sonja Auerbach and Claire Werner worked with disadvantaged youth participating in a Job Training Partnership Act Program in Los Angeles. Included in their materials are more than 40 pages of behavioral objectives and competency lists for achieving desired skills.[28]

Larry Jewell and others studied the effect of noise on the performance of vocational students. They found that as noise intensities increased, reading comprehension decreased, and time to complete assigned tasks increased. They concluded that vocational teachers who try to reduce noise levels in their shops can help their students learn more effectively.[29]

Skills

Skills needed by all vocational students can be divided into several groups: reading and communication skills, English language skills, computer skills, social skills, and job-seeking skills. All the skills imply being able to read well.

Among the most important reading skills are finding the main idea, noting specific details, and using the dictionary and other resource materials. Other necessary skills include listening, speaking, and writing—activities that are interdependent with reading. Frequently, the informal nature of the workplace requires workers to cope with handwritten notes or oral instructions.[30] Many vocational students are seen as incapable of learning a foreign language. An often not-so-subtle prejudice is abroad, even among educators, which suggests that students who elect a vocational technical program are "dummies" who would not be able to succeed in an academic program. This unfounded notion is a denial of important differences in learning styles and frames of mind among students, and a negation of the value of the technical worker, vital for the functioning of our society.

It is essential, in any event, that all vocational students spend time and effort learning at least one "new" language—the language of the workplace. Minimum job requirements demand learning a basic sight vocabulary of the technical terms in a given vocation and whatever additional specialized vocabulary is necessary.

Some vocational students need to learn two new languages—the job language and English. Many immigrants into the United States are placed in occupational training programs to ensure that they will be able to support themselves, or because guidance counselors sense that they will benefit from vocational programs. In America, non-English-speaking students find learning English essential to learning a skill; finding a job; and doing safe, effective work.

After they have become workers, students will need to know how to use external references, understand printed directions, and follow the steps in sequence.[31] They also need to be able to read and interpret a variety of graphics, such as blueprints, drilling prints, layouts, and instruction sheets. Moreover, because the world of work is increasingly going "on-line," a knowledge of computers is required to deal with it adequately.[32] Computers control many industrial processes, analyze such things as electronic circuitry and automobile engines, schedule maintenance and repairs, and keep inventories of parts and tools.

In addition to their work skills, vocational students need interpersonal and job-seeking skills to gain and keep employment.[33] Special instructional units may be required to address the needs of VESL students.

Strategies

Because, in many instances, the talents of vocational students lie in areas other than reading and writing, some vocational students cannot read well enough to succeed in a world of work even where reading and writing are not primary. Vocational teachers need a plan to help these students with motivation to read, vocabulary, purpose for reading, actual reading, discussing, applying, and extending skills.[34]

For students whose talents lie elsewhere than with reading, teachers need to emphasize clear expressions of main ideas, new concepts, and logical relationships. The use of examples and non-examples is important, as is good organization. Students, like the rest of us, find it helpful for their teachers to avoid irrelevant details, and to use simple syntactical sentences involving interesting and motivating materials.

Many vocational teachers excel in finding appropriate materials for teaching content, making or adapting them when good ones cannot be found, using the interest and involvement that the students feel in their trades. Teachers also need to know how to find or adapt reading materials to develop individualized instruction not only for the usual VESL students in the classroom or shop but also for physically handicapped and reading-disadvantaged students.[35]

Because occupational material is written in the expository style, students need to learn to read this style, which they may have encountered less frequently than others.[36] Presenting material with lots of diagrams, charts, and illustrations is most helpful to less-able readers.[37]

To increase comprehension, vocational educators can help students see text structures and organizational patterns, the most common of which are cause/effect, compare/contrast, time order, and simple listing.[38]

The use of immediate and later reinforcement, relevant graphs and pictures, and questions that focus on personal aspects of new applications are also important. Students should use new information as soon as possible; that makes it easier for them to retain it.[39]

The skills of metacognition afford self-monitoring strategies that help all students, regardless of their respective strengths and weaknesses, learn to "understand understanding."[40]

Because much of the communication of the vocational worker is in the casual/intimate style of insiders familiar with the trade, students need to learn three different kinds of vocabulary.

The first of these, ordinary vocabulary, can be taught in several ways:

- by semantic mapping or semantic feature analysis which help students see meaning in words

- by context clues (definition, example, restatement)

- with graphic aids, glossaries, and dictionaries[41]

The second kind is the specialized vocabulary of the trade, often taught in context while manipulating equipment.[42] In the third kind, ordinary words have special meanings that usually are not found in the dictionary.[43] Examples are the mason's "buttering blocks," the electronics technician's "hacking a cludge," a communication technician's "jeeping in a TV," or a welder's "running a bead."

To help solve the problem of finding appropriate materials for their vocational students, some teachers and other educators have used variations of a cloze procedure to match readability levels and reading levels. To develop a cloze exercise, the teacher selects a passage of approximately 250 words from the textbook and leaves the first sentence in the passage intact. Starting with the second sentence, every fifth word is replaced with a blank line. All lines are about the same length. The students are given as much time as they need to fill in the blanks. To arrive at a score, the teacher counts the number of exact words or acceptable substitutes that the student has written. If a student is able to fill in less than 50 percent of the blanks, or is selecting incorrect parts of speech, the material is probably too difficult; hence, additional materials need to be found or developed.[44]

In addition to texts, career-oriented literature (COL), which may include stories about people engaged in the occupation, may be used. Tom Derby, seeing the value of trade materials, listed *The Physician's Desk Reference*, the *Merck Index of*

Chemicals and Biologicals, and *The National Electrical Code* as readable materials.[45]

Because many, even most, vocational students cannot read their school materials by themselves, directed reading activities (DRA) are helpful. Usually, a DRA consists of the following steps:[46]

- establishing background

- building vocabulary

- prequestioning to develop a purpose for reading

- silent reading

- after-reading questioning

- incorporating a reading skill

- enrichment

Vocational teachers have developed a variety of special techniques to help their students read. Larry Mikulecky and William Diehl suggested having students make instructional signs and warning labels. They also suggested having teachers use talk-aloud protocols, saying things such as these:

"I wonder which manual I need to use?"

"This one will probably give me the information I need."

"Let me check the table of contents first."

By verbalizing the procedure, the teacher externalizes a model process that the students can follow on the job.

Mikulecky and Diehl also suggested sending students to job sites to gather relevant reading materials.[47] Maxine Perine gave students five-minute tasks for which they must use job-site materials.[48] M.C. Manuel motivated student questioning with auto magazines, increased student interest in new auto products, and helped develop problem-solving skills by giving a problem that students could solve by using only a book's table of contents.[49]

Strategies that may be especially helpful for students who are learning English are writing safety warnings, carrying on conversation such as would be found in the workplace, requesting help, and reading and writing the names of the tools they see in pictures.[50]

Many authorities suggest techniques such as SQ3R: survey, question, read, recite, review.[51] Shorter, simpler strategies might be more effective with slow learners than this seemingly complex technique because memory and mental processing are required to untangle the mnemonic before one ever gets to the meaning.

Phonics instruction is minimal in the few programs in which it is used, but, in at least one case, phonics is used without regard to whether it is actually needed or not. While phonics instruction may be helpful to those who are diagnosed as having difficulty in identifying words, it is not helpful if the student's difficulty is in comprehension.

The Future of Vocational Education

The passage of the Carl D. Perkins Vocational Education Act of 1984 (PL 98-524) provided a mandate to "improve academic foundations of vocational education students."

"The burgeoning technological revolution requires that more and more employees be able to think critically and solve problems."[52]

"However, reading instruction in the context of vocational education programs is rare."[53]

By juxtaposing these three quotations, we emphasize the need to examine the relationships between academic and vocational education more closely, and the need for reading professionals to become involved in vocational education.

The increasing use of computers in almost all vocations means that the teaching of computer skills must be an integral part of vocational education. Already a number of older auto mechanics are being taught by interactive video instead of by written materials, as auto mechanics becomes a more complex field.

Textbooks written for vocational students seem to be improving. Although textbooks in 1973 were found to be too difficult (101 commonly used vocational textbooks had an eleventh-grade readability level), two recent auto textbooks, Webster (1986) and DeKryger (1986), are much improved. Webster's even includes a vocabulary development program. The earlier texts contained no advance organizers, no subordination, no systematic approach to vocabulary; their readability was poor. These shortcomings have been addressed in recent textbooks such as *Computers Today* by Sanders. It is an attractive textbook containing advance organizers, and important terms are keyed to the pages in context. Two tables of contents are geared to different levels of complexity, and a section called "Other Features and Aids to Learning" is included. These new textbooks may help close the gap between vocational educational needs and the reading demands of the workplace.[54]

Vocational teachers' attitudes towards having to teach reading as well as students' attitudes toward reading, need to be examined more closely with an eye towards finding ways to improve them. James Brown and Gerald Chang suggested a number of steps to help students enjoy reading more.[55] Vocational teachers can begin to see reading-resource teachers as people who can help them find alternative reading materials and new techniques to help their students.[56]

People in general feel threatened by change, and vocational teachers are no exception; teachers' negative attitudes toward change must be addressed. Cooperative efforts by English and vocational teachers are essential, but attitudes must change before cooperation and improvement are possible. The first step, of course, is better communication.

Academic teachers and vocational teachers need to understand and cooperate with each other. It may be possible to legislate changes at teacher-training institutions that would encourage the empathy and cooperation needed to help vocational students succeed in the world of work.[57]

Plumbers, electricians, mechanics, auto body workers, drafters, and workers in all the other trades keep our country flushed, lighted, rolling, shining, squared, and moving. Let's help our students learn to read—it is vital that they succeed.

Notes

1. J. M. Brown and G. Y.-S. Chang, "Supplementary Reading Materials for Vocational Students with Limited Reading Ability," *Journal of Reading 26* (November 1982): 144-49.

2. L. J. Thornton, *Basic Reading Skills and Vocational Education* (Columbus: Ohio State University, 1980).

3. M. M. Dupuis, *et al. Teaching Reading and Writing in the Content Areas* (Glenview, Illinois: Scott, Foresman and Company, 1989

4. D. M. Nielsen and H. F. Hjelm, *Reading and Career Education*. (Newark, Delaware: International Reading Association, 1975): 81.

5. M. D. Siedow, "Reading in Vocational Education: A Review of Recent Literature," *Reading World 23* (December 1983): 158-65.

6. L. J. Thornton *et al. Trade and Industrial Reading Strategies* (Harrisburg: Pennsylvania State Department of Education, 1980).

7. M. D. Siedow, *op. cit.*: 160.

8. G. Steinley, "In the Works: A New Model of Content Reading," *Journal of Reading 27* (December 1983): 238.

9. L. J. Thornton, *op. cit.*.

10. M. M. Dupuis, *op. cit.*

11. R. T. Rush, A. J. Moe, and R. L. Storlie, *Occupational Literacy Education* (Newark, Delaware: International Reading Association, 1986): 25.

12. L. J. Thornton, *Carpentry Literature. Readability vs. Reading Ability* (Utica/Rome, New York: State University of New York, 1978).

13. R. T. Rush, "Occupational Literacy: Requirements and Instructional Response" (1987): 2; Sticht and McFann, cited in D.M. Nielsen and H.F. Hjelm, *Reading and Career Education* (Newark, Delaware: International Reading Association, 1975): 68.

14. R. T. Rush, *et al., op. cit.*; Rush, *op. cit.*

15. L. Mikulecky and W. Diehl, "Reading for Vocational Literacy," *VocEd 58* (August 1983): 34-35.

16. Rush, *op. cit.;* see also B. Davis and N. Woodruff, *Project Trade Related Packets for Disabled Readers. Final Report 1984-1985.* Trenton: New Jersey State Department of Education, 1985.

17. M. M. Dupuis, *op. cit.;* Rush *et al., op. cit.*

18. T. Derby, "Reading Instruction and Course Related Materials for Vocational High School Students," *Journal of Reading 30* (January 1989): 308-16.

19. J. D. Scarborough, "Effects of Text Organization, Visuals, and Activity on Comprehension of Technical Discourse," *Journal of Industrial Teacher Education 22* (fall 1984): 14-26.

20. G. A. Negin, "Logical Connectives in Industrial Arts Textbooks," *Reading Improvement 19* (fall 1982): 1970-72.

21. S. R. Matt, "Reading Teacher's Text Selection for Industrial Arts and Other Technical Fields," paper presented at the annual meeting of the American Reading Forum, (Sarasota, Florida, December 8-10, 1983).

22. G. Fardig and G. West, *Assisting Students in Improving Their Basic Skills. Professional Teacher Education Module Series* (Washington: Department of Education, 1985).

23. M. E. Wonacott and E. Kendall, *Assisting Students in Improving Their Basic Skills* (Washington: Department of Education, 1985).

24. B. E. Parrish *et al. An Industrial Arts Teacher's Primer to Reading* (Tempe: Arizona State University, 1983).

25. P. Incardone, "Help! I Can't Read," *VocEd 53* (December 1978): 51-52.

26. P. Incardone, *Teaching Students to Read Better: Professional Development Series* (Arlington, Virginia: American Vocational Association, 1985).

27. L. K. Gujral *et al. Vocational English as a Second Language for Welding* (Flint: University of Michigan, 1984).

28. S. Auerbach and C. Werner, *Basic Educational Competencies for JTPA Youth* (Los Angeles Unified School District, 1984).

29. L. R. Jewell and C. R. Weston, *Effects of Noise on Reading Comprehension and Task Completion Time: Final Report* (Jefferson City: Missouri State Department of Elementary and Secondary Education, 1979).

30. Dupuis, *op. cit;* Rush *et al., op. cit.*

31. South Carolina State Department of Education, *Teaching Reading in Vocational Education* (Columbia: Columbia Office of Vocational Education, 1984).

32. Derby, *op. cit.*

33. See Nielsen and Hjelm, *op. cit.:* 39; Gujral, *op. cit.*

34. M. H. Perine, "Teaching Reading in Vocational Education" (Michigan, 1980).

35. South Carolina, *op. cit.*

36. Rush, *op. cit.*

37. Rush, *op. cit.*; F. Sofo, "Graphic Literacy: Part II. A Recent Study," *Vocational Aspects of Education 38* (December 1986): 81-84.

38. A. N. Luparelli, *A Reading Program for Technical Education,* paper presented at the annual meeting of the Massachusetts Reading Association (Boxborough, April 1-2, 1982).

39. Fardig and West, *op. cit.*; Rush, *et al., op. cit.*

40. S. Pogrow, "Challenging At-risk Students: Findings from the HOTS Program," *Phi Delta Kappan 71* (1990): 389-97.

41. Rush *et al., op. cit.*.

42. Dupuis, *op. cit.*

43. J. D. Stammer, "Vocational Education and Vocabulary of a 'Third Kind.' Open to Suggestion," *Journal of Reading 27* (October 1983): 70-75.

44. Dupuis, *op. cit.*: 183-86; Luparelli, *op. cit.*; L. J. Thornton, *Review and Synthesis of Reading in Post-Secondary Occupational Education* (University Park: The Pennsylvania State University, 1980).

45. Tom Derby, "Reading Instruction and Course Related Materials for Vocational High School Students," *Journal of Reading 30* (January 1989): 308-16.

46. Dupuis, *op. cit.*: 244-51.

47. Mikulecky and Diehl, *op. cit.*

48. Perine, *op. cit.*.

49. M.C . Manuel, "Vocational Reading Methods," *Journal of Reading 27* (1984): 546-552.

50. Gujral *et al., op. cit.*

51. Perine, *op. cit.*; South Carolina, *op. cit.*; L. J. Thornton, *op. cit.*

52. Mikulecky and Diehl, *op. cit.*

53. Derby, *op. cit.*

54. Derby, *op. cit.*

55. Brown and Chang, *op. cit.*

56. Dupuis, *op. cit.*: 327.

57. Dupuis *et al.*, *Teaching Reading and Writing in the Content Areas* (1989): 334; Rush, *op. cit.*; Siedow, *op. cit.*1984.

Annotated Bibliography

Auerbach, S. and C. Werner. *Basic Educational Competencies for JTPA Youth.* Los Angeles Unified School District, California, 1984. [ED 250 557]

Lists competency statements for young people participating in Job Training Partnership Act programs. Contains more than 40 pages of behavioral objectives and competencies.

Brown, J. M. and G. Y.-S. Chang. "Supplementary Reading Materials for Vocational Students with Limited Reading Ability," *Journal of Reading 26* (November 1982): 144-49.

Lists and describes materials that could be used to help the teachers of special-needs students develop content-area skills.

California State Department of Education. *Learning to Read and Write* series. Sacramento, 1984.

Addresses educationally disadvantaged industrial education students' need for basic skills while they learn their respective trades.

Learning to Read and Write the Automotive Way. [ED 244 091]

Learning to Read and Write the Electronics Way. [ED 244 100]

Learning to Read and Write the Metalworking Way. [ED 244 097]

Learning to Read and Write the Woodworking Way. [ED 244 094]

Cranney, A. G. and W. E. McKell. "Selected References for Reading Skills in Industrial Education," *Journal of Reading 27* (October 1983): 56-60.

Lists sources for teaching reading in high-school industrial-arts courses.

Davis, B. and N. Woodruff. *Trade-Related Reading Packets for Disabled Readers.* Trenton: New Jersey State Department of Education, 1985. [ED 262 163]

Includes activities for students in the areas of assembling, baking, building maintenance, data entry, interior landscaping, and warehousing.

Derby, T. "Reading Instruction and Course Related Materials for Vocational High School Student," *Journal of Reading 30* (January 1989): 308-16.[ED 147 568]

Discusses the need for vocational reading and the impact of PL 98-524 on vocational reading. Looks at materials now available.

DiGise, J. *Reading in the Automotive Trade.* Trenton: New Jersey Department of Education, 1978. [ED 147 568]

Anthologizes articles selected from auto magazines and journals. Comprehension and vocabulary exercises encourage reluctant readers to read.

Dupuis, M. M., J. W. Lee, B. J. Badiali, and E. N. Askov. *Teaching Reading and Writing in the Content Areas.* Glenview, Illinois: Scott, Foresman and Company, 1989.

Discusses teaching essential reading and writing processes and organizing for instruction in the content areas. Offers techniques for learning about students and suggests how reading and writing in the content areas fit into the total school program.

Fardig, G. and G. West. *Assisting Students in Improving Their Basic Skills. Professional Teacher Education Module Series.* Washington: Department of Education, June 1985. [ED 252 702]

Outlines a performance-based teacher education packet for teaching vocational students technical reading skills.

Ferri, K. *From Autos to Stereos: A Collection of Readings.* Trenton: New Jersey Department of Education, 1978. [ED 147 633]

Suggests 35 vocationally oriented articles of general interest to teach basic reading skills to high-school students.

Gujral, L. K. *et al. Vocational English as a Second Language for Welding.* Flint: University of Michigan, 1984. [ED 263 364]

Discusses a curriculum designed for use in teaching welding to adult learners of English as a second language. Includes use of basic welding tools and techniques, social interactions, work behaviors, and pronunciation skills.

Harris, E. and E. Kendall. *Do You Read Me? Prevocational-Vocational Reading Development Activities.* Charleston: West Virginia State Department of Education, 1982. [ED 210 454]

    Helps vocational students with comprehension, vocabulary, word recognition, and socialization.

Hunter, C. F. *Reading for Main Ideas and Details in Electronics.* San Jose, California: San José City College, 1982.

    Describes using actual electronics materials to help improve students' reading skills.

Incardone, P. *Teaching Students to Read Better. Professional Development Series.* Arlington, Virginia: American Vocational Association, 1985.

    Discusses ways vocational teachers can help vocational students improve their reading skills. Includes methods for helping bilingual students.

Jewell, L. R. and C. R. Weston. *Effects of Noise on Reading Comprehension and Task Completion Time. Final Report.* Jefferson City: Missouri State Department of Elementary and Secondary Education, 1979. [ED 159 631]

    Concludes that as noise intensity increases, comprehension decreases and task completion time increases.

Kendall E. L. and R. Chenoweth. *Do You Read Me?* Series. Charleston: West Virginia State Department of Education, 1984.

    Provides games, puzzles, and other activities to help vocational students develop skills in word recognition, vocabulary, and comprehension.

Do You Read Me? Service Supplement: Reading Development Activities Guide, 1984. [ED 237 814]

Do You Read Me? Industrial Supplement: Reading Development Activities Guide, 1984. [ED 237 813]

Do You Read Me? Business and Office Reading Development Activities Guide, 1984. [ED 237 815]

Do You Read Me? Environmental Supplement: Reading Development Activities Guide, 1984. [ED 237 812]

Kessman, W. A. *Building Maintenance: Reading and Language Activities.* Trenton: New Jersey Department of Education, 1976. [ED 118 763]

Covers some basic aspects of building maintenance with the goal of building basic reading skills.

Lamatine, R. *Twenty Trades to Read About.* Trenton: New Jersey Department of Education, 1978. [ED 145 189]

A workbook of instructional materials drawn from twenty trade areas for use by students with reading difficulties. Includes written exercises.

Lee, H. D. "Dealing with Reading in Industrial Arts," *Journal of Reading 24* (May 1981): 663-66.

Discusses reading problems that students may encounter in industrial-arts classes; suggests solutions.

Luparelli, A. N., *et al.* "Basic Skills," *VocEd* 56 (June 1981): 31-38.

Four articles that deal with basic reading, science, and job-search skills.

Luparelli, A. N. "A Reading Program for Technical Education," paper presented at the annual meeting of the Massachusetts Reading Association, Boxborough, Massachusetts, (April 1-2, 1982). [ED 223 967]

Suggests activities to help students develop vocabulary and comprehension skills. Proposes a cloze procedure to match the student's reading level to the level of the materials being used in the shop.

Manuel, M. C. "Vocational Reading Methods," *Journal of Reading* 27 (1984): 546-52.

> Suggests ways to use materials from auto mechanics to motivate students' interest in reading.

Matt, S. R. "Reading Teacher's Text Selection for Industrial Arts and Other Technical Fields," paper presented at the annual meeting of the American Reading Forum, Sarasota, Florida, December 8-10, 1983. [ED 244 235]

> Makes recommendations for selection committees to follow when choosing textbooks for adoption in vocational courses.

Mikulecky, L. and W. Diehl. "Reading for Vocational Literacy," *VocEd 58* (August 1983): 34-35.

> Suggests ways to incorporate on-the-job materials into classroom assignments.

Negin, G. A. "Logical Connectives in Industrial Arts Textbooks," *Reading Improvement 19* (fall 1982): 170-72.

> Reports that the logical connectives in industrial-arts textbooks are different from those in academic textbooks.

Nielsen, D. M. and H. F. Hjelm. *Reading and Career Education.* Newark, Delaware: International Reading Association, 1975.

O'Connor, Frank and Jerry D. Pepple. *An Analysis: Illinois Goals for Learning in Language Arts and Applied Communication Instructional Materials.* Champaign-Urbana: University of Illinois, March 1991.

> Aids teachers and others deciding how to integrate Applied Communication (developed cooperatively by the Agency for Instructional Technology and 42 states and provinces) into English or vocational courses. Details instructional content; correlates each lesson with language-arts learning goals, including students' ability to read, comprehend, interpret, and evaluate written material and understand various forms of literature.

Parrish, B. E. *et al. An Industrial Arts Teacher's Primer to Reading.* Tempe: Arizona State University, Arizon, 1983.

Uses student interest to develop vocabulary and comprehension skills.

Pepple, Jerry D., Constanza M. Valdes, and Dale A. Law. *The Use of Applied Academic Curricula in Vocational Education; Preliminary Results of Teacher Survey, Applied Communication.* Berkeley: National Center for Research in Vocational Education, University of California, 1990.

Reports responses of teachers using Applied Communication (developed cooperatively by the Agency for Instructional Technology and 42 states and provinces), mostly in vocational classes with "average" secondary students. Reports that students generally liked the material and found it interesting, that a majority of the teachers would recommend it, and that students and teachers agreed that the content was important. Suggests team-teaching by academic and vocational teachers.

Perine, M. H. "Teaching Reading in Vocational Education," Michigan (1980). [ED 189 556]

Suggests that vocational education teachers can help their students improve their reading skills by using strategies learned earlier. Offers a plan that focuses on word recognition, vocabulary, comprehension, and study skills.

Pogrow, S. "Challenging At-Risk Students: Findings from the HOTS Program," *Phi Delta Kappan 71* (1990): 389-97.

Reviews a program designed to help students at risk by teaching them to use basic metacognitive skills.

Rush, R. T. "Occupational Literacy: Requirements and Instructional Responses." Wyoming, 1987. [ED 296 283]

Reviews requirements and skills required for occupational reading and writing. Previews a new curriculum called "Applied Communication," developed under the leadership of the Agency for Instructional Technology.

Rush, R. T., A. J. Moe, and R. L. Storlie. *Occupational Literacy Education*. Newark, Delaware: International Reading Association, 1986.

    Discusses occupational literacy requirements and suggests ways of developing occupational literacy competencies.

Scarborough, J. D. "Effects of Text Organization, Visuals, and Activity on Comprehension of Technical Discourse," *Journal of Industrial Teacher Education 22* (fall 1984): 14-26.

    Reports a study to determine the effects of text organization, visuals, and activity on students' comprehension. Found that using each separately was more effective than using them in combination.

Siedow, M. D. "Reading in Vocational Education: A Review of Recent Literature," *Reading World 23* (December 1983): 158-65.

    Reviews literature and suggests improvements that could be made in the teaching of reading in vocational education.

Sofo, F. "Graphic Literacy: Part II. A Recent Study," *Vocational Aspects of Education 38* (December 1986): 81-84.

    Reports a study that concluded that most vocational educational materials include graphs, charts, tables, and illustrations of great benefit to vocational students.

South Carolina State Department of Education. *Teaching Reading in Vocational Education*. Columbia: Columbia Office of Vocational Education, 1984. [ED 233 177]

    Suggests strategies for helping teachers to help students improve reading skills.

Stammer, J. D. "Vocational Education and Vocabulary of a 'Third Kind.' Open to Suggestion," *Journal of Reading 27* (1983): 70-75.

    Suggests that students need to learn a special kind of vocabulary in which ordinary words are given specific job-related meanings.

Steinley, G. "In the Works: A New Model of Content Reading," *Journal of Reading 27* (December 1983): 238-44.
Reviews the Content Processing Model of reading; suggests a revision of it.

Thornton, L. J. *Carpentry Literature. Readability vs. Reading Ability*. Utica/Rome, New York: State University of New York, 1978. [ED 149 128]
Reports that the readability ranges of the literature of carpentry in a significant proportion of the materials examined were not within the reading levels of vocational students.

Thornton, L. J. *Basic Reading Skills and Vocational Education*. Columbus: Ohio State University, 1980. [ED 189 278]
Provides an overview of issues involved in the relationship between basic reading skills and vocational education.

Thornton, L. J. *Review and Synthesis of Reading in Post-Secondary Occupational Education*. University Park: The Pennsylvania State University, 1980.
Reviews issues and problems of reading for vocational education in various areas; calls for further research in the field.

Thornton, L. J., *et al. Reading Strategies Series*. Harrisburg, Pennsylvania: State Department of Education, 1980-81.
Reading guides that help teachers help educationally disadvantages students improve reading skills in their respective subjects.

Cosmetology Reading Strategies, 1980. [ED 192 017]

Medical Assisting Reading Strategies, 1980. [ED 192 018]

Trade and Industrial Reading Strategies, 1980. [ED 192 023]

Clustered Business Occupations Reading Strategies, 1981. [ED 217 135]

Clustered Construction Trades Reading Strategies, 1981. [ED 217 134]

Clustered Health Occupations Reading Strategies, 1981. [ED 217 133]

Data Processing Reading Strategies, 1981. [ED 192 024]

Radio and Television Reading Strategies, 1981. [ED 192 025]

Uberto, J. A. *Readings in Air Conditioning and Refrigeration.* Trenton: New Jersey Department of Education, 1978. [ED 147 491]

    Offers a series of articles selected from trade magazines and journals dealing with air conditioning and refrigeration. Encourages students to read; includes vocabulary and comprehension exercises.

West Virginia Department of Education. *Do You Read Me?* Wheeling: West Virginia Department of Education, 1980.

    Includes games, puzzles, and other activities for most occupations, including service, industrial, and business.

Wonacott, M. E. and E. Kendall. *Assisting Students in Improving Their Basic Skills.* Washington: Department of Education, 1985. [ED 252 701]

    Outlines a performance-based teacher-education packet for teaching basic reading skills to vocational students.

Do You Have An Idea to Share?

Research to Report?

A Cause to Champion?

This excellent book was published by the ERIC Clearinghouse on Reading and the Communication Skills, a unit within the U.S. Department of Education's farflung network of information processing for everyone interested in education.

At ERIC/RCS, we are always looking for high-quality manuscripts having to do with teaching English, the language arts, reading, writing, speech, theater, mass communication, the media, personal communication, thinking, literature, and literacy. We publish original research and scholarship, teaching guides and practical applications for educators and others who work with youth. In conjunction with EDINFO Press and our other partners in education information, we publish books of all kinds within the field of education.

Do you have a novel understanding of some timely issue, an innovative approach to a troubling problem, or an especially effective method of teaching? Does one of your colleagues have something burning to say on curriculum development, professionalism in education, excellence in teaching, or some other aspect of schooling? If so, let us know. We'd like to hear from you. Tell us that reading this book gave you an incentive to get in touch.

Contact:

Warren Lewis
Assistant Director, Publications
ERIC/RCS
Smith Research Center, Suite 150
Bloomington, IN 47408-2698
812/855-5847
BITNET% WWLEWIS@IUBACS

All about TRIEDs

TRIED is an acronym: **T**eaching **R**esources **I**n the **E**RIC **D**atabase. The TRIED series is a reliable alternative to textbook teaching. The name TRIED reflects the fact that these ideas have been **tried** by other teachers, reported in the ERIC database, and have now been condensed and redesigned to be teacher-friendly and student-friendly to the max.

- ❖ A TRIED taps the rich collection of instructional materials and techniques collected in the ERIC database.

- ❖ A TRIED is focused on specific topics and grade levels.

- ❖ TRIEDs include a wide but manageable range of practical teaching suggestions, useful and inspiring ideas, and dependable classroom techniques and effective approaches.

- ❖ TRIEDs save you time by helping you manage the information explosion, serving as your curricular guide, introduction, or reacquaintance to the wealth of the ERIC database, the oldest and largest information retrieval system in professional education.

Because these approaches to teaching and learning come with the ERIC seal of approval—they have been "TRIED and tested" in the classroom—you can appropriate these guidelines for use with your students in full confidence: They are educationally sound, they equip you with the latest and the best ideas, and they work—your students will respond eagerly.

We have kept educational jargon to a minimum, wanting to put the results of the best thinking and planning into your hands in a brief, clean, interesting, easy format. Each lesson is organized under these headings:

- ❖ Source (where you can find the original document in the ERIC database)

- ❖ Brief Description

- ❖ Objective

* Procedures

* Personal Observation

Space is left in many cases for your own notes and comments.

Each **TRIED** volume also contains an activities chart that indicates the focus and types of activities in each lesson (such as collaborative learning, remedial instruction, teacher/student conferencing, games, media, etc.)

An annotated bibliography at the end of each **TRIED** volume contains references to other learning alternatives and additional resources available in the ERIC database.

Writing across the Social Studies Curriculum
by Roger Sensenbaugh.

Provides examples of how to connect many kinds of writing activities with important topics in the social studies; a writing-across-the-curriculum approach. (**T01**) $14.95

Reading and Writing across the High School Science and Math Curriculum
by Roger Sensenbaugh.

"Reading and writing across the curriculum"—when it is done right—helps the science and math teacher in a powerful way to get content and concepts across the students. Contains additional material to help science and math teachers tool up to use imagination, analogies, enriched vocabulary, and the full range of reading/writing technology in science and math classrooms. (**T12**) $16.95

A High School Student's Bill of Rights,
by Stephen S. Gottlieb

Students in school, legal minors, constitute a special class of citizens: people with the same civil rights as everyone else, but not quite. Explores the U.S. Constitution and other bodies of law, focused on precedent-setting legal cases that have dealt with students' rights when they were contested in the school setting. (**T09**) $14.95

Teaching Values through Teaching Literature

by Margaret Dodson.

The literature taught in English classrooms expresses a wide range of religious, personal moral, and social ethical values—and opinions about these values vary greatly.(**T13**) $16.95 Many of the pieces of literature discussed in this **TRIED** correspond to the literature at debate between Charles and Ben Suhor (see below).

Other Titles by ERIC / RCS

Teaching Values in the Literature Classroom (A Debate in Print)

by Charles and Bernard Suhor

"A Public School Perspective" by Charles Suhor; "A Catholic School Perspective" by Bernard Suhor (Bloomington, Indiana: ERIC/RCS; Urbana, Illinois: NCTE, 1992).

The value structures, and many of the specific moral and ethical ideas, expressed in the Western literature that is typically taught in public school English classrooms are rooted and grounded in the religious vision of the Judaeo-Christian tradition. Ought, therefore, the public school teacher, who is in effect a civil servant, paid by the tax-payer to educate school children at the public expense, attempt in any way to teach moral and ethical and religious values? Or ought the teacher to hue strictly to a values-neutral line, neither attacking nor advocating this or that idea or behavior as either moral or immoral, leaving the issue of values clarification strictly up to the student, the student's parent(s), and the student's non-school community?

Bernard Suhor was a teacher of English, religion, and social studies at Redemptorist High School in New Orleans for over 35 years, during which time he served as assistant principal for five years, and chaired both the English and the religion departments. He now teaches English, Latin, and French at Archbishop Rummel High School in Metairie, Louisiana, a New Orleans suburb. In his passionate defense of teaching religious values as enshrined in the literature read in the majority of English classrooms whether public or private, and in his attack on Secular Humanisms of various kinds, Ben Suhor leads the reader to the threshold of a conclusion that moral logic might well take: If instruction in moral and ethical values is good for kids in one school, it's good for kids in another school.

Charles Suhor is Deputy Executive Director of the National Council of Teachers of English, and an experienced high-school English teacher and teacher of English teachers; he is also a distinguished semiotician, a poet, and a jazz drummer. He argues for the teacher's maintaining a position of moral neutrality, resisting the urge to indoctrinate students in any particular set of values, and fostering a classroom atmosphere in which students can explore their own and others' values in a non-judgmental, exploratory fashion.

The Suhors' debate raises again for new consideration a perennially significant question to which neither the Supreme Court nor any of the partisan groups, whether to the Right, to the Left, or down the middle of the political spectrum, has yet found the answer: How do we teachers uphold before our students the moral values and ethical behaviors that our society needs in order to remain civilized, while, at the same time, safeguarding everyone's Constitutional rights?

Teacher Effectiveness and Reading Instruction
by Richard D. Robinson

What are the actual teaching behaviors that real-life teachers use when they are being effective in the classroom?

By answering this question, naturalistic research shows how any reading teacher can apply in his or her own situation the techniques and strategies that, according to the latest and berst findings, make a reading teacher effective.

Includes exercises in self-research, "You Become Involved" instructions, and chapters on managing the reading classroom, establishing an effective environment for reading, and ways of involving the students' parents in the school's reading program. The extensive, annotated bibliography richly documents the resources. (**G25**) $14.95

Ship to:

Name _____

Address _____

_____

City_____State_____ ZIP _____

Phone (_____) _____

Item No.	Quantity	Abbreviated Title	Price	Total Cost
			$	
			$	
			$	
		Subtotal		
Minimum order $5.00		Plus Postage and Handling		
		TOTAL Purchase		

Method of Payment

❑ check   ❑ money order

❑ P.O. # _____

❑ MasterCard   ❑ VISA

cardholder _____

card no. _____

expiration date_____

Make checks payable to ERIC/RCS.

Order Subtotal	Postage/Handling
$5.00 - $10.00	$2.00
$10.01 - $25.00	$3.00
$25.01 - $50.00	$4.00
$50.01 - $75.00	$5.00
$75.01 - $100.00	$6.00
$100.01 - $125.00	$7.00
$125.01 - $150.00	$8.00
over $150.00	$9.00

Send order form to:
ERIC/RCS
Indiana University
2805 E. 10th Street, Suite 150E
Bloomington, IN 47408-2698
FAX (812) 855-7901